Richard Bronk, who has _____
tional politics and econc_____
was born in New York a_____
acquiring a first-class hoi._____
phy at Merton College, Oxford, he trained as a financial
analyst at the Bank of England. In the mid-1980s he became
a pension fund manager in the City specialising in European
equity markets, and from 1991 to 1995 was head of European
equities at Baring Asset Management.

He is now working in the City on the economic and market
implications of Monetary Union in Europe. He is married
with two sons.

Progress
and the
Invisible Hand

The Philosophy and Economics
of Human Advance

RICHARD BRONK

27/9/99
To Brendan
Wishing you the very best
in retirement

[signature]

WARNER BOOKS

A *Warner* Book

First published in Great Britain in 1998
by Little, Brown and Company
This edition published in 1999
by Warner Books

A CIP catalogue for this book is
available from the British Library.

ISBN 0 7515 2660 6

Typeset in Caslon by M Rules
Printed and bound in Great Britain by
Clays Ltd, St Ives plc

Warner Books
A Division of
Little, Brown and Company (UK)
Brettenham House
Lancaster Place
London WC2E 7EN

To Vyvian

Contents

. . . he intends only his own gain, and he is in this, as in many other cases, led by an invisible hand to promote an end which was no part of his intention. Nor is it always the worse for the society that it was no part of it. By pursuing his own interest he frequently promotes that of the society more effectually than when he really intends to promote it. I have never known much good done by those who affected to trade for the publick good.

Adam Smith, *An Inquiry into the Nature and Causes of the Wealth of Nations*, 1776

Acknowledgements

I acknowledge a considerable debt to the authors listed in the notes at the end of this book, whose scholarship and challenging views provided much of the inspiration for this book. My thanks also go to the staff of the London Library and the Bodleian Library for their help, and to Nick Wetton for obtaining permissions to reprint extracts.

I am very grateful to the many friends who made helpful suggestions; to my father and brother for their useful comments; and to Kerrina Commins, who typed the original manuscript with her usual wit and good humour. I owe a particular debt to my agent, Ros Edwards, for believing in the project long before most; to my editor, Alan Samson, whose wise comments have greatly improved the book, and to editor at large Caroline North for her work on the manuscript. My biggest thanks go to my two young sons for showing more consideration for the requirements of a book-writing father than would many of their age; and to my wife, Vyvian, whose contribution to this book in emotional and intellectual terms has been immense.

To all the above I gratefully acknowledge my debt, while – in time-honoured fashion – pointing out that the shortcomings of the book are entirely my own.

Preface to the
Paperback Edition

The struggle between optimism and pessimism is endemic in human thought, and its ebb and flow is naturally affected by the economic and social state we are in at particular times. When this book was originally written, the 'feel-bad factor' was a concept in vogue even in the land of optimism, the United States. But by early 1999, after one of the longest economic and stock-market booms in US history, optimism was back in fashion there. Progress has once more become an article of faith for much of America's business and political élite, apparently driven by the twin mechanisms of scientific advance and the 'invisible hand' of the free market. In some circles, optimistic belief in progress may even be considered a prerequisite for securing further advances – the secular equivalent of the Second Coming, providing everyone with the duty of preparing for the bright future.

In many other parts of the developed world, by contrast, deep uneasiness remains about some of the social and environmental costs of the free-market pursuit of higher economic growth. Moreover, many less developed countries face sharply increased levels of poverty and insecurity as a result of environmental catastrophes and the economic crises and market turmoil which buffeted south-east Asia, Russia and Brazil in 1997 and 1998. These developments cast fresh doubt on the inevitability of worldwide success for the free-market paradigm of economic progress. Indeed, the scale of the global challenges facing us at the end of the twentieth century suggests that, far from it being essential to human advance to believe in progress, it may be necessary to admit that progress is actually in doubt. For belief in inevitable progress can be used as an excuse for overlooking present-day poverty and for ignoring the interests of posterity; it may foster an unsafe assumption that the free market will in time benefit everyone and that our children will be able to sort out any problem we bequeath them, thanks to advances in science and ever-increasing wealth.

Exploring beneath the contradictory surface swells of contemporary optimism and pessimism, this book aims to trace fundamental ambiguities in the concept of progress through its chequered history and to explore two insidious confusions in much of current public debate: one, between progress in welfare and financial measures of economic growth; the other, between ethical considerations of what kind of progress we should aim for and the narrower goals of free-market efficiency. The book should interest those who fear that the goals of human progress are now being dictated by an obsessive quest for efficiency; and those who sense that our conception of human progress is becoming tragically narrowed to include only the maximisation by individuals of material goods which can be valued in monetary terms and provided by a free market, without any reference to non-material values, public goods and a longer-term approach to human welfare.

Richard Bronk
Spring 1999

Foreword

The ladies mourn the loss of that quintessentially American optimism, the dream of perpetual progress, the certainty that all things
would be ever better. That used to be seen as a law of socio-
economics, just as gravity was a law of nature. Every child better off
than his or her parents, every step forward. Now the law no longer
holds.

> Patti Waldmeir, *Financial Times*, 10 February 1996, reporting on
> the Iowa caucuses

The real meaning of this feel-worse factor is that people and politicians have parted company. For more than forty years, the entire
political class has taken it for granted that the central objective of
economic policy is to promote wealth creation; that wealth can be
equated with GDP per head; and that the rate of growth of GDP per
head is, therefore, the litmus test of economic, indeed of national,
success. For both, a high rate of growth has been a symbol of national
virility, a passport to popular approval and, above all, a proxy for the
pursuit of happiness which the American Declaration of
Independence disastrously defined as an inalienable human right.

> David Marquand, *The Observer*, 9 June 1996

These extracts highlight a growing phenomenon in the late 1990s. In
much of the developed world, continued economic growth and rising
material prosperity coexist with an increasingly anxious society, apparently weighed down by 'the feel-bad factor'. As we approach the next
millennium, there is a pervasive sense of uneasiness and pessimism
which puzzles politicians and worries social commentators. Political
leaders continue to promise a brighter future and perpetual progress so
long as we can embrace change and free-market reforms wholeheart-
edly, and thereby pursue economic growth more effectively. But to
many of their electors, it seems evident that high rates of economic

growth, and the ever faster pace of change required to maintain them, are no longer matched by an ever faster pace of human progress.

This book aims to shed light on such pessimism by exploring ambiguities in the general concept of progress, and by focusing on increasing strains in the two-hundred-year-old relationship between economic growth and progress in welfare. In particular, it analyses the growing challenges to the optimistic assumption that the 'invisible hand' of the free market in liberal economies can spontaneously forge an unambiguous link between the individual pursuit of self-interest and progress for society as a whole. These challenges include the rising environmental and social costs of economic growth, many of which the free-market system seems powerless to prevent, and some of which it seems positively to exacerbate.

There is no attempt in this volume to give a fully comprehensive account of the idea of progress or of the nature of economic growth, nor to adjudicate definitively between the rival claims of collective economic planning, on the one hand, and economic liberty, on the other, to be the main driving force behind human progress. Rather, the aim is to isolate and analyse enough of the key features of these concepts to provide some cogent explanations for the growing lack of confidence in progress and the closely associated disillusionment with economic growth. The book is written for non-specialists; by giving a short survey of specialist thinking across several disciplines – including some philosophy, history and economics – it attempts to draw together some of the central issues which face us at the end of the twentieth century. For the compartmentalised nature of modern academic study can make it increasingly difficult, for professionals and the public alike, to consider as a whole the difficult issues facing the world.

The opening chapters offer a general analysis of the nature of human progress, focusing on some of the psychological factors which determine whether or not societies develop a confident belief in progress. There is a brief discussion of different aspects of the broad spectrum of human progress – in particular the central but enigmatic concept of progress in happiness – in an attempt to define those aspects of our lives which are susceptible to unambiguous and measurable improvement. The book then provides an historical context for the current mood of anxiety and pessimism about the future, by describing the key conditions which were required historically for a confident belief in progress, and by exploring some of the central philosophical, religious, scientific and literary currents that have either underpinned or undermined belief in progress through

Economic growth vs welfare (progress in human welfare
Optimism, 'feel-good' factor *pessimism, 'feel-bad' factor*

the ages. Particular attention is given to the theories of the early free-market economist Adam Smith, and to the ethical doctrine of utilitarian philosophers who hold that the aim of society should be to achieve the greatest happiness of the greatest number.

The modern idea of progress has, until the last few years, seemed securely based on an apparently endless advance in scientific understanding and on the exponential wonders of economic growth. Indeed, the remarkable economic growth of the last two hundred years has seemed to provide not only the chief mechanism for delivering human progress, but also the measure of it. The second half of this book focuses more narrowly on contemporary changes in the relationship between economic growth, on the one hand, and human progress, on the other, and argues that limitations in the free-market mechanism are tending increasingly to undermine the positive link between the two. While political debate still usually assumes such a link, there are now strong reasons for believing that, at least in more developed countries, continued economic growth is becoming less of a guarantee of human progress, and that the largely unmeasured costs of economic growth are now rising faster than the benefits. In particular, environmental pressures are burgeoning, and social strains and economic insecurity are on the rise again. With political leaders under pressure to maintain economic growth rates by deregulation and globalisation, the modern pursuit of economic growth seems to be failing increasing numbers of unskilled casualties of change, while also failing to satisfy many of the increasingly middle-class aspirations of affluent societies. Moreover, the purer forms of free-market ideology are linked to a breakdown in the social ethos and to a rise in rampant individualism. It appears that economics and the pursuit of growth can no longer be isolated from the basic questions of human morality.

Central to this story are the increased levels of uncertainty resulting from ever more rapid change and the ever greater complexity of modern life. Belief in the possibility of positive change and in the ability of mankind to forecast, control and engineer such change are prerequisites for a confident belief in progress. However, particularly rapid change can increase the feeling of insecurity and disorientation amongst those sections of society where people must adjust to new circumstances more quickly than their emotional make-up and skill sets allow. At the same time, a fast pace of change can limit the ability of both the environment and our economic systems to adapt sufficiently quickly and smoothly to avoid significant negative consequences. Very rapid change can lead to

Unpredictability

increasingly chaotic and unpredictable results, especially in complex ecosystems, and many economists are becoming convinced that sharp economic shocks can have negative effects not just on societies but on the very economic growth rates they are often designed to enhance. Economies, like the people who inhabit them and the environment in which they operate, adjust best to slow and deliberate changes, with more predictable effects. The uncertainty associated with rapid change reduces both the effectiveness of rational planning and the efficiency of the invisible hand of the free market.

The principal aim of the book is to provide some explanations for the curious phenomenon of growing pessimism in many of the affluent developed countries. The problems facing developing countries are often different in scale and nature, and distinctive cultural beliefs and historical and religious backgrounds may render their reactions to economic growth and rapid change different from those of the West. For this reason, although many of the arguments of the book do apply equally to developing countries, some apply only to the First World. The greater emphasis on developed countries is certainly not intended to imply that the problems of developing countries are relatively unimportant. Indeed, the feel-bad factor in affluent countries still cannot be compared with the deep misery of hunger and disease in many countries elsewhere; and any prescription for enabling the First World to strive for better-quality growth must, of course, take into account the paramount needs of developing countries.

Detailed policy recommendations are not to be found in this book; its more general purpose is to question some of the basic assumptions behind our headlong pursuit, in the name of progress, of higher economic growth and rapid free-market deregulation. It argues that, if human progress is the paramount goal, policy-makers need to pay greater attention to the quality rather than the quantity of economic growth, and need to ensure more gradualism in the changes that societies necessarily undertake. It concludes that the invisible hand of the free market, for all its undoubted power, is not sufficient to ensure the attainment of many of the social goals which are central to our well-being and to an optimistic belief in progress. There remains an overriding need for the free market to be supported by a strong framework of morality, social cohesion and rational government intervention if we are to safeguard the environment, minimise poverty and unemployment and avoid the worst excesses of the rat race. Such a supportive framework must not be jeopardised by a wholesale glorification of individual self-interest, or by the single-minded pursuit of maximum deregulation and trade liberalisation; for if the necessary balance between the free pursuit by individuals of their own self-interest, on the one hand, and social cooperation and strong government, on the other, is destroyed beyond repair, the chances of continued human progress will not be high. Humanity will be left completely at the mercy of the free market – condemned to be its slave rather than its master.

Human progress is the paramount goal

- Quantity (speed, efficiency of economic growth is a major factor

- Quality of economic growth

. The invisible hand of the free market is not sufficient to ensure the attainment of many of the social goals which are central to our well-being, welfare, happiness

To avoid the worst excesses of the rat race we need: a strong framework of morality, social cohesion + rational government interve

CHAPTER 1

Psychology and Definition of Progress

Psychology and Perspective

The idea of human progress can arouse strong passions. To many, it is a self-evident truth that human progress has occurred and will continue; to others, belief in progress represents a failure to recognise that human nature is a constant. Such opposing views reflect the struggle between optimism and pessimism so evident throughout human thought – between the belief that we can improve our lives and a sinking feeling that the core of the problem, our human frailty, is beyond our ability to mend. This struggle between optimism and pessimism derives some of its force from being a feature as much of our views about our own personal predicament as of our views about society as a whole. Tolstoy's central character in his novel *Anna Karenina*, the passionate and restless Levin, expresses this struggle:

> As he saw all this, he began to doubt for a moment the possibility of arranging the new life he had been dreaming of during the drive. All these traces of his old life seemed to clutch him and say: 'No, you're not going to get away from us; you're not going to be different. You're going to be the same as you always have been – with your doubts, your perpetual dissatisfaction with yourself and vain attempts to amend, your failures and everlasting expectation of a happiness you won't get and which isn't possible for you.' This was what the things

② Examples of ambiguity

g.s. Berlin

said, but another, inner voice was telling him not to submit to the past, telling him a man can make what he will of himself.[1]

When applied to society as a whole, belief or otherwise in the possibility of human progress also depends, in part, on the extent to which evil and unhappiness are seen as owing to innate and unchanging disabilities in man. The quintessential Enlightenment view that evil and misery are the result not of innate failings, but rather of ignorance, prejudice and poverty, allows for optimism that the problems of humanity can be solved by greater use of reason, better education and increased material prosperity.

A confident belief in progress seems often to assume that there is a finite set of human problems, which at least in theory admit of a finite and coherent set of rational solutions. But it is far from clear that the different goals, aspirations and values of any society are finally compatible and are in totality even logically susceptible to a perfect solution. In practice, the prosecution of some important goals will tend inevitably to vitiate other deeply held values. So, for example, our pursuit of individual freedom and mobility in personal transport, in the form of the car, clashes inexorably with our wish for a cleaner and quieter environment. Furthermore, in the complex world in which we live, there are many situations in which we simply cannot predict the long-term consequences of our actions. We had no idea earlier in the century that the blameless goal of providing refrigerators for the safe storage of food to hundreds of millions of consumers would create a new and serious problem, by requiring the manufacture of CFCs that would punch a hole in the ozone layer, causing damage to plant life and millions of extra cases of skin cancer. The limits to rational foresight and prediction must limit our confidence in progress. As Isaiah Berlin puts it in his book *The Crooked Timber of Humanity*:

> It is true that some problems can be solved, some ills cured, in both the individual and the social life . . . but any study of society shows that every solution creates a new situation which breeds its own new needs and problems, new demands. The children have obtained what their parents and grandparents longed for – greater freedom, greater material welfare, a juster society; but the old ills are forgotten, and the children face new problems, brought about by the very solutions of the old ones, and these, even if they can in turn be solved, generate

new situations, and with them new requirements – and so on, for ever – and unpredictably.[2]

Belief or otherwise in progress is a manifestation, more generally, of the inherent ambivalence in our relationship with our parents and ancestors. Some societies have worshipped the dead and the past, and such respect is not fertile ground for a confident belief in progress. Legends and rituals aggrandise past figures to the status of heroes, which then represent a constant foil to the frailties of later generations. By contrast, in modern Western man, there is a deep strand of teenage rebellion against the creeds of our fathers, of self-confidence that we can see clearly what they could not begin to comprehend. The rapid progress of science and the huge technological revolutions of our age have reduced our respect for our ancestors, by appearing to reduce the relevance of what they can teach us.

Different generations often espouse quite different values and, even when the values are constant, generations have different points of view from which they apply them. This is important; for progress is as much a subjective and evaluative concept as it is a question of fact. It is necessary to establish which value yardstick we are using to measure whether or not there has been progress, and we must also understand from whose point of view the judgement is being made. As the great philosopher of history R. G. Collingwood pointed out, the older generation often sees new methods as harmful to the lifestyle and customs it holds dear; from its value standpoint or point of view, change is then not progress but decadence. Likewise, the younger generation tends not to make a neutral evaluation of the life enjoyed by the previous generation, but instead 'seems driven to escape from sympathy with it by a kind of instinctive effort to free itself from parental influences and bring about the change on which it is blindly resolved'.[3]

This disjunction of both value and viewpoint between generations results in us normally judging the recent past in the light of our own distinct values, with the consequence that we tend to see recent history as a progressive development towards our current values and our own conception of the good life. It is an obvious truism that the history of the last five hundred years, written from the value standpoint of those in bygone ages who believed passionately in the divine right of kings, or in the paramount value of spiritual over material salvation, would look more like a story of regress than one of progress. In fact, of course, history tends to be written and read from the viewpoint of victorious contemporary values, giving the past the appearance of progress towards the objects of today's value. We judge the significance of past events in terms of their role in the evolution of our dominant goals and of our conception of the good life, and this gives our perception of history a clearer sense of direction than would often have been apparent to those experiencing it at the time.

The gap between the values and viewpoints of different generations increases in proportion to the rapidity of change. Faster social and economic change tends to bring more rapid changes in social values. It also increases the disadvantage felt by those required to adjust to change at a faster rate than they are able to update their skill-base or adapt emotionally to new pressures. As a result, more rapid change will often increase the divergence of view between generations as to whether change represents progress. Furthermore, as technological and economic changes accelerate, the social generations become shorter. Skills and values become out of date more quickly and the ranks of the old and those dispossessed by progress, extend to those barely middle-aged. Without change there can be no progress, but change usually has casualties as well as beneficiaries. A greater rapidity of change, while further underpinning the faith in progress of the beneficiaries, will often increase the number of casualties who will take a more pessimistic view of it.

Some social historians are now arguing that the disjunction of value and viewpoint between generations has become so great that the past is actually dying as a relevant factor in contemporary life. History is seen as irrelevant, the skills of the last generation as useless. At the same time, old customs embodying collective moral wisdom (or prejudice) are wilfully discarded and old communities are sundered by greater mobility. In this environment, it can be argued, it is not just the older generation who may feel disoriented. The young, too, living exclusively in the present, may have no touchstone against which to value the new, and no way, even assuming the will to do so, of making an informed comparison of their way of life with that of past generations. The past is no longer part of their souls and they cannot learn from it. All knowledge becomes contemporary. It is still the case that a farmer who buys a tractor can relate his fortunate position to that of his father or grandfather who had to plough his farm laboriously with horses, his boots heavy with mud; the farmer – doing the oldest job in our societies – still has a yardstick against which to measure change and judge whether it is progress, and he still makes use of some inherited wisdom. It is less easy for a software programmer, conversing with colleagues on three continents on the Internet, working fifteen hours a day out of his City flat, listening to pop music on his Sony

Walkman and consuming takeaway pizzas, to relate his lifestyle to that of previous generations, and to judge its value.

The necessity to recognise different value yardsticks and perspectives applies, of course, within any one generation nearly as much as it applies across generations. This is especially so since change often alters the distribution of benefits both within a single society and between different countries so that, even among those who share the same yardsticks, the judgement of whether or not there has been progress will differ. Self-evidently, progress rarely affects all individuals (or countries) equally, as there are winners and losers in most dynamic situations. What seems to be progress from the point of view of one group or society may appear to be regress from the point of view of another. E. H. Carr, in his book *What is History?*, provides an amusing and down-to-earth example of this point, with a quotation from the historian A. J. P. Taylor:

> All this talk about the decline of civilization, he writes, 'means only that university professors used to have domestic servants and now do their own washing-up'. Of course, for former domestic servants, washing-up by professors may be a symbol of progress.[4]

Frequently, new predicaments may affect those in the vanguard of change differently from those who lag behind. The rapid growth in computer technology in the workplace is a particular boon to those with up-to-date skills. For those with out-of-date or nonexistent skills in the new medium, it may spell marginalisation and job destruction. Similarly, the rapid globalisation of many industries resulting from moves to greater free trade, free capital movements and computer technology is of huge benefit to people with highly prized skills or plenty of capital. To the unskilled worker in developed countries, it is likely to mean fewer jobs and declining rates of pay. When those benefiting from change are in a large majority in any society, we would expect there to be a widespread belief in progress; when only a small minority benefits, one would expect a pervasive feel-bad factor, with optimism confined to the fortunate minority.

The Broad Spectrum of Human Progress

For all the plurality of values and optical distortions of different points of view explored above, the idea of human progress has been a durable, even dominant, concept for most of the last two hundred years. Before we can begin to make a judgement about whether this dominance was justified and whether it may now be waning, we must distinguish between the different kinds of progress contained within the broad umbrella notion of 'human progress'. For certain aspects of human life are more susceptible to unambiguous improvement than others.

Across the broad spectrum of different kinds of progress, it is helpful to distinguish between those aspects of life where the transmission of acquired knowledge and accumulated experience or skill is central, and those aspects which are to a greater extent a function of innate character and abilities, of our biological inheritance. To use a metaphor from the science of evolution, the transmission of acquired characteristics from one generation to another would generally allow for much more rapid change than the slow genetic evolution by natural selection on the basis of random changes in our biological inheritance. The history of knowledge, of science and of material welfare resembles the putative transmission of acquired characteristics. The progress of underlying emotional make-up or of innate artistic imagination, however, if it exists at all, must be closer to the long evolutionary timescale of Darwinian natural selection. Just as our brains are no bigger than they were 10,000 years ago, so too there is no reason to believe that our innate emotional impulses or artistic imagination are different in quality. In most of the spectrum of human activity, of course, there is a combination of accumulations of technique, skills, knowledge, institutions and artefacts, on the one hand, and of almost constant innate impulses and ability, on the other. These two strands – the cumulative and the near constant – are often difficult to disentangle.

Progress in science, technology and medicine is at one end of the spectrum. No one can deny the enormous strides made in the last few hundred years in all three, as the increasing body of knowledge and understanding has led to a snowballing development of new disciplines. The cumulative, even exponential nature of knowledge is clear and, while the impact of this knowledge on our lives is often somewhat ambiguous, the increasing explanatory power of science is matched, to some extent at least, by a growing ability to control the natural world. Ever since Francis Bacon in the early seventeenth century emphasised the key importance of experimentation and of reaching principles inductively from observation of particular facts, truth has, in his words, been 'the daughter of time', not of ancient authority. His early opposition to the sterility of an exclusive focus on deductive reasoning from axioms held to be self-evident by philosophers, and his support instead for scientific experimentation, together with his belief that the true purpose of knowledge is not the satisfaction of speculative contemplation but the improved welfare of humanity, foreshadowed the fruitful direction taken ever since by science, technology and medicine.

Material progress has been the other principal mainstay of the modern belief in human progress. Like knowledge, material prosperity is cumulative and capable, for a time at least, of exponential growth. Rising material prosperity has been the dominant feature of Western societies since the sudden acceleration of economic growth which began some two hundred years ago. From the time that Adam Smith published *The Wealth of Nations*, which examined the origins of wealth creation, the liberal free market he espoused has been seen to deliver an indefinite augmentation of wealth and living standards. Such economic growth has succeeded in making belief in perpetual progress in welfare, if not happiness, the dominant faith of modern man. Moreover, the modern liberal economy has seemed not only to promise the morally attractive outcome of maximising the welfare of society as a whole, but to do so without even requiring individuals to have consciously moral or social intentions. For the 'invisible hand' of the market is seen to lead to the most efficient satisfaction of the wants of different market participants, and in this sense to maximise the social good, merely by harnessing the selfish desires of individuals to further their own ends. In truth, of course, there are important shortcomings in the pure liberal blueprint of economics as a generator of the social good, and these are the subject of the second half of this book. While many political leaders continue to believe that the relationship between economic growth and progress in welfare is very close, it is clear that the links between the two are coming under increasing strain. Economic growth carries with it negative aspects that are not well measured nor always well understood.

Moving across the spectrum from aspects of life dominated by cumulative knowledge, skill and prosperity towards those aspects dominated by more innate human abilities, it is worth starting briefly with notions of progress in art and literature. Progress in art is a dubious concept. The pottery designs of the Minoans in Crete some 3,500 years ago are not inferior to those of Wedgwood china of the eighteenth century; the Impressionists are not better painters than Raphael; Bernard Shaw's plays do not represent a higher form of drama than that of Shakespeare, or William Golding's novels a more developed art form than those of Jane Austen. In each case the artistic conception is radically different, and we cannot describe it as progress in artistic imagination. As E. H. Gombrich points out in *The Story of Art*, each generation of artists sees itself to some extent as in rebellion against the standards and the conception of its predecessors. This provides movement and change in artistic endeavour but it is necessary to avoid, to quote Gombrich:

> naïve misrepresentation of the constant change in art as a continuous progress . . . we must realise that each gain or progress in one direction entails a loss in another, and that this subjective progress, in spite of its importance, does not correspond to an objective increase in artistic values.[5]

Even artistic technique is not always a one-way continuum, with no one for many generations able to rival the brilliant blue of medieval stained glass.

The concept of moral progress is more contentious still. Some argue that apparent moral advance is no more than a new coating of veneer over the unchanging reality of the 'beast within'; others assert that durable systems of restraining ethics can be evolved that guarantee progress in morality, despite the unchanging nature of our underlying emotional impulses; while still others hold that human nature itself is capable of perfection. It is clearly true that social institutions may be improved over time; slavery has been abolished in all civilised countries, and the provision of health care for the poor in developed countries is much improved over that of a century ago. So, too, the European Union, the World Trade Organisation and other multinational bodies have been developed to allow countries to find more harmonious methods than hitherto of resolving their differences and balancing their conflicting requirements. But it also seems clear that individual societies, like international politics, continue to reflect the unchanging realities of human nature, and transient social and cultural fashions, just as much as the rationality of their evolving institutions.

Some Enlightenment thinkers, such as the Marquis de Condorcet, held the optimistic view that man's innate character could be moulded and improved by rational laws, institutions and education; man himself could be perfected as a result of the indefinite advance of knowledge. Some of the early socialists, too, like Robert Owen, thought that bad social institutions were solely responsible for the evil and misery which existed in society, and that social reform could abolish not only poverty but vice itself. Such doctrines of human perfectibility are hard to hold in this most sophisticated but bloody of centuries. The wars of the twentieth century have not only shown the persistence of extreme evil. They have also demonstrated that the awe-inspiring progress of reason in science and technology is, in itself, ambiguous from a moral perspective, being as powerful in the generation of evil outcomes as of benign. The degree of human progress that results from scientific advance or from economic growth is crucially dependent on the underlying moral attributes of those who harness them.

Throughout history, many have believed that moral and spiritual progress is inversely correlated with increases in knowledge and rises in material prosperity. In both the legend of Pandora's box and the Book of Genesis, evil was seen to originate with the fateful inquisitiveness of mankind (or of women, to be more precise). Eating the fruit of the Tree of Knowledge led to eviction from Paradise. In addition, many ancient philosophers, and the Christian Church in several of its guises, have preached asceticism as the best route to greater happiness and progress in morality. Most now would take a more agnostic line on the link between morality, on the one hand, and knowledge or prosperity, on the other; they would assume that underlying human nature does indeed change little, and that while there can be changes for better or worse in the restraining social ethics which guide societies, these changes are not necessarily closely correlated, either inversely or positively, with economic growth and scientific progress. There is, in this view, no necessary direction in human morality. The ethical and social dimension of economic growth is discussed in more detail later in the book, where it will be argued that, on the contrary, the free-market pursuit of greater prosperity may in fact be linked to a sustained *decline* in the morality of our societies.

Of course, in the area of social ethics above all others, variations of value and viewpoint allow very different assessments to be made. In the eyes of some, the breakdown of neighbourhood and of the codes of social morality that went with it, under pressure from rapid economic change, is a calamity; for others it is a welcome release from a suffocatingly cohesive social and moral order and has allowed much greater social tolerance. Nevertheless, there are few value standpoints from which the horrors of modern warfare, the bestiality of the Nazi holocaust or the war in Bosnia do not underline the precariousness of any social and moral progress. In particular, the spectre of World War I continues to haunt the minds of many who would be optimistic – a war waged by European countries at the very apogee of their civilisation; where a cocktail of popular nationalism, modern technology (the machine gun and railway) and a breathtaking failure of imagination on the part of political and army leaders allowed the slaughter of countless millions of innocent men. The spectre is immortalised in the poems of that lost generation, like these lines from a rare survivor, Siegfried Sassoon:

> *Lines of grey, muttering faces, masked with fear,*
> *They leave their trenches, going over the top,*
> *While time ticks blank and busy on their wrists,*
> *And hope, with furtive eyes and grappling fists*
> *Flounders in mud. O Jesus, make it stop!*[6]

Even today a drive across the eerily flattened landscape of Picardy, in northern France, where the main feature is fields of white crosses, can remind us how fragile and precious is the veneer of peace and civilisation.

CHAPTER 2

Progress in Happiness and the Good Life

Central to any discussion of human progress is the contentious notion of progress in happiness. In some people's eyes, the giant strides in welfare, longer life expectancy and increasing material prosperity make it curious to doubt the existence of such progress. But others point out that happiness is an elastic and complex concept and is quite different from the simple meeting of quantifiable material desires and from the more measurable concept of welfare; they argue that this makes comparison between different generations difficult or even impossible. To address this divergence of view, this chapter will first explore briefly the myriad of different meanings contained in our conception of 'happiness', and its relationship to the notion of the 'good life'; secondly, given this clearer definition of happiness, it will assess how logical and practical it is to compare happiness between periods and hence to judge whether there has been progress in happiness. The analysis of happiness and its importance as a goal of human activity is one of the central and most fraught areas of moral philosophy, and must remain largely outside the scope of this book. For our purposes, it is only necessary to give a flavour of the different arguments as they relate to the theme of progress and to the explanation of the feel-bad factor.

Bentham and the early utilitarians argued that happiness should be equated to pleasure and the absence of pain. It was possible, in their view, literally to calculate and compare units of happiness in a society purely on the basis of quantitative factors like the duration or intensity of feelings of pleasure or pain. Such a hedonistic notion of happiness, and one which purports to allow inter-personal comparison in quasi-arithmetical terms, is apt to seem unsatisfactory for two reasons. First, even if happiness is equated with simple physical or psychological sensations, it is difficult to see how the sensations felt by one person could in practice be compared with those felt by another; even on this narrow definition, it would be next to impossible to assess progress over time in the sum of such pleasures across a whole population – unless everyone was connected by way of electrodes and transmitters in the brain to a central monitoring station. Secondly, the definition of happiness as consisting simply of sensations of pleasure and the absence of pain is unconvincingly narrow. This is partly because the notion of happiness seems to include many facets of our experience other than sensations of pleasure, and partly because of the intuitive need to distinguish between different types of pleasure. We would not normally accept that happiness can be secured simply by the absence of physiologically identifiable pain and the presence of physiologically identifiable sensations of pleasure, such as sexual pleasure or drug-induced euphoria, however intense, without reference to the conditions in which these sensations are produced. In part, this is because (as Bentham would allow) certain types and conditions of pleasure are more likely to persist and to be free from unpleasant side-effects. So, for example, the pleasures of a secure and loving relationship have a higher chance of being intense and satisfactory in the long run than those derived from prostitutes or pornography. Likewise, prolonged use of drugs may lead on to the unfulfilled cravings of addictive dependency and a life of crime. But more important than these 'extrinsic' factors, there appear to be 'intrinsic' qualitative differences between different pleasures – between, for example, the pleasures of sex in a stable long-term relationship and the continual casual gratification of the promiscuous; many people would also argue that there is an important requirement for authenticity of experience before pleasurable sensations can be classed as part of what it is to be happy, and would argue, for example, that drug-induced pleasures are not authentic because the use of drugs compromises a person's identity.

Later utilitarians, like J. S. Mill, recognised that Bentham's analysis was too simplistic and, in order to make the 'hedonistic' conception of happiness more convincing, attempted to introduce the notion of the 'quality' as well as the 'quantity' of pleasures. Mill pointed out that some pleasures have an intrinsic quality such that a small amount of them will be preferred by those who have experienced them to a prodigious quantity of a lower-quality pleasure. Most people cannot be happy at the prospect of being a contented drone once their sights have been raised and their eyes opened to the possible richness of a life not given over entirely to sybaritic pleasures. In part, this departure by Mill from simple hedonism was an implicit recognition that happiness has some evaluative content; the prospect and attainment of pleasures will only make us happy when we judge the pleasures to be in keeping with our own sense of self-esteem, with our sense of our own personal identity and with our own ideal of what it is to be a fulfilled person, and when the pleasures are derived from sources which we approve of. Even if it could be proved that there is a drug capable of changing our basic outlook and keeping us on a permanent high in some everlasting orgy, thereby rendering us permanently in the grip of genuinely pleasurable sensations, without a care in the world, most people contemplating the prospect of such a situation from the outside would argue that it would not constitute genuine happiness for them. Control, personal identity, self-esteem and the authenticity and intrinsic quality of pleasures seem to be important to happiness. The later utilitarian development of the concept of happiness away from a crude hedonism has the effect, of course, of making the task of comparing happiness quasi-arithmetically between people and across time even more forlorn. For if the task of comparing the crude physiological sensations of different people is technically unfeasible, it is essentially impossible on any single, objectively derived scale to sum pleasures which vary not only in a quantitative dimension, but also in terms of their intrinsic qualitative worth.

The concept of happiness includes many facets beyond the experience of pleasures, high or low. We often say that we are happy with our life, happily married or happy in our job when we do not mean to say that there is an identifiable, let alone measurable, sensation of pleasure present all the time. To some extent, at least, the concept of happiness seems to contain within it the idea of being pleased with things, achievements or activities. Elizabeth Telfer, in her book, *Happiness*, explores the notion of happiness as an attitude of mind which can include the crucial notion of being pleased with things. This is a much wider notion than enjoyment or pleasurable sensation, and can cover reactions to things not enjoyed in themselves but with which we are pleased because of their possible results. To say that we have a happy life, then, can mean that we are basically pleased with the way things are and with our achievements. This is certainly a much less crude version of happiness defined as a mental state. But, as Telfer points out, this version undoubtedly leaves individuals as the only ultimate authorities of whether or not they are happy; happiness on this account is not an attribute that can be ascribed with objective certainty to people by others. Nor, critically for our enterprise, can it be compared with any precision between people, let alone across generations. One man's happiness might be another's discontent. Happiness, in this version, does not consist of the acquisition of wealth, health or knowledge – all things which can be measured, at least to some extent; instead it is a subjective state, which might or might not be produced by, and be dependent on, more measurable factors.

Some have attempted to define happiness in terms of the satisfaction or fulfilment of desires and wants, and to some extent at least it is a truism that we will not be happy if all our major wants and desires are unfulfilled. In modern liberal economies, this definition is implicit in much of the political debate. It is assumed that, since citizens express their desires and wants in the marketplace (or at the ballot box), they will be happier if more of their wants are satisfied by the measurable phenomenon of economic growth (or by government action). But any definition of happiness in terms of the satisfaction of wants or desires has its problems too. For example, when we choose self-sacrifice to further some cause we hold dear, it does not accord with our normal understanding of the word 'happiness' to say that the attainment of this desired end (or even the prospect of its attainment) is happiness; we desire the ultimate outcome for its own sake, despite the damage its achievement through self-sacrifice will cause to our happiness.

A further objection to defining happiness solely in terms of the satisfaction of wants or desires is that it makes sense to say that a person can change from being unhappy with his lot to being happy with his lot, without any more of his desires or wants being satisfied; he or she can have a more resigned attitude, or a more cheerful disposition, in the face of the same circumstances. In this case, it might be argued that the new more resigned and realistic attitude or cheerful disposition is in effect a lessening of the wants or desires in question, either in number or in intensity. There is a critical distinction between achieving happiness through the satisfaction of desires, and achieving it as a result of removing the desires or reducing their intensity. For if Epicurus was right, and happiness (defined in his case as pleasure) comes in large part from restricting one's desires, ambitions and needs, it may well be the case that the less ambitious civilisations or individuals are the happier ones. The modern world and the modern economy continually creates new desires and wants, as fast or faster than it satisfies existing ones. If happiness is a balance of wants and the satisfaction of these wants (wants being negative and satisfaction of them counting as positive), or if (as Epicurus argued) happiness is the tranquillity which is only possible without the pain of unfulfilled desires, it may be that more primitive societies were happier than those of today. This was certainly the view of Lucretius, the Epicurean poet of first century BC Rome, who argued that contemporary people derive no more enjoyment from their refined activities and goals than did the woodland race sprung from the soil:

> For what we have here and now, unless we have known some-
> thing more pleasing in the past, gives the greatest satisfaction
> and is reckoned the best of its kind. Afterwards the discovery
> of something new and better blunts and vitiates our enjoy-
> ment of the old. So it is that we have lost our taste in acorns.[1]

It is this inflation and escalation of wants and desires which, in Lucretius' words, causes mankind to be 'perpetually the victim of a pointless and futile martyrdom, fretting life away in fruitless worries through failure to realise what limit is set to acquisition and to the growth of genuine pleasure'.[2]

An argument against this anti-development position would be that it is not only the satisfaction of desires and the lack of unsatisfied desires that is important to happiness, but also the character of the desires them-selves and the richness of life. The richness of life was central to Mill's focus on the quality of pleasures. But it is important to realise that the richness of life can be defined by objective criteria independently of the subjective experiences of contentment or pleasure. As the philosopher Anthony Kenny puts it in his article, 'Aristotle on Happiness':

> The notions of contentment and of richness of life are in part
> independent, and this leads to paradox in the concept of hap-
> piness, which involves both . . . The greater a person's
> education and sensitivity, the greater his capacity for the
> 'higher' pleasures and therefore for a richer life; yet increase in
> education and sensitivity brings with it increase in the number
> of desires, and a corresponding lesser likelihood of their satis-
> faction. Instruction and emancipation in one way favour
> happiness, and in another militate against it. To increase a
> person's chances of happiness, in the sense of fullness of life,
> is *eo ipso* to decrease his chances of happiness, in the sense of
> satisfaction of desire.[3]

The definition of happiness given by Aristotle in the *Nicomachean Ethics* has also been very influential. It is important to stress that the Greek word '*eudaimonia*' is not exactly the same as our word 'happiness'; it has a wider meaning of 'well-being' and 'general satisfactoriness'. As Professor of Greek A. H. Armstrong once noted, the '*eudaimon*' man not only feels happy, but it can really be said that all is well with his life. Happiness in this wider sense (as used by Aristotle) therefore equates to something closer to our notion of the best possible life, or the 'good life'. Without going into details, Aristotle's definition of this broader concept of happiness is that it consists of successful activity – the fulfilment of one's distinctively human potentialities. This notion of the achievement of one's potential, of the achievement of excellence in one's principal activities or function, is certainly a feature of our notion of the good life, too, but seems somewhat incomplete on its own; this is especially so if it is intended as an account of happiness. Happiness cannot be defined simply as the successful accomplishment of one's goal or characteristic activity. For it is possible for someone to achieve all his personal goals and realise his potential in key areas and still not be happy. But even if we discard Aristotle's own definition as incomplete, the very notion of the 'good life' is important to the concept of progress in happiness. For there is an important element of objectivity in this general notion of the good life; it is something which, unlike subjective feelings or attitudes, can be judged – to some extent at least – from outside. This is important, since when we talk of progress in happiness, there is often present in the discussion, either implicitly or explicitly, an element of discussion about progress in the realisation of the good life. This good life might include, for us, general welfare and prosperity, the minimisation of pain-inducing situations (e.g., disease) and the ability for men and women to fulfil their potentialities. Such notions of the progressive attainment of the good life come closer to being amenable to genuine objective assessment – between societies and across generations – than are the other more subjective notions of happiness we have surveyed.

It may be useful to allude to just one more of the many arguments about happiness at this stage. We have seen that for Epicurus the key to happiness was tranquillity and the absence of any dynamic process of desire-creation and subsequent striving for desire-fulfilment. For him modern economic growth, with its constant expansion of desires and pressures, would have been anathema. The English philosopher Thomas Hobbes held a very different view. For him happiness involves, to quote Bertrand Russell's account, 'continual progress; it consists in prospering,

not in having prospered; there is no such thing as a static happiness –
excepting, of course, the joys of heaven'.[4] This is a key part of our
modern assumptions about happiness. Modern man is a striving animal,
not easily content with endless repetition in pleasure as in anything else.
Defenders of the modern way of life and of economic growth as the natural promoter of happiness will point to the huge expansion of diversity
and novelty, particularly in the area of consumer goods, and will argue
that, as the old adage goes, variety is the spice of life. However, even if
this is true, it should be noted that the modern economy often constricts
variety in the workplace as much as it expands variety for consumers.
Many jobs become more and more specialised, narrow and repetitive,
with the result not only of inducing more boredom but also of rendering
it more difficult for people to switch from one form of employment to
another – reducing variety still further.

   In summing up this brief discussion of the nature of happiness, it can
be said that no single notion of what constitutes happiness seems complete. It is best to see it as an amorphous and broad umbrella concept –
including within it such subjective notions as sensations of pleasure, the
attitude of being pleased with things, the satisfaction of desires and the
absence of important unfulfilled desires. Because of the amorphous and
indeterminate nature of the concept and because of the ultimate impossibility of making precise comparisons between people – let alone across
generations – about the nature and strength of these subjective personal
feelings, attitudes or desires, it is clear that a rigorous and objective
judgement as to the existence or otherwise of progress in happiness is
bound to remain elusive. The concept of happiness does also include
more objective factors which can be ascribed to people by others, such as
the richness of life, but such objective notions are more often associated
with the concept of the 'good life'. Progress in the realisation of the good
life is a more coherent and quantifiable notion – akin to that of progress
in welfare. The good life can be defined according to the consensus taste
or values of a particular society or group, and then different societies and
historical periods can – at least to some extent – be judged objectively
against this chosen definition, to establish whether or not there has been
progress. This distinction between objective factors (that make up a definition of the good life) and subjective factors (the feelings, attitudes
and desires of individuals) helps explain the radical divergence of views
on whether or not the existence of progress in happiness can be established. Those who argue that there has clearly been progress are usually
closer to making a judgement about the progressive realisation of their

notion of the good life. Those who are sceptical are often focusing on the more elusive subjective factors. It is at least coherent to attempt to judge whether there has been progress towards a particular definition of the good life. It is much less coherent to claim that we can know for certain that our subjective feelings of happiness in themselves are greater or smaller than those of another generation, or that we can, even in theory, make precise comparisons of subjective feelings between people and across generations.

The subjective notions of happiness and the more objective features of the good life are, of course, linked. For most groups or societies will define their conception of the good life as containing those things which they agree tend to lead to greater pleasure or desire-satisfaction, or tend to make us more pleased with life. As a result, care still needs to be taken in making comparisons between periods, since the definition of the good life in one society may be quite different from that prevalent in another, as the recognised sources of enjoyment change, expectations alter and new desires develop. We cannot be sure that changes we see as positive for the development of *our* notion of the good life would have seemed positive to those having a different definition of the good life. This then is another set of hurdles to the establishment of a notion of progress in happiness: not only is there no necessarily very close correlation between the objective elements of a given society's conception of the good life and the subjective experience of happiness by individuals in that society; but also the very conception of the good life can itself change significantly over time. As Collingwood put it:

> Can we speak of progress in happiness or comfort or satisfaction? Obviously not. Different ways of life are differentiated by nothing more clearly than by differences between the things that people habitually enjoy, the conditions which they find comfortable, and the achievements they regard as satisfactory.[5]

Moreover, it is often very difficult to ascertain facts about what people actually derived enjoyment from (or were pleased with) in different generations and hence what they would have included in their notion of the good life. There is a danger that we may project on to the past the sources of pleasure or happiness we recognise in ourselves and our society, and then assess whether or not these sources of enjoyment were present in the past to a greater or lesser extent. We might, for example, see the absence of cars, television or washing machines, and project on to the past the sense of loss we would feel faced by their absence. Alternatively – if of a more romantic disposition – we might see in the past more silence and a slower pace of life and project our envy of that on to the past. But this projection of our feelings and attitudes might not be valid as evidence for the thesis of progress or regress in happiness. It might also mislead us about what earlier generations would have seen as central to their notion of the good life, and what they valued. For values, expectations and sources of enjoyment can all change radically over time, and evidence for these changes is often elusive. In particular, we may underestimate, or occasionally overstate, the enjoyment derived by previous generations from things that have been casualties of change and of the growth of material prosperity – things that may no longer even form part of our consciousness.

Take for example the aesthetic attributes of unspoilt countryside, with its wild flowers, clean air and birdsong. It is generally held that the derivation of happiness from these things is essentially an urban invention or phenomenon, and that the idylls of Theocritus, Virgil and Wordsworth reflect a romantic view of the natural world and country life from a safe distance; it is such urban literati who count the costs of change and of the destruction of the ancient countryside, not the hungry and overworked peasants. There is, of course, something very idealised and unrealistic about the peaceful vision of Arcadia from Theocritus down, with the shepherds rarely working, but playing pipes and listening to the larks and finches sing, with pears at their feet and apples at their side.[6] But is it not strangely patronising to think that primitive or rural peoples did not enjoy many of these things amidst their toil, even if they shared none of the cloying romanticism of the urban poets? Conclusive proof is hard if not impossible to find. But consider, for example, Homer's epic, *The Iliad* – composed in a hard rural age – and notice the aesthetic imagery of the god Zeus' union with the goddess Hera:

> *So speaking, the son of Kronos caught his wife in his arms. There*
> *underneath them the divine earth broke into young, fresh*
> *grass, and into dewy clover, crocus and hyacinth*
> *so thick and soft it held the hard ground deep away from them.*[7]

Many of Homer's similes, too, give glimpses of the natural world and man's care for it. Elsewhere in *The Iliad* there is a beautiful description of a snowstorm which 'stills the winds asleep in the solid drift', enshrouds the mountains and the plains, 'and the surf that breaks against it is stilled'[8] – surely not lines composed in an age without aesthetic appreciation for the natural world. The pottery designs and wall paintings of the Minoan period in Crete, some 3,500 years ago, also suggest aesthetic appreciation; although some are religious in character, many feature animals, plants and gardens full of flowers – with plump partridges in the grass – apparently for their simple aesthetic appeal. And notice the sensuous pleasure taken in flowering meadows and a babbling brook in these lines from the sixth-century-BC poet Sappho, a gentlewoman to be sure, but growing up in the small rural community of Lesbos:

> Here to the pure temple where stands a grove of apple trees and altars smoking with frankincense. Here cool water rustles through the apple branches. The whole place is shaded with rose bushes, and sleep flows down from the shimmering leaves. Here blooms a meadow where horses pasture, rich with blooms of spring, and the wind breathes sweet fragrance.[9]

Her vignette of the moon rising – 'The rosy fingered moon, outshining the stars, pours her light over the salt sea and equally on flowery fields'[10] – shows a similar aesthetic delight in nature.

These quotations suggest that people of the rural past did indeed derive some aesthetic enjoyment from the natural beauty of unspoilt countryside, which is now largely lost in our mechanical age of industrial farming, neon lighting and the noise and pollution of motor traffic. More obviously, rural people could take just as much satisfaction in a job well done as we can. Indeed, the enjoyment derived in a rural age is likely to have come much more often from pride and satisfaction in the successful nurturing of plant or beast, or from the thrill of successfully taming nature, than from simple aesthetic delight. We can also assume that those rural people in the past who were lucky enough to have sufficient to eat may have derived as much, or perhaps more, sensuous pleasure from food as do those in a modern society. Homer's *Iliad* and *Odyssey* are festooned with lengthy descriptions of the preparation and enjoyment of feasts. Those in the present day who are blessed with the chance to eat fish grilled only hours rather than days after it is caught, or fresh lamb chops sprinkled with the perfumed juice from a newly picked lemon, or experience the exquisite biting taste of watercress cut that morning, know that our palates miss out on many of the delights available to more primitive rural peoples living closer to the land. Processed, packaged, transported and refrigerated food is insipid in comparison; modern urban man needs to enliven meals with delicacies because of the very blandness of his basic fare.

Those of unromantic disposition may argue that since rural people chose to move to cities, and still often do so in developing countries, their choice reveals that the attractions of urban life are perceived to outweigh such simple pleasures, and proves that work in factories or offices is seen as preferable to the slog of farming. But the counter-argument is that those who changed their lifestyle by migrating really had no choice, since economic change undercut the rural way of life as a viable option, just as much as it built an attractive and tempting alternative. In one well-documented case, it is evident that a rural civilisation fought hard to maintain its way of life with a passion that was no mere nostalgia. The surviving fragments of speech from the Red Indians of the last century demonstrate the close spiritual bond between people and land, and a love of the land that left them desolate and disoriented without it. In 1833, in happier times, Arapooish, a Crow chief, described lovingly to a fur trapper the delights of his land, 'where the air is sweet and cool, the grasses fresh, and the bright streams come tumbling out of the snow-banks' and where animals are plentiful. His statement ends with the ringing words of satisfaction: 'The Crow country is exactly in the right place. Everything good is to be found there. There is no place like Crow country.'[11] Just forty years later, the majestic herds of buffalo, once numbering thirty million, on which the Plains Indians depended, and with which they had a deep spiritual understanding, were all gone. As Alvin Josephy records in his book, *500 Nations*, the destruction of the buffalo, and the increasing pressure on the Indians to live on reservations, meant the disappearance of the people's way of life and a fracture in the spiritual bond between land and soul. The grief caused is palpable in many of the recorded sayings of the period – as in this impassioned statement by the great Kiowa chief Satanta, or White Bear:

> I love the land and the buffalo, and will not part with it . . . I want the children raised as I was. I don't want to settle. I love to roam over the prairies. There I feel free and happy, but when we settle down we grow pale and die.[12]

To the Red Indians, then, and to many rural peoples, the natural world was the very fabric of their existence and, whether or not it consciously formed part of their conception of the good life, we can assume they derived enjoyment and occasionally deep satisfaction from it: from the freedom of the prairies, from the sweet smell of freshly cut grass or fermenting hay, or from the exquisite taste of newly caught fish. Much that we see as quaint or pretty, like thatched cottages, may have seemed a regrettable necessity in a poor community. But familiarity does not always breed contempt. Modern man still gets a thrill from an accelerating car, despite traffic jams and pollution. Our problem, if we want to attempt to prove or disprove the theory of progress in happiness, is that it is impossible to make meaningful comparisons between, say, the satisfactions derived in one generation from riding free over the prairies and those derived in another from driving a fast car. Nor can we prove that a past generation would, if alive now, agree with our definition of the good life; they might find the absence of a number of factors they valued to be intolerable.

To many, though, scepticism about our ability to establish progress in happiness, or to establish an objective notion of the good life applicable to all generations and ages, is typical of romantic middle-class academics, and has no relationship to the real world. As Wilfred Beckermann argues in his book, *Small is Stupid*, how can the eradication of so many diseases, the transformation of life expectancy, particularly for women and infants, not have had a dramatic impact on human happiness? Does modern anxiety or unhappiness really compare with the pain of watching your child die of TB or scarlet fever?

> To maintain, as do some critics of economic growth, that the conditions today are more conducive to mental anxiety on account of a faster pace of technical progress exhibits either a complete ignorance of what life was really like for working people in the not too distant past or a complete lack of imagination about what such conditions must have meant to the average working man.[13]

There are few who would not have some sympathy with this sentiment. It may be true that the amount of happiness people attain is only very imperfectly correlated with changes in welfare and in their objective circumstances, and it may be true that we have to rely on imagination, not objective facts, to assess changes between generations in the level of happiness. But this need not make us totally sceptical of any notion of progress in happiness at all. There is room for inspired conjecture as to what would have brought happiness or unhappiness to earlier generations, and what would have been included in *their* notion of the good life.

The "good life"
objectively

This is particularly so for such stark issues as childhood illnesses and death in childbirth.

Nevertheless, if we want to move beyond conjecture, inspired or otherwise, to the area of rigorous analysis, it is necessary to confine ourselves to an assessment of progress in welfare, that is, to an assessment of how far we have succeeded in the progressive realisation of *our* notion of what is objectively the good life. Given our values and the sources of enjoyment and despair we understand, it may not be too difficult to construct a list of key items of welfare which most of us in twentieth-century developed countries could broadly agree upon as essential to our notion of the good life; the list would include sufficient food and shelter, health, safe childbirth, educational opportunities, sufficient employment, the chance for fulfilment in work for women as well as for men, law and order, and a clean environment. It then becomes possible, in principle, to set about constructing statistical measures to gauge the degree of progress or regress. The factors alluded to by Beckermann above would, in themselves, make any such assessment of the last hundred years in developed countries come out firmly in support of the thesis of progress in welfare. However, it remains a fraught question whether all the objective factors of welfare, and of our notion of the good life, can in fact meaningfully be weighted and combined into a single index, or statistical series, that enables us to make a unitary assessment of the degree of progress. In later chapters we will return to this question when examining the critical links between progress in welfare and measurable economic growth, and when analysing why these links may now be weakening. By contrast, progress in happiness, as distinct from welfare, cannot finally be central to our analysis. Happiness may be the goal of all our activities. But it should be clear from the discussion above that both the nebulous nature of the concept and the impossibility of comparing rigorously the strength or quality of subjective happiness across generations make assessments of progress in happiness belong not to the realms of analysis but to the domain of imagination and conjecture.

CHAPTER 3

The Early History of Belief in Progress

To arrive at a clearer understanding of the nature of belief in human progress and the conditions required for it, it is useful to consider some aspects of the historical evolution of the modern idea of progress and our belief in it. There is no attempt here to give a comprehensive account of the history of the idea of progress. Such a mammoth task lies outside the scope of this book and has been undertaken by two more qualified authors: J. B. Bury, in *The Idea of Progress*, and R. Nisbet, in *History of the Idea of Progress*. The aim over the next four chapters is merely to highlight certain specific features of the history and philosophy of the idea of progress which can help provide a better understanding of the ambiguities within the concept. This should also enable us to gain a clearer understanding of the reasons for the still inconclusive struggle in the human psyche between optimism that human progress is possible, or even inevitable, and pessimism that the human condition is, in many respects, not amenable to improvement. This chapter analyses five central conditions for a belief in progress, and traces them through the slow and often faltering evolution of such a belief from ancient times up to the sudden burst of optimism in the age of Enlightenment.

Five Conditions for Belief

Any historical survey of the idea of progress – especially one in a few pages – is fraught with limitations and dangers. To the extent that a belief in progress is a state of mind linked to man's optimism and pessimism, one would expect this to vary between individuals and over time in a non-linear fashion. Add to this the dangers of over-interpreting slender pieces of evidence for the subjective beliefs of those in distant generations, as well as the dangers of distorting the truth by selectivity of evidence, and it is clear that a fairly sceptical approach is required. It is interesting to note that the books of Bury and Nisbet come to radically different conclusions. Bury takes the view, with which I would largely concur for reasons given below, that the idea of progress could never become fully fledged or predominant before the Enlightenment in the eighteenth century; by contrast, Nisbet strives valiantly to document the existence of the belief, and even to argue for its prevalence, in the largely hostile terrain of ancient thought and early Christian dogma. Nevertheless, despite all the necessary caveats, five broad conclusions can, I think, be reached about the conditions normally required for a confident belief in progress, and these can usefully be enumerated at the outset.

First, there is a broad correlation between belief in progress and actual experience of *positive change in a single lifetime*. So, for example, in the ancient world, the idea surfaces most notably in fifth-century-BC Athens – the peak of classical civilisation and a period when positive change was great in the timescale of one generation. If the rate of change is imperceptible in any given generation, or if change is clearly for the worse, only the most resolutely optimistic will have faith in progress in the future. But change – however advantageous to some – can also be too rapid, making it more likely that those who are disoriented and disadvantaged will outnumber those who are its confident beneficiaries. Positive change, at a pace which allows the majority within any given generation to benefit, is a prerequisite of a widespread belief in progress.

Secondly, a belief in progress requires a *knowledgeable but critical relationship with the past*. Those societies which worship the dead, or whose cultures are dominated by aggrandising legends of past heroes, will tend to see themselves as pale reflections of a period of past glory and have little conception of progress. The possession of historical facts about the past, as opposed to myth, is necessary for the evolution of a confident and well-founded belief in progress. However, a modern self-confidence *vis-à-vis* earlier generations and the possession of some facts about the past may, of course, mislead people into possessing an exaggerated belief in progress. For facts tend to be unevenly distributed across our perspective of the past. When we do unearth new archaeological or written evidence, it is often disconcerting. Minoan palaces,

3,500 years old, startle by their sophistication. Cicero's letters, 2,000 years old, stun by the 'modernity' of their thought patterns and practical concerns. The more we know about Roman water distribution and sewage systems, the more they impress us with the boldness of their conception and the skill of the craftsmen involved. If we knew more about everyday life in the Dark Ages, might we change the name? At least part of our belief in progress comes from the piecemeal and parsimonious nature of historical facts at our disposal for all periods before the last 500 years.

A third factor normally required for a confident belief in human progress is a widespread *faith in the power of human reason and skills to engineer and control change*. Both Sophocles in fifth-century-BC Athens and Lucretius in first-century-BC Rome – two writers who did to some extent espouse the idea of progress – stressed the key role of man's cleverness and reason. Faith in reason reached its peak in the Enlightenment, when there was a widespread belief in the ability of intellectual progress to lead to the perfectibility of mankind itself. Whilst there has been greater scepticism since the Enlightenment that man and his moral nature can be perfected through the abolition of prejudice and ignorance, the faith in the power of reason and human skills to engineer a different progress – that of welfare – has grown enormously in the nineteenth and twentieth centuries, with the strides made by science, technology, medicine and commerce. Only recently have serious theoretical as well as practical doubts re-emerged about the extent of man's ultimate ability to control, engineer and predict change in his increasingly complex predicament. It is becoming clear again that there will always remain some limits to the power of reason, whether in the field of scientific analysis or that of economic planning.

A fourth feature required for a society in which a belief in progress is to thrive is either a *secular environment or one dominated by a belief in a benign deity*. It is difficult for the idea of progress, on this earth at least, to be dominant in a pre-scientific society in which man's vision of his potentiality is blinded by feelings of awe and insecurity in the face of fearsome and harsh divinities. Most ancient Greeks and Romans, for example, saw life on earth as contingent upon the will of the gods, a will at times mysterious and implacable. Man was insignificant in the face of these powers, and attempts at progress on earth were likely to attract the anger and jealousy of heaven. The relationship of Christianity to a belief in progress is altogether more complex and is discussed briefly later in this chapter.

Lastly, the idea of progress can only take firm root in the *absence of a*

strong belief in a lost paradise and in the absence of a belief in recurrent cycles.
The belief in a lost paradise in the past has been a central concept for
much of Western human history – enshrined in the fables of Greece and
Rome, no less than in the Biblical story of the Garden of Eden. As E. R.
Dodds pointed out in his book, *The Ancient Concept of Progress*, from a
psychological point of view this belief may owe some of its force to the
individual experience of infancy – the time 'when life was easy.'[1] It may
also reflect a parental tendency to project innocence on to their young:

> *But trailing clouds of glory do we come*
> *From God, who is our home:*
> *Heaven lies about us in our infancy!*
> *Shades of the prison-house begin to close*
> *Upon the growing Boy . . .*

Wordsworth

In this poem, 'Intimations of Immortality', Wordsworth also refers to
another very prevalent set of beliefs in human history – that of recurrent
cycles and hence of reincarnation. These beliefs may reflect not just a
primeval desire for another go at life, but also a deep empathy among
rural societies with the unending cycles of nature's seasons, where cyclical change is an integral part of an essentially static system. Belief either
in recurrent cycles or in a lost paradise, like a belief in jealous gods, is
inimical to a confident belief in earthly progress.   *Reincarnation*

   These five conditions, which are normally required for a confident and
dominant belief in progress, can be illustrated further by a brief survey of
four key periods in the history of the slow evolution of the idea: the
ancient world, the early Christian era, the Renaissance and the
Enlightenment. Only in the last of these four periods were all the conditions fully met. They continued to be met in the confident nineteenth-
century age of science, technology and economics.

The Ancient Perspective

It is a commonplace that classical Greece and imperial Rome were
remarkable periods for the flowering of man's intellectual, artistic, practical and political genius. The Greeks were the fathers of Western poetry,
drama, history and philosophy. Their architectural achievements, such as
the Parthenon, and their pottery and sculpture have scarcely been
rivalled since. The Romans ruled much of Europe, western Asia and

North Africa, tying them together with a legal and government structure which was to be a model for centuries to come. They built roads, amphitheatres and aqueducts of remarkable scale and precision. The artistic, literary, military and political achievements of the twelve hundred years or so from Homer to the fall of Rome were to haunt the Western consciousness for much of the subsequent fifteen hundred years as a vision of past glory – a vision which was initially, at least, to hinder a confident modern belief in progress. It may therefore be surprising to many observers that in the ancient world itself the idea of progress, while it was clearly enunciated from time to time, was far from dominant and all-pervasive.

The status of the idea of progress in the ancient world – and the extent of its prevalence – has been the subject of much scholarly debate – not least in Ludwig Edelstein's *The Idea of Progress in Classical Antiquity* and in E. R. Dodds' *The Ancient Concept of Progress*, which have painstakingly brought together many of the references and allusions to the idea of progress in extant ancient sources. It is not necessary or wise in the end to try to make a single definitive judgement about the so-called 'ancient view' of progress. As Edelstein puts it:

> I cannot persuade myself that one all encompassing answer could ever describe adequately the attitude of a civilization that lasted for more than a millennium, or that the forces of progressivism and of anti-progressivism were constants to be computed by adding and comparing bits of evidence as if they were numerals and as if the views embodied in them were independent of time and circumstance.[2]

And yet there is merit in understanding which areas of man's activities were susceptible to a belief in progress in the ancient world and which generally were not. It is also useful to understand the cross-currents which limited the scope and intensity of the belief; for some of them remain relevant to our modern conception of man's predicament.

In a number of extant passages in ancient literature, we do see a clear articulation of a belief in man's gradual rise in the past from a savage to a more civilised state, as a result of his own cleverness, skills and creativeness. Indeed, in fifth-century Athens – a period when positive change was great in a single lifetime in many fields, artistic and practical – this appears to become almost a dominant view. The relative absence of sophisticated recorded history of earlier ages (as opposed to aggrandising mythology) ceased to hinder a belief in past progress, not only because change within a single generation itself engendered confidence but also because of the growing interest in comparative anthropology, as Greeks travelled further afield and came into contact with more primitive societies. So Thucydides, the historian, surmises that the lifestyle of Greeks in the past resembled that of foreigners in his own day.[3] The introduction to his history of the Peloponnesian War includes an astute analysis of the slow evolution in Greece from a semi-nomadic to a modern city-based way of life. In it Thucydides stresses the important role of agriculture, sea trade, economic capital and new fighting practices in fostering progress. Later in his history, he includes a speech from a Corinthian envoy seeking to persuade Sparta of the threat from Athens, which stresses the importance of innovation, and a conviction that new methods will be superior to the old:

> But at the present time, as we have just pointed out to you, your whole way of life is out of date when compared with theirs. And it is just as true in politics as it is in any art or craft: new methods must drive out old ones. When a city can live in peace and quiet, no doubt the old established ways are best: but when one is constantly being faced by new problems, one has also to be capable of approaching them in an original way. Thus Athens, because of the very variety of her experience, is a far more modern state than you are.[4]

Such confidence in the power of new techniques is fertile ground for a confident belief in progress, and we can see in the works of the fifth-century-BC Athenian tragic poets a clear articulation of a belief in man's progress from a past savage state. For example, in Aeschylus' play *Prometheus Bound*, Prometheus boasts of his achievements in raising up mankind, and describes man's earlier pitiful predicament in these words:

> First of all, though they had eyes to see, they saw to no avail; they had ears, but understood not; but, like to shapes in dreams, throughout their length of days, without purpose they wrought all things in confusion. Knowledge had they neither of houses built of bricks and turned to face the sun, nor yet of work in wood; but dwelt beneath the ground like swarming ants, in sunless caves.[5]

The god Prometheus gave man fire but also, in Aeschylus' account, numbers and letters ('wherewith to hold all things in memory'); he taught man to harness animals and sail the seas and instructed them in the art of medicine. In other accounts, the past progress of mankind from cave existence to modern city life is not ascribed to divine assistance but to man's own cleverness and inventiveness. The Ionian philosopher Xenophanes, in the late sixth century BC, had spoken of man discovering improvements, over the course of time, by his own research.[6] Sophocles, in his play the *Antigone*, includes a chorus passage which is virtually a eulogy of man's cleverness.

> Many things are formidable [the Greek word also means 'clever'], and none more formidable [or clever] than man! . . .
>   And he has learned speech and wind-swift thought and the temper that rules cities, and how to escape the exposure of the inhospitable hills and the sharp arrows of rain, all resourceful; he meets nothing in the future without resource . . .[7]

Four hundred years later, in the first century BC, the Roman poet Lucretius – an Epicurean who firmly denied any divine ordering of man's affairs – gives a long description in the fifth book of his *De Rerum Natura* of the laborious rise of mankind from an earlier savage existence; it ends with this ringing description of the power of man's reason and experience in helping to further human progress:

> So we find that not only such arts as seafaring and agriculture, city walls and laws, weapons, roads and clothing, but also without exception the amenities and refinements of life, songs, pictures, and statues, artfully carved and polished, all were taught gradually by usage and the active mind's experience as men groped their way forward step by step. So each particular development is brought gradually to the fore by the advance of time, and reason lifts it into the light of day. Men saw one notion after another take shape within their minds until by their arts they scaled the topmost peak.[8]

The belief in the power of reason and in gradual step-by-step (pedetemptim) advance is central to the modern conception of progress, and in this passage we see a similar view expressed in ancient times. None the less, there were important caveats to Lucretius' optimism, as discussed below, and it is important to note the suggestion in the last line of this quotation that the peak has already been reached, casting doubt on the possibility of progress into the future.

The passages quoted from Thucydides, Aeschylus, Sophocles and Lucretius show the existence in the ancient world of confidence in man's own powers of reason and inventiveness and of a belief in past material and intellectual progress from uncivilised beginnings. However, there were a number of powerful currents in ancient thought and literature – not least in the works of Aeschylus, Sophocles and Lucretius themselves – which either ran directly counter to a confident belief in progress, or crucially confined the scope of what were seen to be legitimate human ambitions. These were: (i) the perceived insecurity of man's predicament in the face of jealous gods; (ii) the linked concept of a proper limit to man's ambition and the danger of overstepping it; (iii) the myths of the golden age, the lost paradise; (iv) the conception of recurrent cycles; and (v) a strong strain in many of the philosophies of the ancient world of denigration of the pursuit of material prosperity as the source of happiness.

Homer's epic poem, *The Iliad*, the earliest extant masterpiece of Western literature, was hugely influential throughout and beyond the ancient era, helping to define the ancient conception of humanity. Its relationship to the idea of progress is a negative one not simply because it is an aggrandisement of past heroes – a study of the godlike men who fought the Trojan War in a bygone age – but, far more importantly, because of its emphasis on the pain and death suffered even by these heroes, the pathos of which is brought into sharp relief by comparing the lot of men with that of the Olympian deities, who live a life of glorious ease. The poem ends not with the sack of Troy, or a celebration of the heroes' victorious achievements, but with a haunting picture of the pain and grief endured both by Greece's finest hero, Achilles, and by his opponent, Priam, King of Troy. Book 24 opens with Achilles unable to sleep, racked with tears and longing for his killed friend, Patroklos:

> *Remembering all these things he let fall the swelling tears, lying sometimes along his side, sometimes on his back, and now again prone on his face; then he would stand upright, and pace turning in distraction along the beach of the sea; nor did dawn rising escape him as she brightened across the sea and the beaches.*[9]

There is then a description of the old King of Troy coming to the camp of the enemy to ransom his dead son, Hector, from his slayer, Achilles. By this device, Homer evokes a memorable picture of the universality of suffering which affects both victor and vanquished. After Priam's suppliant speech to Achilles come the lines:

> *So he spoke, and stirred in the other a passion of grieving*
> *for his own father. He took the old man's hand and pushed him*
> *gently away, and the two remembered, as Priam sat huddled*
> *at the feet of Achilleus and wept close for man-slaughtering Hektor*
> *and Achilleus wept now for his own father, now again*
> *for Patroklos. The sound of their mourning moved in the house . . .*[10]

Before Achilles grants Priam his request, and then dines with his old enemy, Achilles says:

> *Such is the way the gods spun life for unfortunate mortals,*
> *that we live in unhappiness, but the gods themselves have no sorrows.*
> *There are two urns that stand on the door-sill of Zeus. They are unlike*
> *for the gifts they bestow: an urn of evils, an urn of blessings.*
> *If Zeus who delights in thunder mingles these and bestows them*
> *on man, he shifts, and moves now in evil, again in good fortune.*
> *But when Zeus bestows from the urn of sorrows, he makes a failure*
> *of man, and the evil hunger drives him over the shining*
> *earth, and he wanders respected neither of gods nor mortals.*[11]

Homer's stark picture of the universality of human suffering, and of the grief that will inevitably envelop even the greatest of men, is an important counterweight to the confidence in man's power and achievements sometimes expressed elsewhere in ancient thought. No achievement and no intellectual or material progress, however great, can ultimately challenge the central fact of individual human death and suffering.

The ultimate precariousness of man's predicament and the instability of all happiness and success is a theme which runs right through Greek and Roman thought from the time of Homer on. Herodotus – the fifth-century-BC father of history – states:

> For most of those [cities] which were great once are small today; and those which used to be small were great in my own time. Knowing, therefore, that human prosperity never abides long in the same place, I shall pay attention to both alike.[12]

Later Herodotus records Solon's alleged advice to the legendary rich king Croesus, that no man should be called happy until he is dead. For 'often enough God gives a man a glimpse of happiness, and then utterly ruins him'.[13]

Such a belief in the precariousness of the happiness or prosperity of the individual person or city, while undermining an individual's confidence in his own destiny, need not, of course, stand in the way of a belief in the general progress of mankind as a whole. However, in much of ancient thought there is an associated belief which seems more deeply inimical even to the general idea of progress; this is the notion that the gods are prone to be jealous of man's achievements, that there is a proper limit to man's ambitions and that any arrogant attempt to overstep these limits will be punished by divine retribution. So Solon tells Croesus, in Herodotus' account, that God is 'envious of human prosperity and likes to trouble us'.[14] In the *Agamemnon*, Aeschylus' chorus sings of the danger of 'hubris', or arrogance, which brings destruction upon men;[15] and the returning hero – conqueror of Troy – is afraid even to step on a red carpet for fear of bringing the envy of the gods upon his head. The same poet, whose Prometheus boasted of the progress of man, is keen to point out that righteousness attends the poor, not the power of wealth.[16] Similarly, Sophocles follows his praise for man's great cleverness, in the *Antigone*, with a warning that it sometimes leads to evil as well as to good outcomes, and later he states: 'Zeus, what arrogance of men could restrict your power? . . . For present, future and past this law shall suffice: to none among mortals shall great wealth come without disaster.'[17] The same play ends with the words: 'Good sense is by far the chief part of happiness; and we must not be impious towards the gods. The great words of boasters are always punished with great blows, and as they grow old teach them wisdom.'[18]

Four centuries later, in the first century BC, the urbane Roman poet Horace writes of the divine limits placed on man's ambitions in similar terms:

> *No barrier is too high for mortals:*
> *In our foolhardiness we try*
> *To escalade the very sky.*
> *Still we presumptuously aspire,*
> *And still with unabated ire*
> *Jove hurls his thunderbolts of fire.*[19]

Such a view of the proper limit to man's ambitions, and of the incalculable consequences of overstepping this limit, would have made a fully fledged confident belief in perpetual human progress seem almost blasphemous to many in the ancient world. Man's vision of his potentiality was clouded not only by feelings of awe, but by feelings of insecurity in the face of jealous, inscrutable and unpredictable divinities.

The poet Hesiod, writing in the eighth century BC, enunciated another conception inimical to a belief in progress – that of a lost paradise, of the decay of man from a previous golden age. One account, in his poem *Works and Days*, attributes all evil to Pandora, a woman created by the Olympian gods under orders from Zeus who wished to give evils to men, in revenge for Prometheus' unauthorised gift to them of fire. It was Pandora who opened the famous jar, out of which flew all the troubles and misfortunes of mankind, only Hope remaining behind.[20] Another account in this same poem speaks of the decline from a golden age – when man lived free from sorrows, old age and the need to work, and the fields produced food of their own account – to the current iron age. Hesiod foresees further decay, with children no longer honouring their parents, nor hosts their guests, when oaths will no longer be kept and violence and evil will reign on earth.[21] This myth of a lost paradise – mirrored by the Hebrew Bible's account of the eviction of Adam and Eve from the Garden of Eden – must have hampered the early development of a belief in progress. However, even in Hesiod's poem, there is emphasis on the dividends that accrue to man in his fallen condition from hard work, benign competitive rivalry and a greater sense of justice.

Gradually, in the centuries that followed, the myth of a lost golden age gave way to the more progressive views of human history espoused by Aeschylus, Sophocles, Thucydides and Lucretius in the passages quoted above. But the myth of a lost paradise never totally lost its hold on the ancient imagination. In many cases, it became transformed into a vision of the moral rather than the material superiority of the simple past – a vision of the morally upright rural peasant or nomadic herdsman of yesteryear, which resembles the later eighteenth-century vision of the noble savage. Moral regress was increasingly seen as the inevitable counterpart of material progress. So, Plato in the *Laws* looks back to primitive men who, while ignorant of arts and practical techniques, had enough to eat and drink and, above all, were more manly, temperate and just than the men of today.

Hence in those days there was no great poverty; nor was poverty a cause of difference among men; and rich they could not be, if they had no gold and silver, and such at that time was their condition. And the community which has neither poverty nor riches will always have the noblest principles; there is no insolence or injustice, nor, again, are there any contentions or envyings among them. And therefore they were good, and also because of what would be termed the simplicity of their natures . . .[22]

The Roman poet Horace, writing after Augustus had become the first emperor in all but name, expressed even more forcefully the theme of moral regress. Partly to back up Augustan moral reforms he wrote: 'What do the ravages of time not injure! Our parents' age, worse than our grand-sires', has brought forth us less worthy and destined soon to yield an offspring still more wicked.'[23] These lines come at the end of a poem which includes two vivid vignettes contrasted with each other. The first is of the modern woman, obsessed with dancing and coquetry, and sleeping with any man who offers himself, even in front of her husband. The second is of the old rustic stock of Italy who made Rome all that she was:

Not such the sires of whom were sprung the youth that dyed the sea with Punic blood, and struck down Pyrrhus and great Antiochus and Hannibal, the dire; but a manly brood of peasant soldiers, taught to turn the clods with Sabine hoe, and at a strict mother's bidding to bring cut firewood, when the sun shifted the shadows of the mountain sides and lifted the yoke from weary steers, bringing the welcome time of rest with his departing car.[24]

Much of Roman thought and literature in the great days of empire is suffused with this sort of nostalgia for a simple and moral past and with overwhelming respect for the moral and military prowess of earlier generations. Even when Virgil wrote in the *Aeneid* with politically inspired optimism for the new age of Augustus, he did so by referring to a return to a golden age of values that would mirror those of the founders of Rome. Virgil depicts his hero Aeneas – a putative ancestor of Augustus and founder of the precursor to Rome – being taken down to Hades, where he is shown the principal heroes of Roman history to come, including Augustus himself:

> This, this is he, whom thou so oft hearest promised to thee,
> Augustus Caesar, son of a god, who shall again set up the
> Golden Age amid the fields where Saturn once reigned, and
> shall spread his empire past Garamant and Indian . . .[25]

As R.G. Austin notes in his commentary on the *Aeneid*:

> . . . Virgil's words have a special social significance; the Golden
> Age of Saturn symbolised the purity and simplicity of early
> Italian life, the ways that had made Rome great . . . It is highly
> probable that . . . there is an allusion [here] to Augustus' social
> and moral reforms, attempted unsuccessfully in 28 BC . . .[26]

Many ancients believed sincerely in recurrent cycles of human history. Plato in the *Laws* speaks of a series of destructions of mankind, with the need for civilisation to recover each time.[27] So, too, the later Stoic philosophers believed in periodic conflagrations and recurrent cycles where everything that has happened will happen again. Such a view must make all belief in progress more provisional, but need not obviate a belief in some progress between such periods of destruction. Indeed, Plato posits exactly this in his account in the *Laws*. Likewise, Aristotle states in the *Metaphysics* that: 'probably each art and science has often been developed as far as possible and has again perished'.[28] But such a gloomy view does not prevent him from developing a clear conception of cumulative progress in knowledge elsewhere:

> The investigation of the truth is in one way hard, in another
> easy . . . no one is able to attain the truth adequately, while, on
> the other hand, no one fails entirely, but everyone says some-
> thing true about the nature of things, and while individually
> they contribute little or nothing to the truth, by the union of
> all a considerable amount is amassed.[29]

This is a clear expression of the collective progress of knowledge, belonging to humanity considered as a whole. As Edelstein shows in his book, there was a growing confidence, particularly among Hellenistic and Roman philosophers, in the possibility of future as well as past progress in knowledge. Nowhere was this more confidently expressed than in the writings of the Stoic of the first century AD, Seneca. Seneca shared a

N.b:
Seneca quote

general Roman pessimism about the evils that came with the rise of civil-isation, as well as the Stoic conviction in the prospect of the annihilation of the world and the destruction of all man's works. This did not stop him confidently predicting: 'The time will come when diligent research over very long periods will bring to light things which now lie hidden . . . There will come a time when our descendants will be amazed that we did not know things that are so plain to them.'[30] In the same vein, Pliny the Elder in his discussion of astronomy expresses the view that no one should despair of there being continual progress in knowledge from one generation to another.[31]

A belief in past, present and future progress of knowledge was more prevalent in the ancient world than belief in the possibility, or desirabil-ity, of indefinite progress in material prosperity. In part, this was because the dominant philosophers of the age had a strong ascetic streak. Plato's philosophy denigrated the physical world, and Aristotle argued that ratio-nal contemplation was the key constituent of happiness – the ultimate goal of the 'good life'. For the Stoics, the pursuit of virtue was the sole good or goal for the rational man, with material possessions, health and worldly happiness being of no value. Even the hedonistic Epicurus, for whom pleasure was happiness, placed heavy emphasis on restricting the number of desires and on withdrawing from the hurly-burly of commer-cial and city life. Desire for wealth was considered futile, and was thought not only to deprive men of contentment but to lead to conflict and war. Thus the Epicurean poet Lucretius, whose account of man's past progress was quoted earlier, tempers his optimism by stressing the down-side of progress in civilisation – it leads, in his view, to moral regress, strife and discontent – and he articulates a belief in the futility of the pursuit of ever greater pleasure:

> So mankind is perpetually the victim of a pointless and futile
> martyrdom, fretting life away in fruitless worries through fail-
> ure to realise what limit is set to acquisition and to the growth
> of genuine pleasure. It is this discontent that has driven life
> steadily onward, out to the high seas, and has stirred up from
> the depths the surging tumultuous tides of war.[32]

In conclusion, we can say that there was at times in the ancient world a confident belief in progress in knowledge – past, present and future. There was also, however, for much of the period, a widespread pes-simism about the direction of human morality, and a nostalgia for the virtues of the past. In some of the extant sources there is clear evidence of belief in the practical power of man's reason and inventiveness, as well as a belief that there had been, in the past, significant advances in material prosperity, in technology and in the arts. But throughout the period confidence and optimism about the future were, to a great extent, held in check by a strong sense both of the ultimate insecurity of man's predicament and of the futility of the pursuit of material aspirations.

The Early Christian Perspective

The Christian view of the world is so rich and complex that it has always contained within itself elements which appear to contradict each other – some inducing great optimism about the present and future, others answering to a deep pessimism about human capacities and about the scope for any meaningful improvement in our lot here on earth. As Richard Tarnas puts it in his book, *The Passion of the Western Mind*:

> Indeed, on first impression one might discern two entirely distinct world views that co-existed and overlapped within Christianity, and that were in continual tension with each other: whereas the one outlook was rapturously optimistic and all embracing, its complement was sternly judgemental, restrictive and prone to a dualistic pessimism. But in fact the two outlooks were inextricably united, two sides of the same coin, light and shadow.[33]

The loving Father gave his Son that all who believe in him might have eternal life. The word of God was made flesh and dwelt among us; the providential plan of God was reuniting the previously alienated physical world of man with the spiritual world of God. This was the good news. Mankind was now triumphantly liberated from the ultimate insecurity and fear of death which had served to limit pagan optimism about man's predicament. Furthermore, Christianity inherited from Judaism a linear conception of history – seeing in it the unfolding of a single pattern, according to the will of God. This linear conception of a progressive realisation of man's potential was to be a key element in the Western idea of progress. But it is important to note the immaterial nature of the early Christian conception of the goal of history. Secular glory was not meaningful. As Tarnas puts it: 'all true progress was necessarily spiritual and transcended this world'.[34] Indeed, a denigration of the physical world and of the require-ments of the flesh is a constant theme in Christianity. In the well-known passage in the Gospel According to St Matthew (chapter 6) Jesus says:

> No man can serve two masters: for either he will hate the one, and love the other; or else he will hold to the one and despise the other. Ye cannot serve God and mammon . . . And why take ye thought for raiment? Consider the lilies of the field, how they grow; they toil not, neither do they spin:/And yet I say unto you, That even Solomon in all his glory was not arrayed like one of these./Wherefore, if God so clothe the grass of the field, which today is, and tomorrow is cast into the oven, shall he not much more clothe you, O ye of little faith?/Therefore take no thought, saying, What shall we eat? or, What shall we drink? or, Wherewithal shall we be clothed?/For your heavenly Father knoweth that ye have need of all these things./But seek ye first the kingdom of God, and his righteousness; and all these things shall be added unto you./Take therefore no thought for the morrow: for the morrow shall take thought for the things of itself.

A simple exhortation to place spiritual and moral requirements before bodily needs and material progress is central to Christian thinking, but in its optimistic form leaves plenty of scope for the moral and spiritual progress of man – for reform and 'renovation' here on earth.

However, from the beginning there was a darker side to the Christian message which was, for most of the centuries leading up to the Enlightenment, to be deeply corrosive of any conception of progress here on earth. No one spelt out this more pessimistic message with more style and verve than St Augustine (AD 354–430). For him, not only was it folly to seek happiness in physical pleasures, but the flesh and the urg-ings of it were actually evil; an attachment to the affairs of the body was a sign of sin. Moreover, even the goal of moral or spiritual perfection could not, in his view, be secured by man's own attempts to perfect his virtues, but must rely on the divine gift of the remission of sins; man was as nothing before the majesty of God and was in continual need of pardon. For St Augustine espoused the bleak doctrine of original sin; all men and women were born with the handicap of inheriting sin trans-mitted to posterity by Adam's guilt; unbaptised babies were not pure and innocent but almost limbs of Satan; sin had so corrupted man that he had

no right to salvation and no means to earn that salvation by his own application of reason; his sin made him impotent and incapable of
perfectibility or moral advance. This doctrine is the antithesis of the
optimistic Enlightenment view that man's intellectual progress can lead
to a perfection of his moral nature. While the influential heretic
Pelagius – a contemporary of St Augustine – held a more optimistic view
of human nature and saw a positive role for human merit, St Augustine
insisted that man's efforts were fundamentally inconsequential; people
could only be rescued by God's gift of grace and mercy, not by their own
efforts. In part, St Augustine was motivated by the desire to assert a doctrine which could vindicate divine providence; none of the suffering or
fear of death so evident in the world was, in his view, undeserved; all men
were so sinful that they deserved damnation and eternal death. Only by
God's unearned and inexplicable grace and mercy could man be saved. In
this extreme view, there was an arbitrariness about who would share in
eternal torment with the majority of men ('the mass of perdition'), and
who would be chosen to enter the Kingdom of God. Man had good
reason to be insecure about his spiritual as well as his physical future.

A concern to vindicate divine providence may also have lain behind St
Augustine's influential thesis of the duality of the City of God and the
City of the World. Faced with the sack of Rome and the gradual collapse
of the empire, St Augustine was at pains to emphasise that God's promise
of salvation, and his providential plan, related to salvation in the next
world, not in this one. He distinguished between, on the one hand, the
City of God, which was dedicated to the selfless love of God, and whose
inhabitants were predestined to enter heaven after the Second Coming,
and, on the other hand, the City of the World, which was dominated by
man's love of self, his pride and his disobedience, and whose inhabitants
were destined to eternal damnation with the Devil after the Last
Judgement. For St Augustine, any actual state, like Rome, was a blend of
these two cities which would remain entangled and at odds with one
another until the Last Judgement. The citizens of the City of God – the
followers of Christ – would meanwhile live in the material world like foreigners, never truly at home. There is in St Augustine's teaching a deep
pessimism about the ability to resolve the tensions and conquer the evil
present in human society, and a considerable indifference as to the
ultimate value of all secular institutions: 'As far as this mortal life is concerned, which is passed and ended in a few days, what difference does it
make for a man who is soon to die, under what ruler he lives, if only the
rulers do not force him to commit unholy and unjust deeds.'[35] In St

Augustine's view, political structures – even the Roman Empire – are not central to God's providential purpose. James O'Donnell writes in his book, *Augustine*:

> In earthly terms, the vision of human society *City of God* provides is unremittingly bleak, even if indisputable. Most human societies, enamoured with the daydreams of politics, pretend the human condition is better than it is. Men forget history because they do not want to remember that others have gone down paths of prosperity and complacency before them. But in western Christianity since Augustine there has always been a prophetic voice to proclaim the ultimate weakness of human political societies. Christianity offers mankind a hope beside which the gloom of the human condition is as nothing.[36]

Such pessimism about human endeavour was, of course, by no means uniform in early Christianity, or even in all the writings of St Augustine. As Nisbet shows in his book, *History of the Idea of Progress*, there are passages in St Augustine which show a real appreciation for the past advances of human civilisation – although this is not, as most commentators would agree, the abiding impression given by his works, which seem rather to be dominated by a stress on the moral weakness and incapacity of mankind. But there were also some at the time of St Augustine, such as Eusebius and Origen, who took a radically different line and actually sought to identify the Roman Empire with the unfolding of God's providential plan and to give the Christian Empire on earth a sacred significance. Such a sanctification of the existing political order was to become popular again in the Holy Roman Empire of the late Middle Ages. However, the demise of the Western Roman Empire in the fifth century AD may well have inclined most in the Dark Ages and early medieval era to share St Augustine's disparagement of the secular works of mankind, and to share his belief that the historical process here on earth is largely irrelevant to the fulfilment of Christ's kingdom. This does not imply that St Augustine or his followers considered political commitment to good works on earth to be an unimportant duty for a Christian; but, as R. A. Markus puts it in his book, *Saeculum: History and Society in the Theology of St Augustine*:

> His first insistence . . . remained the denial that society was in any way the agency of man's pursuit of his ultimate good. His

downgrading of society by confining it to the sphere of the temporal needs of men in their fallen condition is the counterpart of his secularisation of history.[37]

In conclusion, it can be said that the early Christian view of the world, torn between optimism and pessimism, was at best ambivalent in its relationship to a belief in human progress, and at times overtly hostile to it. There was a strong linear sense of history as the unfolding of a divine plan leading ultimately to the Second Coming of Christ. But unlike its Jewish forerunner, this necessary Christian history did not lead – in most accounts, including that of St Augustine – to a new utopian Kingdom of David here on earth, but to a spiritual heaven which would unfold only after the terrible Day of Judgement and an apocalyptic End of History. Although there were Millennialists who predicted a glorious Messianic age when Christ would reign on earth (as prophesied in the Book of Revelations), they also held that this would only materialise after the destruction of this world and the condemnation of all sinners – i.e., most of mankind – to eternal fire and brimstone. The widespread conviction of the imminence of the Day of Judgement, an apocalyptic End of History and the consequent paramount necessity of pursuing and hoping for salvation in the spiritual afterlife, left little room for a confident belief in a slow, deliberate and linear future progress here on earth. As Bury notes in *The Idea of Progress*:

> For Augustine, as for any medieval believer, the course of history would be satisfactorily complete if the world came to an end in his own lifetime. He was not interested in the question whether any gradual amelioration of society or increase of knowledge would mark the period of time which might still remain to run before the Day of Judgement.[38]

Pessimism concerning man's capacities further limited any notion of progress. Not only was man seen as inherently sinful and reliant for salvation upon God's grace and mercy, rather than his own doomed efforts at reform; even human reason was considered to be of dubious value, when compared to the paramount need for faith and to the superior role of revelation in illuminating truth. So St Paul says in his first letter to the Corinthians (chapter 3): 'For the wisdom of this world is foolishness with God . . . And again, The Lord knoweth the thoughts of the wise, that they are vain.' As O'Donnell notes, the Christian view of the world was very different from the pagan (or the modern) conception: 'Instead of preaching final insignificance but present power, Christianity reversed the polarities and discovered an anthropology pessimistic regarding the capacities of sinful man but optimistic about his fate.'[39] The promised spiritual fate of the chosen few would be glorious, but for a person brought up on St Augustine's teachings, and faced with the fact of the collapse of the Roman Empire, the idea of a secular triumph of human reason and progress on this earth would have seemed as futile and impossible as it was historically untrue.

The Renaissance Perspective

If change was far from positive at the onset of the Dark Ages, and if the magnificent achievements of medieval Europe were slow to unfold – making it difficult for a belief in progress to become dominant in either period – the Renaissance would seem to offer more fertile territory for a belief in progress. For this period saw a second flowering of Western civilisation as vibrant as anything seen in the ancient world. Leonardo, Michelangelo and Raphael in art, Shakespeare and Cervantes in literature, Copernicus, Bacon and Galileo in science, were just a few of the men of genius. The city states of Italy and Holland pioneered new forms of commerce and banking, while three seminal inventions had in their different ways profound effects on thought and history: (i) the printing press allowed an unprecedented flow of ideas with hitherto inconceivable speed; (ii) the mariners' compass made possible the circumnavigation of the world, the discovery of the Americas and contact with Far Eastern civilisations; and (iii) gunpowder heralded the end of feudal and medieval warfare and helped bring about large changes in society. Suddenly, the tempo of history seemed to speed up, and the quality and economic basis of life began to change considerably in a single lifetime. There was a new confidence in human reason and in the independent value of man's enterprise on earth, resulting from the vibrancy of the period's art, commerce and voyages of discovery.

However, despite the period's stunning achievements and actual progress in many fields, and despite the new interest in the secular human condition so evident in the art, poetry, philosophy and rhetoric of the age, confident Renaissance man was still hampered from forming a clear conception of progress by two phenomena: the glorification of antiquity, and the power of the Church. The rediscovery in the late

Middle Ages of broad swaths of ancient literature, philosophy and science was the spark and much of the tinder for the Renaissance. For a long time scholarship became dominated by the rediscovery and elaboration of ancient thought, while much of art sought to portray the mythology and history of the ancient world. This broke the monopoly of Christian images and ideas, and allowed more freedom of thought and expression. But idolisation of ancient civilisation and the past masters hindered a strong belief in man's progress nearly as much as did the tenets of early and medieval Christianity.

John Hale, in his book *The Civilisation of Europe in the Renaissance*, describes the importance of the ancient world to the people of the Renaissance.

> Far in the past, but nearer to their own concerns than the medieval centuries, was a society like their own, lacking only stirrups, the compass, printing, gunpowder, the papacy and the Americas: a society which, thanks to time's tendency to winnow its trivial sources and monuments more thoroughly, appeared to have been peopled by an intellectual and creative master-race. Whatever there was to do, in philosophical speculation, political action or cultural achievement, appeared to have been done, and done with a supreme vigour and accomplishment, among a people whose history not only had the clarity of distance in time but the wholeness of a completed cycle, from obscurity through world empire to barbarian chaos.[40]

Such reverence for a past civilisation not only hindered a strong conception of progress, it heightened the perception that there had been a catastrophic decline in the Dark Ages from this pinnacle of achievement. Not surprisingly, therefore, many Renaissance thinkers emphasised a cyclical view of history. So Machiavelli saw history as subject to '*ricorsi*' – cycles from order to disorder and back to order; fate or fortune had the power to turn states upside down, at will. There was no strong linear conception of secular history; the golden age of the Renaissance came after a thousand years of darkness, to which mankind might return.

The power of the Church remained a second powerful brake on the new confidence in the ability of man's reason to reinterpret and order the world. For while the Church did much to sponsor Renaissance art and classical learning, there were limits to its tolerance of new ideas –

particularly after the Reformation. The radical philosopher Giordano Bruno was burnt at the stake and Galileo was persecuted by the Inquisition. The fateful decision by the Catholic Church to follow Protestantism in reaffirming literal scriptural orthodoxy, in the face of scientific challenges from the new astronomy, set the scene for the great battle which was to follow between science and religion. The gradual victory during the next three centuries of man's reason in science over the orthodox beliefs of religion and the theories of the past masters, such as Aristotle and Ptolemy, would later do much to give man the self-esteem required for a confident belief in human progress.

The Enlightenment Triumph of Progress

In the two centuries between Galileo's momentous astronomical discoveries and the death of Napoleon in 1821, there was a sea change in attitudes and values – particularly in France, Britain and America. It was this sea change, called 'The Enlightenment', that was finally to engender, at least in the minds of most educated people, a confident and optimistic belief in progress both in the past and into the future. At last, the conditions required for belief in progress were all met: there was faith in the power of reason to engineer and control change; there was a more secular atmosphere, as religion lost some of its emotional hold, and as the new sciences weakened the concept of an active and unpredictable divine providence; there was a new critical attitude towards the authorities of the past; and there was positive change evident during the space of a single lifetime.

New horizons on all sides challenged the traditional view of the world. The great age of exploration and colonisation underway since Columbus' voyage in 1492 was slowly beginning to impinge on the Euro-centric conception of the world, with anthropological discoveries of other races – some savage and some, like the Chinese, with an immensely old and sophisticated civilisation. Slowly but surely, too, during the eighteenth and early nineteenth centuries, geological discoveries of fossil remains began to suggest that the Biblical time frame since the creation of the world was far too short. The world was enormous, varied and old. But it was also small and insignificant from the perspective of the new astronomy. The hypothesis of a sun-centred universe – posited by Copernicus and later Galileo to explain more simply the complexities of observed astronomical phenomena – had a far-reaching psychological impact. The emotional shock of the loss of the earth's central position should not be underestimated. As the Marquise in Fontenelle's *Plurality of Worlds* put it: '*Je commence à voir la Terre si effroyablement petite.*'[41]

The traditional man-centred Christian conception of reality began to seem less plausible. At the end of the seventeenth century, Newton propounded his famous theory of gravitation which, together with his simple laws of motion, seemed to explain the workings of the heavens themselves. The rational simplicity of this new, scientific, mechanistic conception of the universe compared starkly both with the complexity of the earlier Ptolemaic system, still insisted upon by the Church, and with the ornate and static heavens of Dante and of religious art. Reason seemed to be triumphantly challenging faith in the traditional Christian picture of the world. Furthermore, if the universe was largely explicable in terms of immutable laws of nature, this appeared to many (though not to Newton himself) to weaken the scope for an active divine providence.

A growing secular confidence and even, in some influential quarters, an outright rejection of the dogma of religion were key features of the Enlightenment. This new confidence allowed people to develop a sense of their own worth and of the human potential for improvement and progress, by liberating them from a St Augustine-style feeling of dread and guilt. For as Norman Hampson writes in his book, *The Enlightenment*: 'The cardinal fact in religious experience had hitherto been the Fall. Man, born in sin, made his erring way through this vale of tears, with eternal damnation the final destination of the great majority.'[42]

Perhaps the most extreme expression of the new attitude to religion came from the French philosopher Baron d'Holbach in his *Common Sense, or Natural Ideas Opposed to Supernatural*, published in 1772. For him theology was 'revered solely because not understood', and was 'only the ignorance of natural causes reduced to system'. His most bitter remarks are reserved for what he saw as the social ill-effects of religion:

> Infested with frightful phantoms, and guided by men interested in perpetuating its ignorance and fears, how could the human mind have made any considerable progress? Man has been forced to vegetate in his primitive stupidity; nothing has been offered to his mind, but stories of invisible powers, upon whom his happiness was supposed to depend. Occupied solely by his fears, and unintelligible reveries, he has always been at the mercy of his priests, who have reserved to themselves the right of thinking for him, and directing his actions.

Thus man has been, and ever will remain, a child without experience, a slave without courage, a stupid animal, who has feared to reason, and who has never known how to extricate himself from the labyrinth where his ancestors had strayed. He has believed himself forced to groan under the yoke of his gods . . .[43]

The great French *philosophe* Voltaire, while not an atheist, also held that the social effects of religion were often pernicious and an obstacle to progress. If the prejudice induced by some religious dogma and by religious wars could be conquered by reason, in a new era of religious tolerance, man's predicament would rapidly improve.

The new science not only weakened the authority of the Church and of traditional Christian teaching; it led to a more general rebellion against the authority of ancient texts, a revolt in particular against the dominance of Aristotle. Gone was the Renaissance idolisation of the ancients which had been, as we have seen, an obstacle to a belief in progress. As Bury records in *The Idea of Progress*, Descartes was proud to have forgotten his Greek, while Joseph Glanvill – writing in 1668 in defence of the new Royal Society in London – delighted in repudiating Aristotle and in stressing the utilitarian importance of modern science. Bury quotes Glanvill as arguing that we should be more grateful to the unknown inventor of the marine compass 'than to a thousand Alexanders and Caesars, or to ten times the number of Aristotles. And he really did more for the increase of knowledge and the advantage of the world by this one experiment than the numerous subtle disputers that have lived ever since the erection of the school of talking.'[44]

Such liberation from slavish devotion to the past masters allowed a new confidence in man's capacity for progress in science. Fontenelle, who for sixty years was the secretary of the French Academy of Science at the time of Louis XIV, and who did much to propagate the new science in the salons of Paris, explicitly held the view that an endless progress in knowledge was possible. Increased experience and methodological improvements would continue to help new generations build on the discoveries and learn from the errors of earlier generations.

It is hard to overstate the extraordinary degree of new-found confidence in the power of reason which resulted from the new science, as can be illustrated by this extract from the French political writer Anne-Robert-Jacques Turgot, in his discourse, *On the Successive Advances of the Human Mind*, written in 1750:

At last all the clouds are dissipated. What a glorious light is
cast on all sides! What a crowd of great men on all paths of
knowledge! What perfection of human reason! One man,
Newton, has submitted the infinite to the calculus; has
unveiled the nature and properties of light, which, while
revealing to us everything else, had concealed itself; he has
placed in his balance the stars, the earth and all the forces of
Nature.[45]

There was also increasing optimism that the new sciences would allow
men to control nature better and improve health and happiness. As
Benjamin Franklin put it in a letter to Joseph Priestley in 1780:

The rapid Progress true Science now makes, occasions my
regretting sometimes that I was born so soon. It is impossible
to imagine the height to which may be carried, in a thousand
years, the power of man over matter. We may perhaps learn to
deprive large masses of their gravity, and give them absolute
levity, for the sake of easy transport. Agriculture may diminish
its labor and double its produce; all diseases may by sure
means be prevented or cured, not excepting even that of old
age, and our lives lengthened at pleasure even beyond the
antediluvian standard.[46]

Fontenelle had not extended this new confidence in the power of human
reason beyond the realms of science and knowledge; convinced of
progress in knowledge, he was sceptical about social or moral progress.
Bury sums up Fontenelle's view with typical succinctness:

The world consists of a multitude of fools, and a mere handful
of reasonable men. Men's passions will always be the same
and will produce wars in the future as in the past. Civilisation
makes no difference; it is little more than a veneer.[47]

Even Benjamin Franklin followed his ringing eulogy of the power of science with the plaintive exclamation: 'O that moral science were in as fair
a way of improvement, that men would cease to be wolves to one
another, and that human beings would at length learn what they now
improperly call humanity!'[48]

However, many Enlightenment figures did crucially extend belief in the power of reason into the social, political and even moral domain. Most, including Franklin of course, believed passionately in the possibility of political progress through the rational perfection of government; many also championed the view that reason could perfect man's very nature, leading to genuine moral progress. Abbé de St Pierre was one of the first French writers explicitly to argue that reason could be used to perfect the science of government, and to engineer both social and moral progress. Reason should, he argued, be applied to ethics and politics as much as to the physical sciences; rational improvements to the science of government and to the art of regulation could lead to a golden age of greater happiness and to the abolition of war. He even argued for an early league of nations in Europe, with rational arbitration to settle all disputes. Another French philosopher, Claude-Adrien Helvétius, held that differences in people's moral characters were a product of circumstances and environment; morality could therefore in principle be perfected by wise laws, rational institutions and good education. It was Condorcet, writing during the French Revolution, who epitomised most clearly the optimism about the perfectibility of man and the scope for human progress on all fronts – material, scientific, moral and political. In his famous treatise, *Sketch for a Historical Picture of the Human Mind*, written in 1794, he aimed to prove 'that no bounds have been fixed to the improvement of the human faculties; that the perfectibility of man is absolutely indefinite' and to show 'by what ties nature has indissolubly united the advancement of knowledge with the progress of liberty, virtue, and respect for the natural rights of man'. Condorcet prophesied: 'The time will therefore come when the sun will shine only on free men who know no other master but their reason.' The rule of reason would, he thought, rid the world of tyranny and superstition, increase equality, improve health, prosperity and happiness and even lead people to exercise voluntary birth control 'rather than foolishly to encumber the world with useless and wretched beings'.[49]

The American and then the French revolutions, initially at least, engendered an enormous surge in optimism, both inside and outside these two countries, that reason could help evolve new forms of government which would embody and give effect to 'certain inalienable rights' – life, liberty and the pursuit of happiness. As Priestley wrote in a letter to Edmund Burke:

> How glorious, then, is the prospect, the reverse of all the past, which is now opening upon us, and upon the world . . .

> . . . Thus will reason be the umpire in all disputes and
> extinguish civil wars as well as foreign ones. The empire of
> reason will ever be the reign of peace . . . when men shall beat
> their swords into plough shares, and their spears into pruning
> hooks, when nation shall no more rise up against nation, and
> when they shall learn war no more. This is a state of things
> which good sense, and the prevailing spirit of commerce,
> aided by Christianity and true philosophy cannot fail to effect
> in time.[50]

Such unalloyed and extreme optimism did not survive the Terror which
followed the early stages of the French Revolution and which claimed
Condorcet's life among many others. The guillotining of 1,100 people in
Paris and the perversion of the noble aims of the revolution during the
later years of Napoleonic autocracy sapped the naïve human idealism of
many, including the young Wordsworth, and weakened the hold of the
new doctrine of human perfectibility. However, belief in the progress of
morality was by no means lost for ever – playing its part in the great
social reforms of the nineteenth century. The abolition of slavery, the
enfranchisement of ordinary men and (later) women and the introduction
of universal education were all, to some extent, motivated by a desire to
boost human dignity and improve the moral stature of mankind. The
early socialism of Robert Owen, the Lanarkshire mill-owner, also
reflected the belief that current social institutions were responsible for
vice as well as misery; social change could banish both from the world. In
our own century, idealism about the perfectibility of man has struggled to
survive the horrors of World War I and the Nazi holocaust. Man's capacity for evil seems as great as ever. Social reform has, of course, continued
apace in this most bloody of centuries, but more with the aim of fostering
progress in welfare and equality than with any illusion that it would in
itself lead to the perfection of men's moral faculties. Optimism about the
power of reason to generate continuous improvement in the moral sphere
was not in the end to be the main motor of the modern belief in progress.

Even within the Enlightenment period itself there were, of course,
widely differing views about the idea of human progress. Some influential thinkers stood opposed to the increasingly optimistic faith in the
power of reason alone to generate human progress. At the extreme, Jean-
Jacques Rousseau held that 'our minds have been corrupted in
proportion as our arts and sciences have made advances toward their perfection', and he expounded the Romantic idea of the noble savage.[51] We

shall explore this view, and the wholesale Romantic reaction against the belief in rationalistic progress, in the following chapter. We shall also examine the views of those thinkers, such as Kant, in the Enlightenment and beyond, who – while firmly believing in progress towards a more rational state of affairs – argued that ambition, greed and pride play a greater role in furthering such progress than reason itself. A hybrid view, which gave an important role to both reason and self interest, and which laid particular stress on the importance of the freedom of the individual to pursue his own economic advantage, was especially popular in the British libertarian tradition. Its most brilliant exponent was Adam Smith, who argued, in *The Wealth of Nations*, published in 1776, that progress was made possible by harnessing the creative power of self-interest in a framework of rational institutions, the rule of law and personal freedom. He believed that free markets could, through the operation of the decentralised 'invisible hand', lead to the most efficient satisfaction of the various wants of different market participants, each bent on pursuing their own rational self-interest, and so maximise the welfare of society as a whole. As Hampson remarks, this theory 'seemed to eliminate the traditional Christian conflict between virtue and acquisitiveness'.[52] While Smith himself repeatedly stressed the importance of moral sentiments as well as self-interest and liberty, his influential economic analysis was increasingly taken to promise unbounded progress in welfare and an indefinite augmentation of wealth – a morally desirable solution for society – without the need for the moral perfection of the citizens of that society. The way was open for the truly modern conception of progress, the focus of which is not human perfectibility but the combination of continued progress of reason in science and technology and a concomitant surge in economic growth and material prosperity. These two versions of progress – technological advance and economic growth – seemed to promise to all mankind a sure material route to progress in happiness and social welfare.

CHAPTER 4

The Philosophy of Progress

The Enlightenment period saw a huge upsurge in optimism about man's capacity for self-improvement and about the power of his reason to further the progress of mankind. Such optimism about the progressive power of human reason was, of course, by no means universal. Romanticism and nihilism are just two of several broad strands of thought which in their milder forms have been subversive of the conception of rational progress towards a happier life, and in their more extreme forms have denied altogether the possibility or the meaningfulness of such progress; these movements are the subject of the second part of this chapter. But even among those thinkers who have shared a confident belief in human progress, there has not been, by any means, one single conception – either during or since the Enlightenment. The first section of this chapter highlights five central philosophical areas of disagreement among those who have espoused doctrines of human progress: between those who believe progress to be an inevitable process, with a definable and predictable goal, and those who think that belief in a happy ending to history is an act of mere faith; between those who discern necessary laws of progress, and those who see progress simply as reflecting the interplay of various factors, the outcome of which is uncertain but has hitherto been largely positive; between those who assign the major role in generating a better future to the use of reason by individuals or societies, and those who emphasise the importance of antisocial or even irrational motives, such as avarice or pride; between those who, while agreeing that liberty is central to progress, disagree as to whether liberty should be defined as collective empowerment, or as individual freedom of choice and freedom from coercion; and, finally, between those who see progress as the unfolding of an international universal destiny for all mankind, and those who believe that the only true progress is through national self-expression and the development of national values. These five central and interconnected areas of debate and disagreement have consciously or unconsciously dominated the philosophical evolution of the idea of human progress over the last 250 years.

Five Disagreements

The first key area of debate centres on the wide divergence of views as to the certainty or otherwise of progress, particularly as regards the future. Some have believed that human progress in the future is inevitable and that it has some predictable and desirable destination. The Jewish conception of a progressive, divinely guided history, culminating inevitably in the coming of the Messiah to bring a golden age here on earth, is one influential version of this. So, too, is the Christian version – the predestined Second Coming and Last Judgement, with the promise of an otherworldly salvation for the elect few. These are very specialised notions of human progress – where advances in knowledge, prosperity and social progress here on earth are largely irrelevant. There is, however, a similar notion of inevitable progress to a predictable and supposedly desirable end, in the nineteenth-century philosopher Hegel's doctrine of the dialectic of History and the End of History. This was to have a profound influence on secular thinking, not least because it was later absorbed by Marx, in his theory of the inevitable arrival of the communist Utopia. Hegel's doctrine has been espoused more recently by Francis Fukuyama, in his controversial book *The End of History and the Last Man*.

Fukuyama argues that at the end of the twentieth century, it is increasingly plausible to see history as a single coherent, intelligible and evolutionary process with a definable purpose. Like Hegel and Marx, he also believes that an End of History is in sight. This is not to be seen as the end of important events, but as the point where 'there would be no further progress in the development of underlying principles and institutions, because all of the really big questions had been settled'. Whereas for Marx this point was to be reached with the communist state, Fukuyama's thesis is that the spread of liberal democracy and free-market economics to the greater part of the world constitutes the End of History.

Liberal democracy and liberal economics alone, he argues, can resolve the overwhelming desire by all individuals for recognition – because they alone provide for universal and reciprocal recognition. He sees the collapse of alternative political and economic conceptions – chiefly communism and fascism – as evidence for his thesis of the inevitable triumph of liberal democracy, and claims that they failed because they did not allow for universal and reciprocal recognition. Fukuyama also argues that science is increasingly the regulating mechanism of history, and that its advance is leading to an increasing homogenisation of all societies; by establishing 'a uniform horizon of economic production possibilities', it is making the unfolding of a truly global End of History more certain.[1]

By contrast, many of us would adopt a more sceptical position and be unwilling to postulate a single intelligible process of history, or any inevitable conclusion to it in the future. We may grant that there has been an important *de facto* ascent of man in the past – in particular progress in knowledge, science and welfare – but be unwilling to project this ascent as an inevitable feature into the future, with a definite happy ending. If the theory of progress involves more than just a conviction of past progress in what we judge to be a desirable direction – if it also involves a prophecy of further development in a desirable direction into the future – then many of us would agree with J. B. Bury that:

> . . . it cannot be proved that the unknown destination towards which man is advancing is desirable. The movement may be Progress, or it may be in an undesirable direction and therefore not Progress. This is a question of fact, and one which is at present as insoluble as the question of personal immortality. It is a problem which bears on the mystery of life.
>
> Moreover, even if it is admitted to be probable that the course of civilization has so far been in a desirable direction, and such as would lead to general felicity if the direction were followed far enough, it cannot be proved that ultimate attainment depends entirely on the human will. For the advance might at some point be arrested by an insuperable wall.[2]

In the end, for Bury as for most of us, a belief in progress into the future is an act of faith – which we either have or do not. There is no certain outcome to the endless human struggle for progress.

A second, and closely related divergence of view concerns the mechanism behind human progress. Those who have believed in its inevitability have generally held that there are laws of progress, like laws of nature or mathematics. This was the view of Auguste Comte in the mid nineteenth century, with his three stages of man, and of Herbert Spencer, who claimed to have discovered laws governing the upward course of social evolution. Spencer held that evolution was necessarily progressive, and that it was a universal process governing the social affairs of man, no less than the biology of species; evolution must gradually push human life towards higher states of organisation and complexity, through the mechanism of the gradual adaptation of man to his civilised environment. Hegel's quite different theories were of more lasting influence. His famous dialectic of history may not be easily intelligible to most of us, but his core belief that history is not a chapter of accidents but a purposive moving forward of certain principles has been very influential. Hegel's theory of dialectical change is notoriously difficult, and in this context need only be explained as the supposed process by which the human spirit sees the conflicting elements within its complex situation gradually resolved; history is the logically necessary working out of spirit, or *Geist*, coming to know itself; the End of History is when we have reached the point at which there is nothing left to be resolved – when spirit has reached a full and rational state of self-understanding. Marx borrowed much of Hegel's philosophy of history – while dropping the focus on *Geist* and the weird metaphysics – and spoke of materialist laws of historical development working with 'iron necessity' towards communism. For Marx, man's destiny was realised through the dialectic of inevitable class conflict.

However, the dominant strand of Western thought over the last 150 years has been hostile to the idea of laws of inevitable progress. It has come, for example, to see Spencer's philosophy of inevitable social evolution as a misreading of the long time frame of genuine evolutionary adaptation – which relies on the exploitation of random changes rather than on the inheritance of acquired characteristics – and a misreading of the essentially opportunistic nature of Darwinian evolution. In the natural world, later evolutionary adaptations are not necessarily superior to their predecessors in any objective sense other than their ability to survive. Nature has no necessary direction or purpose which it can lend, by analogy, to history. Indeed, Western thought has become increasingly sceptical of there being any single dominant purposive pattern to history. It has come to regard Hegel's all-encompassing spirit as an unnecessary and unconvincing fantasy and to see the process of history as not governed by inevitable laws of progress, but driven by the natural interplay of forces; so, a typical modern model of progress will regard the cumulative power of knowledge as promoting man's control and understanding of the world, and as interacting with the creative power of the free pursuit by individuals of their own self-interest, to generate economic growth and social progress. Such an interplay of factors is regarded as making progress into the future increasingly likely, but by no means assured.

A determinist view of history, like that of Comte or Hegel, appears to ignore the role not only of individual freedom of choice, but also of contingent events – the impact of random chance events like the fact of Hitler or Napoleon's existence, or the mental state of the leader with his finger on the nuclear button. However much we may discern patterns in history, most of us would argue that chance events have significant and crucial power to change the course of history and to derail human progress. Indeed, some believe that chance events dominate the course of history, and would answer affirmatively Isaiah Berlin's question: 'Can history be a mere purposeless succession of events, caused by a mixture of material factors and the play of random selection, a tale full of sound and fury signifying nothing?'[3]

Within the dominant sceptical tradition of Western thought, whether any individual retains confidence in future progress, or sinks into despair, becomes ultimately a question of that individual's inherent optimism or pessimism. We can detect no inevitable purpose or destination, and although many of us still hope it is valid to extrapolate forward from mankind's huge *de facto* triumphs in the past to a brighter future, optimism depends on an element of faith and hope.

A third major area of philosophical disagreement concerns whether or not the application of reason, and particularly the collective use of reason, should be seen as the central determining factor in the progressive development of a more rational and moral society. Some have stressed the importance of other factors in bringing about progress and the development of humanity. So, for example, Turgot held that individual passion and ambition were necessary to further progress; indeed he argued that, without 'unreason' and injustice, there would have been no progress at all. Bernard de Mandeville, too, in his allegorical poem, *The Fable of the Bees* (1714), made a shocking, if humorous, defence of the importance of the vices of avarice, luxury and pride in leading to prosperity and success. Perhaps the most striking theory of this kind was that of the great German philosopher Immanuel Kant, in his essay *Idea of a Universal History*. Kant sees history as the development of the hidden potential of the human species for reason, morality and freedom. But he argues that this development is brought about not by the conscious rational plans or well-intentioned reforms of human societies, but by the antagonism within societies, by the conflict induced by evil antisocial motives and by the desire of men to dominate one another. His subtle argument defines this antagonism as 'unsocial sociability': men wish to dominate each other but need each other as partners in conflict. It is such conflict, Kant argues, which enables mankind as a whole to develop its talents. He does not see the conscious goal of this conflict as being greater happiness or contentment; indeed, he sees it as necessary to progress that men aim for more than contentment: 'Thanks be then to Nature for this unsociableness, for this envious jealousy and vanity, for this unsatiable desire of possession or even of power! Without them all the excellent capacities implanted in mankind by nature would slumber eternally undeveloped.'[4] George Bernard Shaw, in his *Man and Superman*, was to express a similar thought: 'The reasonable man adapts himself to the world; the unreasonable one persists in trying to adapt the world to himself. Therefore all progress depends on the unreasonable man.'[5] In his essay *Perpetual Peace*, Kant does foresee a time of ever-lasting peace, but he argues that in the meantime war is the most important spur to human development. Many later German thinkers, like Hegel, also accorded considerable importance to war and conflict as moulders of humanity. After the world wars of the twentieth century, this is a less popular view.

By contrast, there is a strong strand of pure rationalism in Western thinking – essentially a broad set of beliefs which share the assumption that the central questions of humanity, as well as those of the physical universe, can at least in theory be solved by reason alone; if we could only (individually and collectively) find the right answers, life lived according to these rational solutions would represent a huge leap forward, a Golden Age of peace and prosperity. From Christian and social democrats to socialists, many have believed – in various ways – that the right rational answers if enacted in government policy would lead to a more perfect and virtuous society. At its most extreme, some French thinkers of the Enlightenment believed that human nature itself could be perfected and that war could be abolished by the application of reason to ethics, by improved education and by the creation of more rational institutions and better cross-border treaties. So, Condorcet, writing during the French Revolution, believed that intellectual progress would lead to the destruction of prejudice, and the progress of liberty and virtue, and that the continuing process of enlightenment would lead to perpetual social progress, to the end of war and of inequality and to the advance of humanity towards truth and happiness. It is unfortunate that such a pleasingly optimistic visionary was arrested by Jacobin revolutionaries and died in prison before his famous work on progress was even published. But some of this Enlightenment optimism lives on in the French and German political figures responsible for the creation of the European Union of today. They still hold that rational blueprints can avert war, change history and engineer social progress.

It should be noted that there has also been – especially in British and American thought – a hybrid view which, while optimistic about the role of reason in science and the rule of law, has also stressed the importance of harnessing other less attractive facets of the human character in order to foster progress. In this tradition, human reason may be used to greatest effect, even from the point of view of society, when it is in the service of the individual's selfish quest for advancement or glory. Liberal economics has, since Adam Smith, argued that the free-market mechanism ensures that competition and the rational pursuit of self-interest by individuals furthers the economic progress of society as a whole. Even those who have not had complete faith in the ability of the free market to establish social harmony and maximise the social good have often been concerned to harness effectively the creative power of self-interest and competitive rivalry, while placing them within a framework of rational institutions, government action and a strong ethical code. Despite the fact that political and economic debate has continually raged about how far the individual pursuit of self-interest needs to be guided and curtailed by collective rational planning, most people in the West would agree that both reason and selfish motives have a crucial role in promoting human progress. As Alexander Pope exclaimed in his optimistic *An Essay on Man*:

> *Two Principles in human nature reign;*
> *Self-love, to urge, and Reason, to restrain.*[6]

The fourth closely connected area of debate about progress concerns the nature of liberty and its role in promoting human advance. There have been few commentators since the Enlightenment who have not at least paid lip service to the importance of freedom, but there have been radically different interpretations of what is meant by the word. Following Hegel and Marx, many thinkers have essentially defined freedom as the collective empowerment of people through their participation in a rational state. In this view, freedom becomes defined not as individual freedom of choice nor as freedom from coercion by others, but as the chance to live in a state which individuals can accept as an expression of their own rational will. Freedom, in other words, becomes the sublimation of the individual will to that of the perfect rational state. Marxist definitions of freedom also involve an economic dimension: people are not seen as genuinely free unless they have equal (and hence collective) control of the economic means to exercise their choices. Scepticism in Western liberal democracies about such collective definitions of freedom has been heightened by fear that a Hegelian or Marxist belief in the inevitability of progress towards a perfect rational state – that is, in the inevitability of the evolution through dialectical change of a rational state which transcends all conflicts and allows complete harmony between the wills of the individual and the state – can encourage governments to dispense completely with individual freedom from coercion and with other ethical constraints. The perceived importance and inevitability of the desired goal may leave those who do not fit neatly into the dialectical movement in a precarious moral position. The twentieth century history of totalitarian states has made us more wary of such conceptions than Marx or Hegel saw reason to be.

By contrast, the dominant Western liberal consensus has stressed the paramount importance of individual freedom of choice and freedom from coercion. All democracies have championed the freedom to participate in government, and most have also sought to enshrine in law certain individual rights which seek to secure for individuals some inalienable areas of freedom of action and thought. Progress has, in part, become defined in the liberal tradition as the gradual extension of these individual freedoms and rights. The central problem for liberal democracy, however, is that one person's right to freedom of action may clash with another person's right not to be harmed. J. S. Mill, in his essay, *On Liberty*, famously argued that individuals should have complete freedom of action so long as their actions do not harm other people. But in our increasingly interconnected and congested world, many people argue that surprisingly few actions by individuals are without important consequences for others. The crucial debate has centred around what role democratic government should have in trying to ensure greater harmony of interests between members of society, and what role government should have in forging the best social and environmental outcome for society as a whole. So, for example, those who believe that collective rational planning can arrive at the right answers to society's problems in the field of economics are more likely to wish to allow government a large role, even at the expense of the freedom of the individual to pursue his or her own economic advantage. By contrast, those who, like Turgot and Kant, champion the progressive power of ambition and rivalry will tend to accord paramount importance to the ability of individuals to compete freely in pursuit of their own glory. Likewise, those who believe, as Adam Smith did, that the invisible hand of the free market operating in conditions of natural liberty is best placed to further the interests of society as a whole will tend to emphasise the key importance of economic liberalism, and the dangers of government intervention. For such thinkers, the chances of continued progress will best be safeguarded by deregulation, small government and global free trade – that is, by the maximum extension of economic liberty which is seen as compatible with the requirements of justice and perfect competition. We will return to this key debate in later chapters.

The fifth and final area of controversy that can usefully be highlighted in this brief survey of the philosophy of progress is the sharp divide between those who have seen progress as a universal phenomenon – as the expression of a single international destiny for all mankind – and those who have stressed the importance of national self-expression and development. We have already alluded to the fact that many French Enlightenment thinkers believed that war could be abolished and mankind live in harmony, if only the right rational blueprint could be devised. For them the goals of humanity and the cultural values of civilisation were timeless and universal. Reason could find universal answers to the problems of humanity, in the same way that it had discovered the laws of the physical universe. Condorcet even held that Europe was in essence a single society, while another French Enlightenment figure, Chastellux, argued that the interests of all nations were ultimately the same and could be reconciled on rational principles. The German philosopher Johann Herder was the leading figure in a German reaction to this predominantly French universalist thinking; the reaction was, of course, linked to German resentment of French political and military domination in the eighteenth century, as well as to resentment of the cosmopolitan arrogance of the French world view. For Herder, there was a paramount importance in national self-expression, in each nation or *volk* living according to its own customs and values, singing its own national song and developing according to its own distinctive historical rhythm. Progress was the realisation of nationhood; and international progress was development towards a collection of independent *volk* units, learning to live in harmony with each other – but each respecting its own traditions. The values of different peoples and their individual conceptions of happiness were all equally valid. Herder did not believe that human nature was uniform, but rather that each race had different innate psychological characteristics; the ultimately pernicious nature of this essentially racist view did not occur to Herder, who never personally stressed the idea that one race might be superior to others. His concern was to fight for the right for individual *volk* units to live their own lives and express their own values, and not to be subordinated to an international culture and destiny emanating from Paris.

Isaiah Berlin, who applauds Herder for demonstrating what he holds to be the fallacy of seeing history as 'a single universal process of struggle towards the light', sums up the implications of Herder's thought in his book, *The Crooked Timber of Humanity*:

> If free creation, spontaneous development along one's own native lines, not inhibited or suppressed by the dogmatic pronouncements of an élite of self-appointed arbiters, insensitive to history, is to be accorded supreme value; if authenticity and variety are not to be sacrificed to authority, organisation, centralisation, which inexorably tend to uniformity and the destruction of what men hold dearest – their language, their institutions, their habits, their form of life, all that has made them what they are – then the establishment of one world, organised on universally accepted rational principles – the ideal society – is not acceptable.[7]

This clarion call for national self-determination has obvious relevance to many of the current economic and political arguments surrounding the European Union and the European Monetary Union project in particular. Euro-sceptics like Messrs Portillo and Redwood in the UK might echo the words of Herder or Berlin; for they see further European integration as a fundamentally damaging attack on national sovereignty, a denial of a nation's ability to control its own destiny and fly its own flag. By contrast, Chancellor Köhl of Germany has described further European integration as 'a question of war and peace in the twenty-first century', and argues that the absence of continued integration would lead to retrogression and nationalism. In part, this current debate reflects a philosophical divide which goes back to the schism between the Enlightenment thinkers of eighteenth-century Paris – who passionately believed that rational blueprints and treaties could foster progress and allow countries to live harmoniously together and banish war forever – and the German romantics from Herder on, for whom national self-expression and autonomous development were paramount. Ironically, in post-World War II Europe, the leadership of Germany is firmly in the Parisian Enlightenment camp, and both the French and German élites want to keep it that way. The torch of national as opposed to international destiny and progress has passed to the right of the UK Conservative Party and other European right-wing splinter groups. Of course, the passions and motivations behind each side of the debate are hugely complex. For part of the impetus for European integration comes from a Continental desire to protect and build a European alternative to an American-dominated world culture and to an all-pervasive liberal economic order which – as Fukuyama points out – is fast leading to the homogenisation of world cultures and politics and the creation of a 'global village'. Many Europeans would argue that the dictates of free trade and free-market economics will ultimately be more destructive of national spontaneity and variety than the voluntary creation of a federal union of European states. They would argue that it is not the pooling of European sovereignty but the globalisation of trade that is causing individual European cultures to be swamped, national languages to be increasingly supplanted by pidgin English, and national working practices to be harmonised to the dominant US standard.

Counter-currents: Romanticism and Despair

The most important broad strand of Western thought that is subversive of the conception of rational progress towards a happier life is Romanticism. Romanticism covers a broad spectrum of beliefs and values, but common to them all is a conviction that there is much to be valued in human life that is *not* the product of rational intellect. The Romantic outlook consists of a set of conscious and unconscious reactions against the growing dominance of secular rationality – against the rationality of empirical science and against the Enlightenment faith in the paramount role of reason in guiding men's affairs and perfecting their natures. In its later stages, it is also a reaction against the soulless aspect of industrialism and of the growing centrality of material aspirations in a modern economy. Richard Tarnas, in his book, *The Passion of the Western Mind*, argues that the medieval and Renaissance dichotomy between reason and faith and the seventeenth-century dichotomy between secular science and Christian religion became in the eighteenth and nineteenth centuries a more general schism between scientific rationalism and the Romantic outlook.

> Because both temperaments were deeply and simultaneously expressive of Western attitudes and yet were largely incompatible, a complex bifurcation of the Western outlook resulted. With the modern psyche so affected by the Romantic sensibility and in some sense identified with it, yet with the truth claims of science so formidable, modern man experienced in effect an intractable division between his mind and his soul.[8]

To some extent this bifurcation remains essential to any modern understanding of human aspirations and human happiness. There is a part in all of us that doubts that an entirely rational world of scientific analysis and carefully codified material aspirations can answer to our innermost needs. We recognise – at least from time to time – the truth proclaimed by Romantic artists, musicians and poets, that there is a transcendent value in emotion, love and nature.

The central early figure in the creation of the Romantic outlook was, of course, Rousseau. He was crucial to its evolution, for three main reasons. First, he stood firmly opposed to the dominant beliefs of the French Enlightenment – to its faith in the efficacy of reason in perfecting humanity and to its belief in the progress of civilisation. Rousseau championed the reverse view, that mankind has been corrupted and made more unhappy by civilisation. He asserted the nobility of the savage, and argued that primitive society was better adapted to human happiness, freedom and dignity. The evil of inequality entered society with agriculture and the private ownership of land. Civilisation imparted a passion for appearances and affectation in place of the simple and sincere discourse of rustic folk. In Rousseau's words:

> Our minds have been corrupted in proportion as our arts and sciences have made advances toward their perfection. Shall we say that this is a misfortune particular to our times? No gentlemen, the evils arising from our vain curiosity are as old as the world.[9]

The idea of the noble savage and of moral regress since primitive times has been, since Rousseau, a cultural counterpoint to optimism about human progress – the ideal of innocence balanced against the ideal of civilised sophistication. From the writings of Diderot, in the eighteenth century, to the paintings of Gauguin, in the nineteenth, the image of innocent happiness on the Pacific island of Tahiti – where social practices seemed to be based on human instinct rather than on artificial convention – had a particular cultural resonance.

Rousseau was important, secondly, as an early exponent of an essentially totalitarian conception of the ideal relationship between individual and state. His blueprint for modern man was his *Social Contract*, published in 1762. The memorable opening line was: 'Man is born free, and everywhere he is in chains'; but his influential and dangerous solution was for citizens to enter into a social contract. This involved 'the total alienation of each associate, together with all his rights, to the whole community'. The fundamental principle of this community was to be that 'each of us puts his person and all his power in common under the supreme direction of the general will'. The general will is defined as what is common among the interests and wills of all the individuals in the society, so that the fulfilment of the general will would lead to the greatest collective satisfaction. The existence of such a general will is no utopian musing in Rousseau's account. For his social contract stipulates that refusal by individuals to obey the general will should, in some cases, be punishable by death. Men should be 'forced to be free'.[10] This conception of freedom – so far from the libertarian ideal of *individual* freedom – and this complete identification of individual and state were to have unfortunate echoes in the ideological history of Europe over the following two hundred years.

Rousseau was influential, thirdly, in championing the view that man's natural intuitions and feelings, unfettered by the conceptions of civilisation, were the best sources of morality. He argued that the inner voice of nature, the conscience or the heart were preferable to the head, and were more likely to serve the common interest than the selfish promptings of reason. The rules of conduct were written by nature in the soul; if only we followed these, undiverted by the norms of civilisation and reason, we would, he argued, be happier and morally superior. In his book *Emile*, he elaborated a new scheme of education for children, in which they were to be allowed full scope for individual development surrounded by nature and protected from the corrupting influences of civilisation and philosophers.

Most philosophers operating in the empirical tradition have been sceptical about these ideas. Bertrand Russell, for example, disposes of the

claim that beliefs based on the natural emotions of the heart can in themselves be sources of a genuine morality, with two objections:

> One is that there is no reason whatever to suppose that such
> beliefs will be true; the other is, that the resulting beliefs will
> be private, since the heart says different things to different
> people. Some savages are persuaded by the 'natural light' that
> it is their duty to eat people, and even Voltaire's savages, who
> are led by the voice of reason to hold that one should only eat
> Jesuits, are not wholly satisfactory.[11]

But if natural religion never convinced most philosophers, it remained
nevertheless a powerful cultural and artistic undercurrent.

The gentler manifestations of the Romantic movement, like the
poetry of Wordsworth, reflected some of Rousseau's themes. For the
English poets, as for many of the great Romantic musicians, poets and
novelists of the nineteenth century, it was not so much that progress
didn't exist, or that reason had no remit, but rather that the idea of
progress was based on a rationalist, utilitarian, economic, technological
conception of the world which was narrow and ignored much that was of
the essence of humanity. They saw nature not as something to be tamed
and used, nor only as an object of beauty, but as expressive of spiritual
meaning and as an educator of the soul. For them, the mysteries of love
and death, of dreams and imagination were the central facets of life – the
core of being human. The Romantic movement also brought about a
profound shift in aesthetic taste. Neoclassical architecture – rational
designs of perfect harmony – gave way to a revival in the Gothic. Tastes
in landscape, as reflected in poetry and painting, shifted from ordered
and tranquil pastoral scenes to alpine crags, torrents, caves and primeval
forests. The quintessential Romantic vision might be that expressed in
Coleridge's dream poem 'Kubla Khan':

> *But O, that deep romantic chasm which slanted*
> *Down the green hill athwart a cedarn cover!*
> *A savage place! as holy and enchanted*
> *As e're beneath a waning moon was haunted*
> *By woman wailing for her demon-lover!*

While such mild forms of Romanticism – vital but tame expressions of
the ideal of innocence and of the aesthetic and moral importance of the

emotions and nature – have represented an important cultural counter-weight to the idea of rational human progress in our technological and materialistic age, they have not had the power to derail the idea alto-gether. But the Romantic movement also had uglier aspects. Not only, in the writings of Rousseau, had it planted the seeds of a totalitarian con-ception of the state; it also had even more extreme exponents for whom the value of the free expression of the human will was transcendent over the mere utility of reason or the happiness of the common man. One of the most memorable expressions of this idea is to be found in the poetry of Byron, whose aloof heroes are portrayed as proudly defying the shallow world, as in this extract from *Lara*:

> *There was in him a vital scorn of all:*
> *As if the worst had fall'n which could befall*
> *He stood a stranger in this breathing world . . .*

> *Too high for common selfishness, he could*
> *At times resign his own for others' good,*
> *But not in pity, not because he ought,*
> *But in some strange perversity of thought,*
> *That swayed him onward with a secret pride*
> *To do what few or none would do beside.*

For Byron, as for a number of the Romantics, Napoleon was the supreme hero; his evocation of him in *Childe Harold's Pilgrimage* (Canto III) is a per-fect example of the influential Byronic hero – a man of superhuman energies, a wronged and suffering genius, at odds with the common herd of mankind:

> *He who ascends to mountain-tops, shall find*
> *The loftiest peaks most wrapt in clouds and snow;*
> *He who surpasses or subdues mankind,*
> *Must look down on the hate of those below.*
> *Though high above the sun of glory glow,*
> *And far beneath the earth and ocean spread,*
> *Round him are icy rocks, and loudly blow*
> *Contending tempests on his naked head,*
> *And thus reward the toils which to those summits led.*

Byron's verse was hugely influential on the continent of Europe, inspiring, among others, the German philosopher Nietzsche. Nietzsche's thought has many parallels with the music and subject matter of the operas (particularly *The Ring*) of Wagner, of whom he was a great admirer and a friend until they quarrelled. For Nietzsche, modern progress was decadence, and he was equally scathing of the politics and morality of the majority. He abhorred democracy as leading to the morality of the lowest common denominator, and ensnaring the great and noble in the rules designed for the common herd; all that is admirable and good is to be found only in the superior élite. He attacked Christianity as furthering the underdog and encouraging the survival of those who cannot stand on their own two feet. Furthermore, he believed that morality is not absolute and is not laid down by some impersonal objective rationality, but that there is a plurality of valid perspectives and values. Indeed, he thought the loss of belief in God and in an objective religious morality – 'the death of God' – could allow the birth of Superman. Superman is Nietzsche's Byronic hero, the man who lives according to the dictates of his untrammelled will for power and creates his own values. Nietzsche saw life as a work of art, the leader as supreme artist.

Though Nietzsche himself became insane, his powerful writings have not only had enormous influence on literature, but have also found unfortunate resonance in the world of politics. His works were read by Mussolini and he was the favourite philosopher of the Nazis. The horrors of World War II, of Stalin and Hitler, have shown us the horrific potential of the untrammelled will to power and of a Superman as supreme artist. However, they must also instil in us, as Fukuyama argues, an understanding of man's craving for recognition and self-assertion. If we deny the importance of this drive, we may create the conditions for Nietzschean monsters. Indeed, Fukuyama tempers his conviction that liberal democracy is the triumphant End of History by wondering whether men will be content forever with a life of material accumulation, and whether the tame struggles allowable in a prosperous democracy will be sufficient to cater for their desire for glory and a chance to prove their valour. In his article, 'On the Possibility of Writing a Universal History', he comes to the following disquieting conclusion:

> . . . it seems unlikely that all men will be content to become such contemptible creatures, preoccupied with endless consumerism and petty self-interest. They are, after all, human

beings with pride, and they will rebel at the prospect of a world bereft of ideals and struggle. And if they cannot struggle against injustice and oppression because the world has somehow become 'filled up' with successful democracies, then they may well seek to struggle against justice, peace, and prosperity.[12]

The worst excesses of Romanticism may still have the power to reverse the direction of human affairs from progress to regress.

During the twentieth century, the threat to a confident belief in human progress has manifested itself, not only in Nietzschean delusions themselves, but also in a growing psychological and cultural reaction of despair, prompted by the horrors of war. Despair at the bestiality of man has combined with a growing sense of alienation in our increasingly technological societies, and with feelings of emotional and spiritual insecurity as the old moral certainties of religion, king and country wither away. The prevalent pessimism in some circles – particularly between the world wars – is expressed in these lines from W. B. Yeats' poem 'The Second Coming':

> Things fall apart; the centre cannot hold;
> Mere anarchy is loosed upon the world,
> The blood-dimmed tide is loosed, and everywhere
> The ceremony of innocence is drowned;
> The best lack all conviction, while the worst
> Are full of passionate intensity.[13]

In twentieth-century philosophy, the existentialist movement's view of life as 'an impassioned freedom towards death' and the nihilist rejection of all justifications for morality are extreme expressions of this failure of confidence in man's destiny. Man is seen as alone in a universe blind to human concerns. At the same time, much of art has ceased to be figurative, harmonious or even coherent; where it is figurative, it tends to be concerned with human suffering – like Munch's famous *The Scream* (1895) – or with the elemental passions of fear and hate, as in Picasso's works, like *Guernica*. In literature, Albert Camus' influential novel, *The Outsider* (1946), highlights the absurdity of existence, the arbitrariness of events and the solitary detachment of the human condition, while the works of Samuel Beckett typify feelings of spiritual desolation and utter loneliness which seem to deny the validity of all human endeavour.

Beckett's monologue *Malone Dies* opens: 'I shall soon be quite dead at last in spite of all', and the later volume in the same trilogy (*The Unnamable*) ends with: '. . . where I am, I don't know, I'll never know, in the silence you don't know, you must go on, I can't go on, I'll go on.'[14]

CHAPTER 5

Progress in the Age of Science and Technology

Belief in human progress reached its apogee in the hundred years before 1914 and, despite the nightmare of two world wars, soared again in the generation immediately following 1945. Widespread and confident belief in progress rested firmly on two pillars: that of progress in science and technology on the one hand, and of material progress and economic growth on the other. These were two forms of progress that seemed undeniably cumulative, and together they appeared to promise a sure material route to advances in happiness and social welfare for all mankind. This chapter begins with a brief survey of some key features of scientific and technological progress during the last two hundred years which helped initially to engender a widespread confidence and optimism about the future; it then analyses the slow re-emergence in this century of doubts about the ability of mankind ever fully to understand or control the natural world, as well as the growing anxiety about whether society can learn to direct wisely the enormous power given to it by scientific innovation.

Evolution and Progress

We live in an age which has long grown accustomed to expecting that medical and other problems will, in due course, be susceptible to scientific solutions. We have come to expect that we will continue to be swept along on a tide of innovation and discovery designed to make our lives easier, longer and more productive, and our universe more intelligible. It is easy to forget the enormous psychological impact that the early triumphs of science and technology had on contemporary perceptions of the human predicament. We noted earlier the extraordinary impact that the new cosmology of Copernicus and Galileo, and the physics of Isaac Newton, had on the collective consciousness of the seventeenth and eighteenth centuries. But even the shock of this relegation of the earth to peripheral status was eclipsed in the nineteenth century by the Darwinian revolution.

The theory of evolution, which had been slowly gaining ground for several decades, burst into popular consciousness with its brilliant exposition in Charles Darwin's *On the Origin of Species by Means of Natural Selection* (1859) and later in his *The Descent of Man* (1871). Darwin emphasised the struggle for existence, and argued that new species arise gradually by a process of natural selection. A hostile environment ensures that, among a population with innate variations, the fittest and best adapted are most likely to survive and pass on their advantageous variations to their offspring. In this way, particularly when the environment itself is changing, the natural selection of the most advantageous random variations can gradually result in the evolution of a new species. In the early twentieth century, the science of genetics, echoing the earlier work of Gregor Mendel, explained the existence of random variations as the product of spontaneous genetic mutations, and provided firm evidence for the process of inheritance of genetic characteristics.

Even before genetics provided a convincing mechanism to account for Darwin's theory, the idea of evolution he did so much to propagate had profound effects on contemporary views of the human predicament. Already the discoveries of geology had suggested an immeasurably longer time scale for the earth's existence than that suggested by the Bible. Now, just as earlier the earth had been demoted to the status of one planet in a vast universe, man himself was in danger of being relegated to the status of the latest form of ape, at the end of a long process of evolution. However, as Peter Bowler describes in his book, *Evolution: The History of an Idea*, the impact of the theory was complicated for many years, even after Darwin's work was published, by the existence of different conceptions of evolution. Many evolutionists did not accept the random character of Darwinian natural selection. Among these were some who continued to believe in evolution by design, with man the very pinnacle of creation, thanks to God's benevolent providential design; evolution was, in this view, one of the laws of nature designed by God to carry out his ultimate purpose. As the detail of Darwin's theory gained acceptance, such views had to contend with the fact that natural selection via the survival of the fittest is a harsh mechanism entailing untold suffering, and therefore appears to be an odd law for a benevolent God to use as his instrument.

Many other evolutionists, like the avowedly materialist Herbert Spencer, had a strong conviction that evolution, however harsh a process, is essentially progressive. According to Spencer, evolution is a law of nature which ensures that matter becomes increasingly complex, with life evolving into higher states of organisation. Spencer was important because he held that this universal progressive process governs the social affairs of men no less than the biology of species; evolution must gradually push human life towards higher states of organisation and complexity, through the mechanism of the gradual adaptation of man to his civilised environment. As a result, Spencer thought it vital that nature should be allowed to evolve unhindered, and argued for a social policy of *laissez-faire*, on the grounds that this would guarantee human progress. In this view, evolutionary success becomes the only criterion of correct conduct, while the ability to adapt and conform to the requirements of social evolution becomes the prerequisite of progress. Spencer argued for eliminating barriers to individual initiative, in order to foster a successful society. Such views came to be termed social Darwinism – a broad collection of right-wing *laissez-faire* beliefs which argue that progress would be guaranteed if the fittest were allowed to prosper unfettered.

The theory of evolution, therefore, did much in the nineteenth century to foster and complement the dominant belief in progress. However, it did so as a result of a non-acceptance, or a fundamental misreading, of Darwin's own version of the theory. As Bowler points out:

> The concepts of hierarchy and progress, however, were those most threatened by the details of Darwin's theory. Branching evolution made it difficult to define how one form could be ranked higher or lower than another, especially when some apparently 'low' forms have survived over vast periods of time. Natural selection worked toward adaptation, not progress, and was opportunistic in its exploitation of new avenues of development. If these points were accepted at face value, much of the late nineteenth century's evolutionary philosophising would be worthless.[1]

Contrary to the views of Spencer and others, Darwinism seems to entail that there is no *necessary* direction or purpose in nature. Later evolutionary adaptations are not necessarily superior to their predecessors in any objective sense other than their ability to survive. Some successful evolutionary adaptations may be very simple and unattractive. Change is not necessarily for the better.

The great biologist T. H. Huxley argued forcibly both against attempts to see in evolution evidence of divine design, and against Spencer's use of evolution as a theoretical basis for a *laissez-faire* ethic. If evolutionary change is not necessarily progress in nature, why should change be inevitably progressive in society? It was, in Huxley's view, quite wrong to subordinate human morality to an ethic of 'evolutionary' success. There is nothing necessarily noble and progressive about the natural struggle for survival, which can involve great suffering and lead to the survival of successful brutes. Humanity consists of protecting and helping the weak, not eliminating them, and of fostering love and charity as well as encouraging the drive for success. In the years following Huxley's attack, Spencer's theories fell into disrepute, not least because of their reliance on the increasingly discredited theory of the inheritance of acquired characteristics; his philosophy came to be seen as a misreading of the long time frame of genuine evolutionary adaptation, which relies on the exploitation, over many generations, of random changes in the genetic make-up.

Evolution does not provide a necessary law of human progress. At best, it represents an analogy to the changes in human society, and one which if properly understood is more likely to underline the random, directionless nature of change than to emphasise any necessarily progressive attributes. Among many twentieth-century thinkers – such as the existentialists and the nihilists – Darwinism did indeed help to underline the meaningless of nature, the pointlessness of human existence and the ubiquity of suffering.

If the idea of evolution itself had a complex relationship to belief in progress, Darwinism nevertheless represented one of the greatest advances of theoretical science. Together with a myriad of other theoretical advances in the nineteenth and early twentieth centuries, in chemistry, physics, astronomy and biology, it helped to foster a strong belief in linear and cumulative progress in knowledge. As human reason gradually triumphed over the great mysteries of life and the universe, self-confidence in the ability of human reason to explain and control nature, so evident among the Enlightenment thinkers, spread far more widely, making society as a whole more critical, even scornful, of the past masters; it also left less and less room, even at the popular level, for superstitious belief in an unpredictable God in control of everyday events and men's physical lives on earth. To be sure, many continued to interpret the new rational explanations of the workings of the universe and nature in a religious light, as revealing the glory of divine reason and the perfection of God's rationally coherent creation. However, such a belief in a benign deity – operating through the great intelligible laws of nature and showing His love by granting man the ability to understand these laws and to use that knowledge to improve his lot – did not represent the sort of obstacle to a confident belief in progress here on earth that had been provided by the pagan religions and by the earlier Christianity of St Augustine and the Middle Ages. Furthermore, as the triumphs of science and technology increased confidence that mankind could discover materialistic explanations for everything, and could control nature to create a paradise on earth of material prosperity, Christianity gradually lost its grip on Western thinking as an all-embracing conception of life. It became increasingly a religion of personal morality and spirituality which had to accommodate itself to a secular culture of increasingly materialistic objectives, explanations and standards. Slowly but surely, moral and spiritual progress and the securing of the afterlife ceased to be even notionally the paramount concerns of the majority in society. The pursuit of happiness became an inalienable right, while the pursuit of improved prosperity and social welfare on earth, and the advancement of secular learning, became the key civic duties. Christianity had to be content with providing a moral and spiritual dimension to the headlong pursuit of a material heaven on earth. This more materialistic view of the world, combining belief in indefinite progress in knowledge with expectations of an endless rise in material prosperity driven by technology and economic growth, allowed a secular idea of human progress to triumph.

The Triumph of Technology

The giant strides in the theoretical sciences no doubt had a more direct effect on the outlook of educated élites than on the views of ordinary working people. However, the advances in applied science and technology – which by the beginning of the twentieth century had touched the lives of nearly everyone in the Western world – induced a more general sense of optimism about the future and confidence in the power of human reason. If, by portraying humanity as a mere accident of evolutionary history, Darwinism diminished man's status, the tidal wave of technological inventions in the nineteenth and twentieth centuries, and the increasing power of science to help man control the natural world, seemed enormously to enhance it. It was an irony that in the same century in which most people came to realise that the story in the Book of Genesis could not be a literal account of the Creation, the Biblical view (expressed in Genesis Chapter 1) that man had been granted dominion and mastery over the rest of nature became, thanks to the new technologies, more true than it had ever been: 'And God blessed them, and God said unto them, Be fruitful, and multiply, and replenish the earth, and subdue it: and have dominion over the fish of the sea, and over the fowl of the air, and over every living thing that moveth upon the earth.'

From 1800 onwards the speed of technological change was breathtaking and inspiring. The catalogue of technological advance is a commonplace and needs only the briefest survey here. In the nineteenth century, the power of steam and coal was harnessed to run factories, sparking the Industrial Revolution. Steam navigation and railways dramatically collapsed the distances on earth, opening up new horizons and fostering an enormous growth in trade around the globe. Gas lighting started to conquer the darkness of night, while better sanitation and clean piped water defeated the scourge of cholera and dysentery. The bicycle provided the individual with a cheap and practical alternative to travel on horseback or foot. During the last hundred years, cars have given previously undreamed-of personal mobility, and air travel has made the global village a reality. Electricity has brought bright lighting to almost every home in the developed world, and ushered in an era of cleaner factories and transport. Refrigeration has allowed a giant extension of man's diet. The typewriter, the mechanical adding machine and, more recently, the word processor have transformed office life, while telecommunications have given us the ability to talk around the world. Computers have granted mankind previously inconceivable computational and information storage capacity. Cinema, radio and television have established a global entertainment industry and culture, and brought varied entertainment, live sporting events, music, drama and the world's news into the living rooms of millions of ordinary homes. Over the last fifty years, washing machines, electric irons, vacuum cleaners and microwaves have transformed the nature of household work. Nylon and plastics have brought cheaper clothing, and greatly increased the availability of all manner of cheap and durable consumer goods. Most crucially of all, medical science has been responsible for enormous improvements in human welfare; vaccines have all but eliminated diseases like TB, polio and smallpox, which had ravaged communities for centuries; anaesthetics and antiseptics have made surgery less painful and safer; and antibiotics offer cures to many previously fatal illnesses, such as pneumonia and blood poisoning. Life expectancy worldwide has risen in the last thirty years alone from 53 to 66 – progress indeed.

For most of the period since 1800, such impressive and life-transforming developments produced significantly positive changes in welfare for much of humanity, often within the span of each single generation. The all-pervasive and seemingly benign nature of most of the changes, and the rapidity of improvements to still young technologies, quickly established a world where 'new' was seen as almost synonymous with 'better'. The accelerating pace of technological and medical advances increasingly seemed to suggest the possibility of an indefinite progress in health, welfare and material prosperity for everyone.

Many of the changes wrought by technology did, of course, cause hardship to some in the period of transition, and produced losers as well as winners. Particularly traumatic was the revolution in agriculture in the nineteenth and early twentieth centuries. Yields began to rise slowly in the eighteenth century as a result of the enclosures, the introduction of crop rotation and the use of new crops (e.g., sugar beet and the potato); but it was the impact of technology which really transformed the productivity and nature of agriculture beyond all recognition. The railways and steam navigation allowed huge farms to be established in the Midwest of America and in South America, and enabled them to compete directly with European farmers. At roughly the same time, new steel ploughs and the invention of mechanical reaping and threshing machines all greatly increased productivity and reduced the requirement for manpower. Horse-drawn reapers could do the work of many men using the traditional scythe. During the early to mid-twentieth century, the tractor and later the combine harvester, together with automatic milking machines and industrial farming of poultry and pigs, further reduced the requirement for human labour; and in the years following World War II, the growth in the use of fertilisers and pesticides, the move to monoculture farming and the introduction of higher-yielding strains led to dramatic increases in yields per acre and per man. As a result of all these changes, there was an enormous displacement of human labour. Whereas in 1850 60 per cent of the working population in the USA was involved directly in agriculture, by the 1990s the number was less than 3 per cent.

This rapid transformation of a rural way of life that had persisted largely unchanged for centuries caused real hardship and distress among many of those bearing the brunt of the forces of change, and also caused considerable economic dislocation. It did not, however, seriously undermine a widespread belief in progress. In part, this was because of the huge boon represented by the increase in the availability of food; plentiful cheap food eliminated starvation in many parts of the world, and allowed for large sustained increases in population; by reducing the price of essentials, it also increased consumer purchasing power, thereby fuelling economic growth. In part, too, the virtual demise of agricultural employment left the creed of progress undented because of the new opportunities which presented themselves to most of those displaced by change. The growing numbers of factories needed more labour, the railways needed staff and the engineering works needed extra skilled craftsmen. The new frontiers of the Americas also allowed many of those displaced by technological change to build a new life. Indeed, the 'Wild West' mentality and the new transcontinental railroads came to symbolise in America the onward march of progressive civilisation, triumphing over barren empty space and the 'savage' tribes of Indians. The western frontier represented the opportunity for enrichment that was, according to the American dream, available to all. With effort and willpower, a new future could be built out of nothing.

The Re-emergence of Doubt and Uncertainty

By the beginning of the twentieth century, man seemed genuinely empowered, by the advances in knowledge and the new technologies, to engineer positive change across many aspects of human life and to sustain this progress by the power of his own reason and ingenuity. The human race might soon be able to control its own destiny and reach a golden age of material bliss, of health, wealth and happiness. However, after 1914, there re-emerged significant challenges to such confidence in the progressive power of science and technology. As Richard Tarnas points out in *The Passion of the Western Mind*, these challenges took two forms – those internal to the world of theoretical scientific research, and those external to it in the form of the morally and practically ambiguous consequences of scientific and technological advance. There were new doubts about the nature and scope of progress in knowledge itself and, more importantly, there was increasing anxiety about whether mankind could be trusted to use the enormous extension of power granted by science to good effect and to the benefit of the majority.

It was in the new physics that the internal challenge to the old certainties of eighteenth- and nineteenth-century science first appeared;
the simplicity of Newtonian physics was challenged by Einstein's Special
(1905) and General (1916) Theory of Relativity and by the theories of
quantum mechanics, especially Heisenberg's Uncertainty Principle
(1927). Einstein's Special Theory argued that as bodies get faster, particularly at speeds close to the speed of light, they become shorter and
heavier. This led him to conclude that mass and energy are two different
aspects of the same thing, as expressed in his famous equation $E = mc^2$.
The counter-intuitive nature of this equivalence of mass and energy was
matched by his development of the notion of a four-dimensional space-
time continuum which, in his General Theory, he showed to be 'curved'
under the gravitational influence of mass. Space and time were no longer
absolute independent coordinates. Moreover, when two observers are in
relative motion, Einstein proved that they will make different judgements as to what is happening at any particular moment. From the
perspective of one observer something can be happening which is still in
the future from the perspective of the other. Modern physics has thus, in
one sense at least, eliminated another basic distinction, that between
past, present and future. In the field of quantum mechanics, Heisenberg,
in his famous Uncertainty Principle, stated that there is a fundamental
limit to the accuracy with which one can simultaneously measure both
the position and momentum of a particle, and a similar limit to the accuracy of simultaneous measurement of energy and time. At subatomic
levels, accurate measurements of these factors will always yield uncertainties in the values obtained, and Heisenberg held that this irreducible
uncertainty reflects the fact that the act of measuring a system interferes
with it. The only certainties at this level are probabilities. For
Heisenberg, atoms and elementary particles formed 'a world of potentialities or possibilities rather than one of things or facts'.

These brilliant discoveries of physics and mathematics represented in
one way a further huge triumph of human reason and another leap in the
progress of knowledge, opening up the whole awesome field of nuclear
physics. But with these and other associated discoveries, much of the
easy intelligibility and simplicity of the Newtonian conception of the
universe began to dissolve. In summing up the impact of the new
physics, as well as the new Freudian theories of the non-rational promptings of the bestial unconsciousness of man, Tarnas writes:

A certain irreducible irrationality, already recognised in the human psyche, now emerged in the structure of the physical world itself. To incoherence was added unintelligibility, for the conceptions derived from the new physics not only were difficult for the lay-person to comprehend, they presented seemingly insuperable obstacles to human intuition generally: a curved space, finite yet unbounded; a four dimensional space-time continuum; mutually exclusive properties possessed by the same subatomic entity . . .[2]

From the 1920s on, the theoretical frontiers of most sciences have become increasingly unintelligible not only to ordinary people but even to scientists operating in different fields. Knowledge has become more and more specialised and compartmentalised. There continues to be progress in knowledge, of course, but the new knowledge increasingly paints a picture of a world of almost unfathomable complexity and counter-intuitive oddity. Furthermore, knowledge is now expanding at such a rate that it has become impossible for any individual human being to comprehend more than a tiny fraction of the key scientific theories on offer or data available. Now that computers can, in seconds, do calculations which would before have taken scores of mathematicians years to complete, the speed of discovery and the intricacy of scientific findings is fast growing beyond anything imaginable just a few decades ago. As scientists become more specialised and cease to speak a language that others can understand, popular faith in them is increasingly turning to suspicion. It is also becoming harder for the scientific community itself to exercise any control over, or even to keep an overall grasp of, the direction in which their knowledge might be leading.

The tendency of scientific theories, even those as respected and well established as Newton's, to be superseded and found either incomplete or plain wrong has undermined the degree of certainty attached to scientific discoveries. Scientific knowledge itself is increasingly recognised as a provisional collection of shifting paradigms. The philosopher Thomas Kuhn highlighted the need for humility about scientific knowledge. While not denying the cumulative impact of discovery, he argued that all research and observation is theory-laden, in the sense that scientists operate within a paradigm (or dominant set of theories) to which they feel emotional loyalty and which colours the way they observe data and the experiments they judge to be worth doing. Only when facts that run directly counter to the paradigm become numerous and very obviously anomalous is a paradigm crisis precipitated and a revolution in scientific thinking made possible. This revolution will of course allow more to be explained than was possible before, and thus will represent progress, but it may well call into question conclusions which were long held to have been settled. Progress in knowledge is far from being a simple accretion of facts; the process, rather than being linear, is fitful.

A more recent internal challenge to the intelligible and progressive picture of scientific knowledge is that posed by the new scientific theories of chaos and complexity. Einstein may have already called into question the idea of a clockwork universe, and quantum mechanics may have posited an irreducible uncertainty at subatomic levels, but it was the new theories of chaos and complexity which emphasised the unpredictability of much of our everyday environment. Chaotic systems are those where the outcomes cannot be predicted at the outset, because the most minute changes in initial conditions will cause radically different outcomes. The 'butterfly effect' in the context of weather is the classic image of chaos, with the flap of a butterfly's wing able to make the difference between a hurricane occurring or not occurring. The meteorologist Edward Lorenz, when modelling weather patterns, noticed that very simple mathematical equations were capable of generating enormously complex but unpredictable patterns very similar to those of the world's weather. Of most importance, he noted that very small differences in inputs (e.g., a rounding error in his program – 0.506 as opposed to 0.506127) could lead to catastrophic differences of outcome. These outcomes could be explained after the event, according to simple laws, but not predicted beforehand. The behaviour of weather, of clouds, of waterfalls, of fluid dynamics, of traffic on congested roads and of a dripping tap all display at times chaotic attributes. Recently, a number of scientists centred around the Santa Fe Institute in New Mexico have, as M. Mitchell Waldrop explains in his book, *Complexity*, been seeking to extend their understanding of the dynamic properties of complexity across a wide range of disciplines. They are exploring the similarities in the behaviour of many complex systems in physics, biology and, most interestingly for our purpose, economics, where there appears to be 'spontaneous self-organisation' 'at the edge of chaos'. In particular, they are investigating the impact of positive feedback or increasing returns and of non-linear relationships in economic systems. In many areas, it is recognised that the old certainties of equilibrium states and predictable linear reactions are not a good model of real-life dynamic systems. In the study of both ecosystems and economics, there is a growing realisation that humanity is part of what Waldrop calls 'an ever-changing, interlocking, non-linear, kaleidoscopic world' where if we 'try to take action in our favour without knowing how the overall system will adapt . . . we set in motion a train of events that will likely come back and form a different pattern for us to adjust to . . .'[3]

The very complexity of the world in which we live not only limits the extent to which we can make theoretical predictions, it also crucially limits the extent to which we can hope to control our predicament. This provides one of the principal external challenges to confidence in scientific-led progress. All too often our solutions to problems in the natural world, medicine or economics are now seen to create new problems which we were not able to predict because of the complexity of the systems being tampered with. We will return to this subject later in the book.

Ever since World War I when new technologies – in particular the railway, the machine gun, the submarine and the torpedo – were seen to lead to the more efficient slaughter of innocent people, and since World War II when the Nazi regime perverted the cause of science, and the Allies developed the first two atomic bombs and dropped them on Japan, it has become increasingly clear that the awe-inspiring progress of reason in science and technology is, in itself, neutral from a moral perspective, being as powerful in the generation of evil outcomes as of benign ones. Nor is the growing ambiguity of the external effects of technological and scientific change limited to the theatre of war. Many of our most prized developments have come with an enormous human or environmental price tag. So, for example, the motor car has caused a huge increase in pollution, noise and congestion. Moreover, as our power to alter our environment and even ourselves becomes immeasurably greater, there is growing anxiety about our ability to control and use this power wisely.

The area of genetic engineering represents a good case in point. As scientists set about mapping the thousands of genes that constitute our very nature, it may soon become possible to turn off the genes responsible for many of the most feared illnesses still to plague us. But at the same time as this good outcome becomes feasible, it may also be possible to engineer genetically the kind of children we want – to direct evolution itself. For many this prospect is morally repugnant and contravenes our residual feelings that there is a necessary limit to human aspirations. In the area of biotechnology, advances such as the creation of transgenic plants containing their own insecticides, or of transgenic pigs which can produce much-needed anticoagulant drugs for humans, raise different sorts of problems – both scientific and ethical. Do we really know enough about the medical and environmental impact of crossing species boundaries? Are we not in danger of creating new, more danger-ous problems as we solve the old ones? A slightly different sort of example is the controversial injection of genetically engineered growth hormones into cows to increase milk supply, which not only prompts important questions of health and safety but also, like many other such developments, raises profound social, economic and ethical questions. If cows are injected to produce 20 per cent more milk, when the supply is currently adequate, many small farmers will inevitably go bankrupt or need to be bailed out by public subsidies. It would not be the first time that a company was making money selling a product that had effects which cost the taxpayer many millions of dollars or pounds. Jeremy Rifkin, in his book, *The End of Work*, cites another example which is trou-bling from a moral and ethical point of view; it is now possible, thanks to genetic engineering, to produce vanilla in a laboratory at a fraction of the cost of importing it from Madagascar where it provides labour-intensive employment for the 70,000 peasant farmers who are growing it naturally. A decision by a First World biotech company on whether to market the product will have an instant effect on the way of life, and maybe even survival, of tens of thousands of people on the other side of the world.

The scientists and entrepreneurs involved in such projects are usually scornful of what they see as 'ill-informed' prejudice about the latest tech-niques and technologies. They can point to the fact that some people have always feared new technologies – e.g., radio waves in the 1920s – and that positive change has almost always involved costs for some, as well as ben-efits for the majority. They can also argue convincingly that in many cases the new biotech applications will prove to be significantly less dangerous than more traditional and familiar techniques. Transgenic plants contain-ing their own toxic insecticides will probably be far less damaging to the environment and to human health than was the wholesale aerial spraying of DDT forty years ago, and will supersede many of the complex chemi-cal pesticides still in use, which themselves all too often have greater health and ecological side effects than originally predicted.

However, general unease about the ever greater scientific power – in biotechnology, computing or other areas – to transform our world is not all irrational and is shared by many scientists themselves. The unease springs in part from the speed of development in so many areas at once which threatens now to become so rapid and all-pervasive that, far from breeding increased confidence in mankind's power, it threatens to induce greater feelings of insecurity and disorientation. This is especially true amongst ordinary people who are forced to adjust to new circumstances and ideas more quickly than the social structures to which they belong can adapt or their own skills and attitudes can evolve. Furthermore, as we shall explore later in the book, a very fast pace of change can limit the ability of both ecosystems and economic systems to adapt to large-scale changes sufficiently quickly and smoothly to avoid significant negative consequences, while many recent developments so profoundly tamper with these complex systems that the danger of inadvertently causing damaging, unpredictable and even chaotic results must be increased. Finally, there is the vexed question of the lack of controls over the direction taken by technological change.

The directions taken by the theoretical sciences, and more importantly the timing and nature of the practical applications of new theoretical discoveries – applications which increasingly shape mankind's destiny and which radically transform the day-to-day lives and prospects of people throughout the world – are under no effective overall control. It is rare that decisions to develop and apply new technologies are the product of careful, democratically controlled cost-benefit analysis; the changes that transform or disrupt our lives are not usually planned, or even initially desired, by the countries and peoples they affect. Governments do, of course, control their own vast military research programmes and do make sure there is some accountability in publicly funded research. They also insist on licensing new pharmaceuticals and pesticides. But to a great extent the direction taken by scientific and technological research is, as it always has been, the result of a myriad of piecemeal decisions taken worldwide by sponsoring companies and by individual specialists who are keen to further their own area of expertise, their own reputation and, in the case of companies, their own profit. The freedom of scientific research is one of the cornerstones of liberal democracy and has been an important factor in the success of such research. But the lack of democratic control over the direction taken by much groundbreaking research and technological innovation is seen by some no longer as a guarantee of intellectual freedom and disinterested excellence in the pursuit of the truth, but rather as itself a cause for unease. In part, such doubt reflects a lower degree of confidence that the ever more rapid and far-reaching advances in scientific knowledge and technology will necessarily foster human progress or provide further ammunition in the fight against ignorance, disease and poverty. It also reflects a growing gulf of understanding between specialists and non-specialists and, in some cases, a growing inability of even specialists to understand the implications of their work outside their own area of specialisation.

Such unease is further increased by a gradual breakdown in the old 'Mertonian' norms of scientific research. As Tom Wilkie explained in *The Independent* of 28 May 1996, Robert Merton in 1947 set out five norms which encapsulated the moral and social values which it was generally agreed should govern the scientific community; these were: communality, universality, disinterestedness, originality and scepticism. The fear is that these values of open collaboration, of being motivated solely by the search for the truth and of being subjected to scrutiny in the open by a process of public verification are under threat from the increasing commercialisation and privatisation of science. More and more of the research carried out today is sponsored by private pharmaceutical, biotechnology or engineering companies. They are naturally more interested in patenting new discoveries than in publicising them and opening them up to public scrutiny and debate; and they are intent, of course, on speedily developing commercial applications to ensure a pay-back on their investment. Influence over the direction taken by science and technology increasingly rests in the same place as influence over that other powerful motor of change – economic growth – namely in the free market. In later chapters we will be considering, more generally, to what extent the free market has the ability to deliver the socially most beneficial outcome, particularly in areas where the long-term effects of interfering with complex systems are difficult to fathom.

An area of increasing concern in the medical world is the rapid evolution of 'superbugs' – new strains of old diseases which are resistant to all known antibiotics. The profligate use of antibiotics, itself of benefit to the pharmaceutical companies, is speeding up the evolution of resistant strains of bacteria by drastically altering their environment; this then provides new opportunities for ground-breaking research and drug developments. The pharmaceutical companies are in a lucrative race to stay ahead of the forces of nature, but many biologists fear it is a race that may ultimately be lost. Meanwhile, from society's point of view, the development of new, more expensive and powerful antibiotics and other drugs capable for a time of combating the continuously evolving resistant strains represents an additional burden on health-care costs. In this case, as in many others, 'development' does not objectively represent 'progress' so much as an additional cost to be paid for the privilege of standing still in health terms. Medical science, like pest-control technology in agriculture, needs to be increasingly ingenious in finding ways to cope with the unpredictable side effects of earlier progress.

Francis Fukuyama argues, in his book, *The End of History and the Last*

Man, that science is increasingly the regulatory mechanism of history, and that its advance is leading to an increasing homogenisation of all societies; by establishing 'a uniform horizon of economic production possibilities', it is – like the global free market which harnesses it – breaking down national differences and creating an international destiny for all mankind. To the extent that this is true, it makes it all the more crucial for the worldwide stability of the next decades that this new destiny – evolving under no overall control – benefits the majority of mankind, and not just a tiny élite in the West. There is plenty of room for doubt and pessimism on this score – not least in the area of labour-saving technological innovation.

Jeremy Rifkin, in his book, *The End of Work*, highlights the effects of technological change on employment prospects. It is this aspect which will increasingly determine whether or not technological advance is seen as conducive or detrimental to human progress. His thesis is that the latest wave of technological advance in the workplace – in particular the computer revolution – threatens employment as never before. Whereas, in the past, the mechanisation of agriculture happened at a time when new manufacturing industries could and indeed needed to absorb millions of extra workers, and the gradual automation of factories in the forty years after World War II happened at a time when a burgeoning service and retail sector was happy to employ displaced labour, it is far from clear, in our own time, who will be in a position to absorb redundant labour now that the computer revolution is hitting virtually all forms of employment at once. Factories are increasingly using not only robots but also computer-aided design and computer-based inventory control. At the same time, the service sector is seeing bank clerks replaced by automatic tellers, and telephonists and secretaries by voice-mail and the word-processor, while the retail sector is using point-of-sale banking and inventory control, thereby bypassing accounts departments and wholesalers. In countless clerical and managerial functions it has become possible to eliminate layer after layer of human labour, as complex processes are catered for by simple software programs, operable by many fewer people. After initial implementation difficulties, computer technology is in most companies helping to usher in an age of 'lean production', of 'corporate re-engineering' and of 'de-layering', which has hit middle-management job opportunities as hard as those of the unskilled, or even harder in some cases.

For nearly two centuries machines have been replacing muscle power; now they are increasingly able to replace brain power too. Complex skills can be transferred to a computer program, eliminating the need for technical craftsmen. Computers can store, handle and transmit data far more efficiently than the labour-intensive management and filing systems of companies a decade or two ago. Already computers can speak, hear, read and understand; soon they may even develop consciousness. When they can do everything other than serve hamburgers with a smile, or clean windows, how will society meet people's ambitions and aspirations in the field of work?

The optimists will, of course, point out that in the vibrant US economy of the late 1990s unemployment has fallen to historically low levels, and that not all the new jobs have been part-time, low-skill, low-paid and insecure, since important new job opportunities have been created in the 'growth' industries; Rifkin, however, argues that these openings in new high-technology sectors are rarely available to more than a small, highly educated élite. For example, he points out that the biotechnology industry has so far created relatively few new jobs in the USA, certainly when compared with the large numbers shed since the early 1980s even by such fast-growing and traditionally labour-intensive industries as telecommunications. He argues that there is a very real prospect that a large proportion of the workforce of the world will find it impossible over the next few decades to find secure, well-paid employment; this could, at some point, lead to economic depression, as purchasing power and confidence collapses, and it will almost certainly create enormous tensions between the haves and the have-nots. Rifkin describes in lurid terms what he sees as the widespread prospect of walled-off ghettos for the new ultra-rich, protected by security guards and cameras, while the inner cities descend into a downward spiral of crime and despair. (One in four young black men in the USA is already on probation or in prison.) To guard against such social dislocation, he suggests that it would be preferable to turn the new technologies to our advantage, and to reverse the trend towards higher unemployment in Europe and increasingly poorly paid underemployment for many in the US, by substituting increased leisure and lower working hours for everyone. He also advocates programmes designed to use surplus labour to help rebuild communities before it is too late.[4]

We will return to many of these pressing questions later in this book when analysing the extent to which economic growth and the free market can, on their own, ensure social and environmental stability and progress. The ethical question of the distribution of wealth and income is crucial to the story – for if there is to be a dominant belief in progress and a general optimism about the future, it is crucial that change benefits more than a tiny minority. The speed of change is also an essential factor in determining whether change represents progress or damaging dislocation. So, for example – if introduced slowly enough to allow people to adjust economically, politically and emotionally – productivity-boosting technology can indeed lower prices, increase consumer purchasing power and so allow more growth in output, more employment and more leisure, according to traditional theory. If introduced too quickly, however, such new technology can lead to untold economic distress, with an important negative 'shock' impact on confidence and growth.

Progress is not possible without some change, but it does not follow that the fastest progress is delivered by the fastest possible rate of change. If time for deliberation and adaptation continues to be compressed by an ever accelerating pace of technological and economic change, man may again come to be overwhelmed by feelings of insecurity and by a sense of the uncontrollable nature of his predicament. Whereas the ancient Greeks and Romans attributed the precariousness of their lot to fearsome and inexplicable Olympian divinities, our sense of insecurity may be attributed, in part, to fear of the activities of the gods we have designed for ourselves – the gods of science and technology and of free-market economics. Their power is awesome and needs to be appeased by more than token sacrifices. At the same time, the age-old forces of nature continue to show a disquieting ability to fight back and surprise us with unpredictable reactions to our interference. The gods of science and free-market economics are engaged in a cosmic battle with the unpredictable forces of Mother Nature; as time goes by, we seem to have less rather than more control over the outcome of this battle.

CHAPTER 6

The Age of Economics and the Maximisation of Happiness

The great strides in science and technology seemed until recently to be a key pillar of the modern idea of progress, representing the onward march of human reason and the cumulative increase in man's ability to understand, predict and control the world in which he lives. The apparently unstoppable advances in science provided a mechanism of progress which was much more intuitively compelling to most observers than the abstruse Hegelian (or Marxist) dialectic of history. The direction of human history was seen to be the product of the triumph of scientific thinking.

This was, however, only half the story. For since the beginning of the Industrial Revolution, the progress of science and technology had been intimately linked to the phenomenon of economic growth. Technological advance was a vital contributory factor to economic growth, and it was economic pressures and incentives which, in turn, provided much of the impetus for technological advance. Scientific advance and economic growth were together seen to be responsible for giant strides in the material welfare of mankind, and so to constitute twin motors of progress. Furthermore, if economic growth provided an additional mechanism of progress, the measurement of that growth in money value terms seemed to provide a measure of progress in human welfare, an objective standard of human advance.

This chapter explores the philosophical importance of the theories of the economist Adam Smith, and of the ethical school of utilitarianism, in establishing conceptual links – both genuine and misleading – between the idea of human progress, on the one hand, and economic growth in a free-market system, on the other. Later chapters of the book will then focus on certain shortcomings in the powerful free-market mechanisms and in the established measures of economic growth, which can help to explain why – even in the triumphant free-market economies of the West – faith in the power of economic growth to deliver human progress is now waning, causing a new crisis of confidence.

Adam Smith and the Invisible Hand

Economic growth did not move centre stage or become an important object of intellectual study until the eighteenth century, when in Britain and a handful of other European countries, commerce and industrialisation were beginning to grow in a rapid and sustained manner. It has been estimated that economic growth may have averaged only 0.1 per cent per annum between the years 500 and 1500, equivalent to output approximately tripling in a thousand years. A growth rate of ten times that pace (over 1 per cent per annum) was achieved by Britain in the eighteenth century, resulting in significant rises in output and material wealth in the lifetime of a single generation. This represented the first stirrings of a powerful new phenomenon. Between 1870 and 1990, real GDP per capita in the UK (i.e., output after adjustment for both inflation and population growth) rose more than fivefold. In today's world, inflation-adjusted or 'real' growth of 2 per cent per annum is considered pitiful, even though 2 per cent growth triples output in just fifty-five years – a feat which took a thousand years between 500 and 1500.

A succession of economists have sought to explain the phenomenon of economic growth. Perhaps the most influential of these has been Adam Smith, who published his great work, *An Inquiry into the Nature and Causes of the Wealth of Nations*, in 1776, the same year as the American Declaration of Independence. Adam Smith was already well known for his book, *The Theory of Moral Sentiments*, published in 1759 while he was professor of moral philosophy at Glasgow. In this earlier work, Smith had placed considerable emphasis on the role of 'sympathy' and the desire to win approval from others in creating the social bonds that tie society together; he also gave a central place to the notion of the 'ideal' impartial spectator, which explained the working of individual conscience as the ability we have to imagine how others would see and judge us if they 'knew all'. It was from a background of such broad-ranging analysis of morality and social influences that Adam Smith, unlike most of his modern counter-parts, approached the study of economics. Economics was not at that time seen as a science divorced from the humanities and from a broader analysis of mankind. Despite his breadth of vision, however, Smith is chiefly remembered as a proponent of what Christopher Lasch, in his essay 'The Age of Limits', calls the liberal 'paradox of a virtuous society based on vicious individuals',[1] and as having demonstrated the possibility of a morally acceptable economic outcome without the need for moral motives.

While there is plenty of evidence that Adam Smith saw his economic analysis as complementing rather than supplanting his ethical analysis, there is undoubtedly a switch of emphasis between his two major works: *The Theory of Moral Sentiments* emphasises the role of sympathy, imagination, desire for approval and benevolence in forming socialising attitudes and creating a cohesive society; *The Wealth of Nations*, by contrast, stresses the importance of self-interest, or self-love, as the driving force behind the development of cooperation and mutual dependence in society:

> It is not from the benevolence of the butcher, the brewer, or the baker, that we expect our dinner, but from their regard to their own interest. We address ourselves not to their humanity but to their self-love, and never talk to them of our own necessities but of their advantages. Nobody but a beggar chuses to depend chiefly upon the benevolence of his fellow citizens.[2]

Smith saw the division of labour as the necessary precondition for economic growth and rising prosperity. This division of labour was itself, of course, closely connected with technological developments, which, by providing new tools and machinery, encouraged greater specialisation of labour. New technology and specialisation together allowed for considerable and cumulative increases in productivity and output. But Smith pointed out that the division of labour was only allowed for by the evolution of market exchange:

> This division of labour, from which so many advantages are derived, is not originally the effect of any human wisdom which foresees and intends that general opulence to which it gives occasion. It is the necessary, though very slow and gradual, consequence of a certain propensity in human nature which has in view no such extensive utility; the propensity to truck, barter, and exchange one thing for another.[3]

In Smith's account then, the process of market exchange – without which the all-important division of labour is impossible – is not itself the product of human reason, but rather of an innate propensity to exchange. His book nevertheless constitutes a reasoned plea for deliberate action to be taken to extend the scope of market exchange and to make it as free from interference as possible. For he held that the scope for the division of labour, and hence for sustained economic growth, was constrained by the size of the market. To pursue higher economic growth it was, in his view, essential to pursue a policy of free trade in order to maximise the possibilities of exchange. This would encourage a country to specialise as much as possible in the industries in which it had a particular advantage, and to benefit from importing cheaper versions of other products in which it did not have an advantage from those countries that did. The plea for free trade was, as we shall see, only one aspect of his general insistence on the virtues of *laissez-faire* economics.

In his analysis of economic growth, Smith stressed the importance of saving and the accumulation of capital, and of the investment of that capital either in more labour or in more productivity-boosting machines, both of which can lead to a permanently higher level of production. While emphasising the importance of parsimony and prudence, Smith argued that: 'the principle which prompts to save is the desire of bettering our condition, a desire which . . . comes with us from the womb, and never leaves us till we go into the grave'.[4] Such self-interest will lead every individual to employ his capital where it is expected to produce the greatest possible returns, thereby maximising the output of society as a whole:

> As every individual, therefore, endeavours as much as he can both to employ his capital in the support of domestick industry, and so to direct that industry that its produce may be of the greatest value; every individual necessarily labours to render the annual revenue of the society as great as he can. He generally, indeed, neither intends to promote the publick interest, nor knows how much he is promoting it. By preferring the support of domestick to that of foreign industry, he intends only his own security; and by directing that industry in such a manner as its produce may be of the greatest value, he intends only his own gain, and he is in this, as in many other cases, led by an invisible hand to promote an end which was no part of his intention. Nor is it always the worse for the society that it was no part of it. By pursuing his own interest he

> frequently promotes that of the society more effectually than
> when he really intends to promote it. I have never known
> much good done by those who affected to trade for the pub-
> lick good.[5]

This passage is one of only two explicit references in Adam Smith's work to the invisible hand, but the image has come to stand more generally for his insistence that a free, competitive market allows the natural interplay of individual self-interest to further the wellbeing of society as a whole. The invisible hand is a metaphor for the free market's ability spontaneously to reconcile and balance the requirements of competing individuals pursuing their own self-interest in such a way that self-interested behaviour can unintentionally promote the economic interests of society as a whole. Classical economic theory has developed this intuition of Smith's into a sophisticated analysis of how an entirely free market, through the free movement of prices, can match supply and demand, allocate resources in the most productive way (taking into account the expressed wants of all market participants), and thereby ensure an outcome which fully exploits all the potential benefits from market exchange to the mutual advantage of all the participants in the market.

Smith's faith in the socially beneficial nature of the free-market mechanism even extended, interestingly, to a belief that it could reduce inequality. Much inequality was, he thought, the result of distorting regulations. So, for example, he thought that a free market could lead to a balance between the unattractiveness of work and the attractiveness of the reward (i.e., the most dirty and dangerous jobs would attract the highest pay). Moreover, in his other famous reference to the invisible hand, in *The Theory of Moral Sentiments*, he explicitly argued for the redistributive effect of market exchange – what we would today call the 'trickle-down effect':

> The rich ... consume little more than the poor, and in spite of
> their natural selfishness and rapacity, though they mean only
> their own conveniency, though the sole end which they pro-
> pose from the labours of all the thousands whom they employ
> be the gratification of their own vain and insatiable desires,
> they divide with the poor the produce of all their improve-
> ments. They are led by an invisible hand to make nearly the
> same distribution of the necessities of life, which would have
> been made, had the earth been divided into equal portions

among all its inhabitants, and thus without intending it, without knowing it, advance the interest of the society, and afford means to the multiplication of the species.[6]

As we shall see later in the chapter, while modern economic theory has been able to prove with rigorous mathematics some elements of Smith's conjecture that competitive markets can optimise the public interest, it has failed to substantiate his view that competitive markets will tend to promote equality of wealth or income. Indeed, much of the economic debate over the last two hundred years has focused on the conflict between the requirements of market efficiency and those of distributive justice.

Adam Smith was, of course, very conscious of the fact that the ability of the free-market mechanism to promote the economic wellbeing of society – despite each market participant being motivated primarily by self-interest – crucially depended on several important conditions. First and foremost it depended, in Smith's analysis, on the existence of a full measure of natural liberty and the absence of constraints on market activities arising from regulations. He argued that 'the natural effort of every individual to better his own condition, when suffered to exert itself with freedom and security, is so powerful a principle that it is alone, and without any assistance . . . capable of carrying on the society to wealth and prosperity'.[7] The necessary freedom included the absence of government regulations, which he held to be 'subversive' and which he saw as retarding rather than accelerating 'the progress of the society towards real wealth and greatness'. In Smith's view, regulations and government interference not only distort markets and capital flows; they are also based on a fundamental misconception or delusion, namely that any government can possess the requisite knowledge or wisdom to direct the industry of private people in a beneficial direction:

> The statesman who should attempt to direct private people in what manner they ought to employ their capitals would not only load himself with a most unnecessary attention, but assume an authority which could safely be trusted, not only to no single person, but to no council or senate whatever, and which would nowhere be so dangerous as in the hands of a man who had folly and presumption enough to fancy himself fit to exercise it.[8]

This ringing call for a *laissez-faire* system of government foreshadows the modern free-market criticism of state planning. The Nobel Laureate F. A. von Hayek and others have argued that even democratic governments cannot accurately ascertain what is in the public interest. This can only be articulated by the actual choices made in a free-market context by self-interested participants. The free market alone, the argument goes, can capture and condense the knowledge dispersed among countless individuals, and allow for the 'public interest' to be perceived and met.

In Adam Smith's analysis, the existence of natural liberty is not on its own sufficient to ensure that the free market can further the interests of society; certain other important conditions have to be met. Most importantly, man is to be free to pursue his own interest only 'as long as he does not violate the laws of justice'.[9] The efficient operation of the free market depends, Smith argued, on the establishment by government of a framework of laws and rules (property rights, commercial law, etc.). Smith also granted government several other key roles, notably the defence of the realm and the provision of certain public goods and services. Many modern right-wing Conservatives may be surprised to note that their patron saint clearly argued that some public works had to be the province of government; for, as he argued, certain public goods are not amenable to production by free-market capitalists because 'the profit could never repay the expense' to those individuals who create or maintain them, even though the public works concerned 'may be in the highest degree advantageous to a great society'.[10]

It is interesting to note, too, that Smith abhorred monopolies of all sorts, as vitiating the important requirement for perfect competition; he understood that the free market could only deliver optimal economic allocations when there were no impediments to perfect competition. He was convinced, however, that, within a proper framework of law and in the absence of distorting regulations, competition itself could control monopolistic tendencies – another example, unfortunately, of his over-optimism about the power of the free market. Indeed, many would now argue that the conditions of perfect competition are inherently unstable given the existence in reality of positive feedbacks, i.e., the tendency for success to be cumulative; winners in the technology race or the market struggle appear often to be able freely to establish a dominant position, control prices and raise barriers to entry in such a way as to frustrate competition.

Although Smith did not foresee this problem of the tendency for competition to be self-eliminating, he did anticipate other problems. Perhaps most remarkably, despite his optimism about the benefits of economic growth and free-market competition, he did warn that the division of labour would have the unfortunate side effect of making the work of specialised labourers in the factory monotonous and repetitive to an extent which, he argued, would impair their moral character and intelligence. To alleviate this alienating effect on the worker of industrialisation and specialisation, he advocated widespread public compulsory education to give citizens the intellectual and moral wherewithal to withstand the pressures of industrialisation. More generally, while Smith does not stipulate in *The Wealth of Nations* specifically social and moral conditions for the efficient operation of the free-market mechanism (other than a system of justice), it has been cogently argued that his central interest in *The Theory of Moral Sentiments* in the role of sympathy, benevolence and self-restraint suggests that he implicitly assumed, even in *The Wealth of Nations*, the context of a cohesive and morally disciplined society. For many commentators, it is exactly this implicit social and moral context for the benign operation of the invisible hand which is now missing; and its absence is seen to be undermining the validity in the contemporary world of Smith's thesis that the self-interested pursuit of private gain can, in economic affairs, best serve the public interest.

Adam Smith's message was an optimistic one: so long as there is genuinely free competition within a framework of justice, the self-interested pursuit of private gain will lead to greater public benefit. In the years that followed publication of *The Wealth of Nations*, the conditions which Smith had stipulated (in particular, the need for perfect competition) – and the implicit moral context which he, as an Enlightenment moral philosopher, had assumed – were not as well remembered as his central message of the power of the invisible hand. It was this image which entered Western consciousness and helped underpin faith in human progress. Here, apparently, was a mechanism capable of delivering human progress without the need for benign human motives; gone was the requirement for the moral perfection of man as a precursor to the establishment of a better world. Gone, too, was the requirement that human reason should be able to plot and plan the way forward and develop a perfect system of government capable of promoting the public interest. Instead, the public interest would be sure to arise, prosper and grow given the simple conditions of natural liberty, a system of justice and a strong dose of self-interest.

Many economists and political figures since Adam Smith have not shared his optimism, though none has succeeded fully in dislodging it. Thomas Malthus (1766–1834) was opposed to the optimism not only of Smith but of Enlightenment thinkers such as Condorcet. He argued that it was inevitable that increases in population would overtake increases in the supply of food, since population growth was naturally exponential, while the growth in food supply was necessarily more constrained; he further argued that only vice, misery and starvation were likely to be able to keep the population down to a level where the food supply was just sufficient. So far, of course, the dire predictions of the first edition of his *Essay on the Principle of Population* (1798) have not proved correct: technological gains and geographic expansion have allowed a gigantic increase in world food supply which has more than matched a huge increase in world population, the scale of which would have surprised even Malthus. In addition, in some parts of the world, the combined effects of increased prosperity and cheap birth control have enabled the population to stop growing. In his own time, however, Malthus' predictions did much to deflate extreme Enlightenment optimism.

One of Adam Smith's most illustrious successors, the economist David Ricardo (1772–1823), was also notably less optimistic about the impact of economic progress. Under Malthus' influence he believed that, however prosperous the economy, the wages of workers would not rise above subsistence level because of population pressures (the 'iron law of wages'). Nor did he believe that company profits would rise inexorably either; rather, he argued that landowners alone would be the beneficiaries, as food shortages led to higher land prices, higher rents and higher food prices; these would in turn entail higher subsistence-level wages and hence serve to lower company profits. It was to avoid such an eventuality that Ricardo argued so forcefully for free trade, which he argued would lower grain prices and prevent them from escalating again.

In time, the pessimism of Malthus and Ricardo was contradicted by the enormous *de facto* strides in economic growth and material prosperity in the nineteenth century, and by the concomitant growth in food supplies. In the latter part of the century, the principal criticisms of the free-market theories of Adam Smith and others were directed not so much at their insistence that the free market was able to generate greater wealth, but at the failure of the market to ensure an equitable distribution of that wealth, or to provide public amenities. By then, most governing political parties – even those fully committed to capitalism – had recognised the importance of the provision of public amenities such as sewers and paved roads. Full *laissez-faire* policies had led to the explosive growth of industrial cities without adequate provision for sanitation or clean water supplies, and the devastating effects on the health and productivity of workers were increasingly obvious. The average life expectancy of a male born in Manchester in 1850 was only twenty-five years. The need for social reform was also recognised, and laws were passed, for example, to ban child labour and to legalise trade unions so that they could fight for a shorter working week and better conditions. By 1914, the area of necessary government interference was generally agreed to be larger than in a pre-industrial age.

Many on the left of the political spectrum, of course, went much further – focusing on the need to reduce inequalities of wealth and income and to eliminate absolute poverty. This was the essence of the socialist and Marxist challenge. Socialists and Marxists remained convinced of the importance of economic growth and increased output to improved well-being, but looked for alternative means to those provided by a liberal free market for distributing the benefits of growth. Given the overwhelming importance socialists attached to redistribution, social reform and regulations to protect labour, they sought to jettison much of the freedom given to markets in the early nineteenth century. Following the slump of the 1920s and 1930s and the famous Keynesian critique of free markets, most non-socialist economists and politicians also came, for a time, to accept the case for some government intervention in the economy to maintain a level of demand compatible with full employment. Public planning and regulation became fashionable once more.

To some extent, the counter-revolution against pure *laissez-faire* government has been enduring. But at its extreme, where the market allocation mechanism itself was replaced by full-scale state planning, the socialist alternative proved a disaster – as Smith would have predicted. One only has to consider the failures of the centrally planned economies of the Soviet Union and Eastern Europe in the forty years after World War II to see how enormously complex and important is the process of the allocation of resources. Classical free-market economics assumes that an economy will – if left to operate freely – quickly find a competitive equilibrium, i.e., a set of prices for all goods in the economy which will ensure that demand in every market is equal to supply. This set of prices is said to 'clear' the markets, while achieving an efficient (though not necessarily fairly distributed) allocation of goods across all market participants. This insight into the power of the market mechanism seems to hold true in most circumstances. In general, the free market has shown itself admirably capable of achieving an efficient allocation of the resources required for production and of ensuring the production of the goods and services which consumers actually want. Moreover, the price system does this in a decentralised manner. It is the market mechanism and the signals given by prices which ensure that consumers can, for example, buy lightbulbs of the right size, fitting, voltage and shape for their appliances; no one and no government department could estimate and plan to cater for all the variations in demand or supply. Central planning appears incapable, no matter how big the civil service, of allocating resources with anything like the efficiency of Adam Smith's invisible hand. This is the powerful and crucial kernel of free-market economics. Twentieth-century history suggests that, without the market mechanism, a complex modern economy cannot cater efficiently for the variety of consumer preferences, and cannot generate meaningful material progress.

The enormous importance of this efficient allocation role for the market mechanism has, however, often resulted in a complacent disregard for the limitations of the free-market system. It is these limitations which have the capacity – particularly if poorly understood – to turn the free-market mechanism from being the most powerful motor of human progress into being a threat to human welfare and the public interest. In the remainder of the book, we will explore some of the more pervasive shortcomings of the free-market mechanism as a generator of human progress. Many of these shortcomings relate to the way markets actually operate in practice in our increasingly congested and complex world. Others, though, relate specifically to the primacy given in recent years to the free-market pursuit of economic growth as a political and even moral goal.

Utilitarianism and Economic Values

In the late twentieth century, economics has gradually supplanted political and moral philosophy as the leading intellectual inspiration in the modern quest for progress. Moreover, this supremacy has coincided with economics coming to be treated by its professional practitioners as essentially a science. In particular, much of the economic analysis that lies behind public policy now relies on complicated mathematics operating within a framework of formalised assumptions. The importance attached to mathematical rigour has had two principal effects: first, it has resulted in the requirement, if the mathematics is to work, for concrete assumptions or premises, which are often lost to the lay person and may not be questioned sufficiently even by those operating within the arcane formulae of the 'science'; these premises may include such dubious assumptions as the possession by market participants of perfect foresight, and the absence of positive feedback mechanisms in markets. Secondly, the perceived importance of mathematical rigour has led economists to concentrate on what can be measured and converted into commensurable numerical values (chiefly money). Both these effects can result in economics becoming gradually divorced from the richness, complexity and even irrationality of everyday life. More critically still, the professional tendency to categorise economics as a 'science' has reinforced the gradual formal separation of economics from the study of ethics.

Modern economics has become the scientific study of what is feasible, of how the market interaction of human beings works, and of how this interaction can be made more efficient – what Amartya Sen, in his book, *On Ethics and Economics*, calls 'the engineering approach'. In itself, there is nothing invalid in this approach, as long as the premises on which the 'science' is based bear a close relationship to the reality of human societies. But in assuming this narrow 'engineering' focus, and in formalising the distinction between the science of economics and the study of ethics (the study of what we ought to do), economics has surrendered any valid claim to help us choose the ultimate goals of human endeavour (the province of ethics). It may seem strange, then, that increasingly the deliberations in economics about what is feasible in a market context have come to be seen by society at large as a blueprint for what *ought* to be done, not just in expediting the achievement of politically and ethically predetermined social goals, but in ordering and defining the selection of goals and values in the first place. Questions of efficiency have frequently come to take precedence over those of morality. Moreover, characteristics assumed in economic models have, because of the primacy of economic policy in the political arena, begun insidiously to alter and constrain our broader view of the human character and predicament. So, for example, the assumption in economics that all market behaviour is self-interested, and the 'proof' that this can be compatible, in an efficiency sense, with the public interest may, unconsciously at least, have encouraged an undervaluation of benevolence and of social cohesion, and encouraged the growth of rampant individualism and – by extension – antisocial versions of self-interested behaviour. In environmental issues, the inability to place an objective monetary value on, for example, the beauty of the countryside may have encouraged detrimental impacts on it to be ignored. Similarly, the economists' habit of financially discounting the value of future consumption to give a financially quantifiable 'present value' builds in a presumption against taking the interests of future generations in any particular resource on a par with those of today – surely an ethical question. At the same time, the fact that externalities, such as pollution, are left out of the market mechanism and out of measures of economic growth – combined with the theory that additional regulation tends to reduce the efficiency of the market – has encouraged the view that pollution can generally only be tackled at considerable cost to 'the public good'. Likewise, since all interference in the market designed to improve distributive justice will also tend to reduce the efficiency of the free market, the existence of this trade-off between equity and efficiency will often be used as a political argument for ignoring all distributional questions, in the interests of maximising efficiency. This is particularly important in the free-trade debate; for even if greater free trade can be shown to boost wealth in total, the speedy extension of free trade can lead to very critical distributional questions within societies, and these are generally ignored in the unrelenting modern quest for greater efficiency.

The discussion of the invisible hand has already provided one explanation of why the science of economics has been allowed to dictate many of our political goals and influence our moral values, and of why it has implicitly been thought acceptable to subordinate ethical considerations – of what kind of human progress we want – to the narrower considerations of economic efficiency. For, at least on a superficial reading of Adam Smith, the invisible hand of the free market seems to economise on the need for moral values and public policy, with the market system apparently capable of delivering a morally and politically acceptable economic outcome – the furtherance of the public interest – without the need for the system's participants to have either overtly moral motives or agreed social goals. In the remainder of the book we will be considering many reasons why it can be argued that, on the contrary, the free market does in fact require a cohesive social context and a strong moral and political framework if it is to deliver the social good. However, it is useful first to consider a philosophical doctrine closely related to free-market economics, namely utilitarianism. For this doctrine and popular misreadings of it have reinforced the perception that the free market can itself guarantee a morally desirable economic outcome, and that the scientific pursuit of free-market efficiency should therefore be accorded the status almost of a moral goal.

Utilitarianism had its origins in the Enlightenment period. Its principal early pioneer was Jeremy Bentham, who published his influential book, *An Introduction to the Principles of Morals and Legislation* in 1789 (thirteen years after Adam Smith's great work). The book begins with the memorable lines:

> Nature has placed mankind under the governance of two sovereign masters, pain and pleasure. It is for them alone to point out what we ought to do, as well as to determine what we shall do. On the one hand the standard of right and wrong, on the other the chain of causes and effects, are fastened to their throne. They govern us in all we do, in all we say, in all we think . . . The principle of utility recognises this subjection, and assumes it for the foundation of that system, the object of which is to rear the fabric of felicity by the hands of reason and of law.[11]

The doctrine of utilitarianism which Bentham espoused has since been developed in many subtly different forms, but a number of features are common to most of them.

First, the only intrinsically good or ultimately valuable thing in human states of affairs, and the sole ultimate goal of right action, is held to be – depending on the various versions – either pleasure and the absence of pain, or *happiness*, or *desire-satisfaction*. The goodness of a state of affairs is entirely determined by the amount of pleasure, happiness or desire-satisfaction it contains. The property of an object which tends to produce this pleasure, happiness or desire-satisfaction is called its 'utility'.

Secondly, the moral value accorded to actions, motives, institutions, laws, etc. is entirely dependent on their *consequences*, i.e., on the extent to which they actually contribute to the promotion of the pleasure, happiness or desire-satisfaction of human beings. Although there may be practical difficulties in predicting the consequences of an action (or even in ascertaining what they are after the event), moral judgements are seen as simply technically difficult calculations of the utilitarian value of consequences; they do not involve an appeal to any inherent value – customary or religious – in particular motives or types of action. The value of actions is entirely a function of their utilitarian consequences. A feature of such a consequentialist position is that, ultimately, *ends justify means*. Rights designed to protect an individual from being used as a means to an end against his or her own will do not, in this account, have paramount value. So long as the utilitarian consequences of ignoring someone's rights (including the precedent effect) have been taken into account, a utilitarian will be forced to accept that if violating that person's rights allows, all things considered, for more happiness or desire-satisfaction overall, the rights should be ignored. Rights are not valuable in themselves, but only insofar as they help to maximise utility. So, for example, in an economic context, the right some would accord to human beings not to live in wretched poverty could not be honoured by a utilitarian if he was convinced that by ignoring that right he would minimise poverty and maximise utility overall. The sacrifice of some individuals' welfare for the good of the greatest number is not prohibited by utilitarian philosophy.

Perhaps the most well-known description of the utilitarian principle is that the best action is the one which leads to the '*greatest happiness of the greatest number*'. Adding the assumption that morality requires us to do our best, most utilitarians argue that an act is morally obligatory if it leads to more pleasure or desire-satisfaction than alternative actions. Utilitarianism is, in most forms, a blatantly maximising or optimising ethical doctrine. The best outcome is the greatest possible happiness of the greatest number. The importance of the *maximisation* of the goal of human activity is one of utilitarianism's most indelible contributions to the modern psyche, and is an important element in the modern notion of progress.

One great appeal of utilitarianism is that it claims to provide *a common currency* for all moral judgements. Every action is to be judged in terms of the amount of pleasure or desire-satisfaction created, and moral conflicts are to be solved by empirical calculation of the effect of the different alternatives on the total amount of what is valuable, i.e. happiness, pleasure or desire-satisfaction. For this task to be even theoretically possible, utilitarianism requires that amounts of happiness, etc. are commensurable (i.e., that all instances of happiness, etc. in various actual or potential states of affairs can be assigned a unit value which can be arithmetically compared between people and across time). This feature of pure utilitarianism implies that it must be possible to reduce all pleasures, all types of happiness and all desire-satisfactions to a one-dimensional standard which admits of no variations other than in quantitative terms, such as intensity, duration, etc. But happiness is an amorphous concept which includes within it a variety of subjective notions, such as sensations of pleasure, the attitude of being pleased with things, the satisfaction of desires and the absence of important unfulfilled desires. It is clear that it is ultimately impossible even for an individual to quantify accurately or make commensurable his own subjective feelings, attitudes and desires, let alone for anyone to make precise comparisons between people and across generations. As a result, a rigorous or objective utilitarian judgement about the best course of action seems bound to remain elusive, in the same way as rigorous judgements about the extent of progress in happiness will always be impossible. The very appeal of utilitarianism – that it seems to provide a clear and unambiguous answer to moral dilemmas – arises from the fact that it fails to take account of the complexity and variety of human goals, aspirations, desires and enjoyments. Its apparent completeness as an ethical doctrine is an illusion based on the misconception that ultimately all values are commensurable in a single unit of account, not unlike money. A simplistic economic view of the world can similarly appear to assume that the variety of human values can be reduced to a simple index of monetary value.

Preference or desire-satisfaction accounts of utilitarianism raise a particularly interesting problem from the point of view of economics. Since they normally imply that all desires are commensurable in value terms, they appear committed to treating the satisfaction of desires which have been artificially created (e.g., by advertising) as on a par with that of innate desires or preferences; they also have no easy way of eliminating irrational or antisocial desires from the equation. Some utilitarian accounts try to avoid this problem by retreating to the position of valuing only 'true' – i.e., fully informed and rational – desires; but this idealisation destroys much of the original purpose of defining the utilitarian goal in terms of the satisfaction of preferences instead of by the amount of happiness or wellbeing. For a value system based on satisfying actual desires or preferences appears to provide a politically attractive and relatively practical blueprint for action – namely, to maximise the satisfaction of preferences as actually revealed in the ballot box, the opinion survey and the marketplace. By contrast, if there is seen to be a need to pre-define what constitutes acceptably rational or 'true' desires, the link is broken between the utilitarian goal and the politically enticing project of meeting the actual desires of actual people. The distinction is important for economics: the market may optimise the satisfaction of actual preferences (rational and irrational) as revealed in the market; it cannot selectively optimise only the 'true' or fully rational preferences, nor even register the unexpressed 'true' preferences of market participants. It is also important to note that the impartiality of simple utilitarian accounts between types of desires is mirrored by impartiality as to who has the desires. In this sense, utilitarian doctrine is very impersonal; its impartiality does not allow us to give extra weight in utility calculations to those close to us, such as family or fellow countrymen; our duty is to maximise the happiness of all. The impartiality can also extend, in some accounts, to giving equal weight to the desires of future people – a feature of utilitarianism which, as we shall see later, is not mirrored in the operation of the free market.

Another important feature of utilitarianism is that it demands that we take the pleasure, happiness or desire-satisfaction of the greatest number into account. In the eighteenth or early nineteenth centuries, it was close to being a revolutionary thought that the interests or desires of the poor should be as important as those of the rich, and that everyone should form the denominator in the equation of happiness. However, this wide franchise does not take utilitarianism as far towards equality as might be thought. Although it provides for everyone to be given equal weighting in the utility calculation, it does not necessarily provide for everyone to end up with equal total utility. Indeed, if sacrificing the happiness of the few would help maximise the overall happiness of the greatest number, then so long as the few are included equally in the calculation, the utilitarian must approve. The utilitarian can only argue for redistribution of a given quantity of goods by arguing that money and goods have a diminishing marginal utility – i.e., that the first unit of goods delivers more units of happiness than do later ones; this allows him to argue that it would maximise utility to redistribute goods from the overfed rich to the starving poor until such a point that their marginal utility is equalised. But, of course, if the goods in question could be shown to produce no more extra (i.e., marginal) happiness for a poor group than for a relatively rich group, there would be no utilitarian argument for redistribution of happiness itself to a point where total utility is equalised.

Many utilitarians have supported their assertion that the moral goal ought to be the greatest happiness of the greatest number, by arguing that all individuals do in fact pursue their own happiness as the goal of all their actions. They are 'pleasure machines', deciding on action by reference only to what is expected to maximise their own pleasure and utility. It is not, of course, necessary to hold this view about human motivations in order to accept utilitarianism as an ethical doctrine; in other words, one does not need to believe that human *motivations* are directed solely toward one's own happiness to believe that the *moral value of actions* should be defined by their consequences for the welfare of everyone. Utilitarians may indeed believe that individuals can rationally aim to promote an end wholly unconnected with their own happiness (e.g., self-sacrifice in battle), so long as their actions promote the greatest happiness of the greatest number. However, the narrow picture of individuals as self-interested personal utility maximisers has acquired considerable importance because it has been built into modern economists' models and assumptions of what constitutes the rational behaviour of 'economic man'.

Given these features of utilitarianism, its importance to the story of progress is twofold. First, despite all the problems associated with it, the 'greatest happiness' principle has been hugely influential – especially when taken as a rough guide to public policy. As a result, it has inevitably had a considerable impact on attitudes towards human progress. Modern ideas of progress frequently include the notion that the goal of human activity should be maximised – the more the better – and that the goal to be maximised is happiness. People's rights and the nature of their motives are often seen as having only derivative value, according to their actual contribution to the desired outcome – the maximisation of happiness. Modern conceptions of progress also implicitly assume that it is possible, if not to construct a rigorous calculus of quantifiable units of happiness, at least intuitively to measure in commensurable value terms progress towards the utilitarian goal. Secondly, utilitarianism is important to our theme because it has become so embedded in the fabric of economic theory and practice. As a result, economics, and specifically free-market economics, appears to share many of the attractions of utilitarianism, while also sharing many of its problems. It is the link between free-market economic theory and utilitarian philosophy which has helped to make it respectable to ignore overt ethical considerations in much of free-market economic theory and practice; it is this link, too, which has, subconsciously at least, helped to engender a widespread misunderstanding about the ethical and welfare significance of the free-market mechanism and about the implied content of measures of economic growth.

The concept of utility is central to much economic market theory. It is important to distinguish here between utility in general and marginal utility in particular, which is the increase in utility derived only from the last unit of a good to be used or consumed. The law of diminishing marginal returns assumes that the more of a good a consumer has, the less utility he derives from each extra unit. The marginal (i.e., extra) utility derived from consuming the third Mars bar of the day, for example, will be much lower than from consuming the first; and that derived from the fifth (in one day) is likely to be negative. In such a situation it may therefore be advantageous to an individual to swap some of his five Mars bars for other goods which have a higher marginal utility to him. Late-nineteenth-century economists, including Léon Walras and W. S. Jevons, argued that in a free market individuals will continue to exchange goods until the point at which the ratio of the respective marginal utilities they derive from each good is equal to the ratio of the prices at which the goods are exchanged. At that point no market participant can gain further advantage by continuing to exchange.

It is important to note, however, that in a free market each individual can only exchange goods or money to the level of his initial distribution of goods. Those poorly endowed to begin with can maximise the efficiency of their use of this poor endowment, but cannot by free-market exchange improve their utility beyond this. And yet the law of diminishing marginal utility would suggest that the redistribution of extra goods to the poor would be expected to yield more total utility. Some utilitarian economists have therefore argued that, given the diminishing marginal utility of income or goods to individuals, and given the further assumption that all individuals have an equal capacity to derive utility from income or goods, the goal of maximising total utility requires a move towards income and wealth equalisation. It would be necessary, of course, to take account in the utility calculus of the disincentive effects of income equalisation; but once these effects had been taken into account, if greater income equality could be shown to increase happiness compared with a market-efficient, but less equal outcome, then redistribution would be morally desirable to a utilitarian.

Since the 1930s, economic theorists have in general significantly watered down the utilitarian content of their models, following Lionel Robbins' attack on the practical impossibility of making utilitarian calculations. There is, as he pointed out, no way of making strict interpersonal comparisons of utility or happiness; one cannot be sure, for example, that the redistribution of £1,000 from a rich person to a poor person would in fact improve the utility of the poor person by more than it reduced that of the rich person. Robbins and others, motivated no doubt partly by a desire to remove their 'science' from the rocky shores of income redistribution ethics, therefore sought to replace a strictly utilitarian programme with a superficially less contentious goal – the so-called 'Pareto efficiency' criterion: this criterion, invented by Vilfredo Pareto in 1894, states that an optimum position is one in which, given a set of tastes, resources, income, abilities, etc., it is impossible to move to another market allocation which would make someone better off, but nobody else worse off. In other words, a Pareto-efficient state is one where no one's utility can be raised further without reducing the utility of someone else. This is a criterion of market efficiency which determines the most efficient allocations possible in a context of free exchange by mutual consent, *given an initial distribution of income and abilities*. As such, of course, it falls well short of the full utilitarian goal, which does allow for some people to be made worse off for the greater good. Pareto efficiency remains a utilitarian concept to the limited extent that it involves judging the consequences of actions in terms of their success in maximising – in a narrow efficiency sense – the satisfaction of (market-expressed) preferences. But the appeal of the Pareto efficiency criterion for economists is precisely that, because it does not allow for any trade-off of even an iota of one person's utility or preference-satisfaction in favour of anyone else's, it requires no comparison between one person's utility and another's, and no computation of the total level of preference-satisfaction in alternative states of affairs. It merely represents the optimisation of all market-expressed preferences to the point where no further *mutually advantageous* exchanges are possible and hence nobody could become better off without someone else becoming worse off. By according great importance to this notion of Pareto efficiency rather than to the broader utilitarian goal of maximising happiness, modern economics has served to draw a sharp but often ignored distinction between 'positive' economic questions of efficiency (which are catered for) and 'normative' questions about just distribution and utility maximisation (which are not).

Now, it so happens that a number of economists (especially K. Arrow and G. Debreu in the 1950s) have succeeded in proving mathematically that if every market in the economy is a perfectly competitive free market, as defined by a set of important conditions – i.e., no positive economies of scale, no future uncertainty, no externalities and no monopolies – the resulting equilibrium throughout the economy will be Pareto-efficient. In this limited-efficiency sense, modern economists have succeeded in proving Adam Smith's first intuition with regard to the invisible hand, that a perfect free market can ensure that the pursuit of individual self-interest or preference-satisfaction, as expressed through the market exchange mechanism, will increase the benefits of society taken as a whole. However, it is important to be clear that this result is not the same as having proved that the pursuit of self-interest in the free market leads to the greatest utility of the greatest number. It merely shows that *if* the important conditions attaching to the model are met, a free market can lead to the most efficient optimisation of stated market preferences, within the constraint of being unable to alter each person's initial endowments of abilities and income. This result sidesteps the whole issue of whether or not the public interest could be further promoted by redistribution of these initial endowments. It should also be noted that the modern proof that a genuinely free market is Pareto-efficient emphatically does not prove Adam Smith's second intuition, that the invisible hand would lead to significant equalisation of benefits through 'trickle-down' effects.

Although there can be a Pareto-efficient outcome for any initial distribution, this does not entail perfect neutrality towards the idea of redistribution on the part of free-market economics. This is because it is generally argued that redistributive activities by the state constitute interference in the free operation of the market and will therefore tend to upset the capacity of the market to deliver an efficient outcome. There is, in other words, an equity/efficiency trade-off. Efficiency will be maximised, according to free-market theory, by the absence of interventions and interference (including redistributive activities); but maximising efficiency by minimising interference may be at the expense of forgoing the opportunity to maximise utility, *if* there is a very unequal initial distribution of income, abilities, etc., and *if* the law of diminishing marginal utilities holds – as seems intuitively likely; an extra £1,000 will undoubtedly produce more happiness for a family on the breadline than for a billionaire tycoon. However, utilitarian philosophy and economics have both failed to come up with a feasible method for comparing utilities between people by which they could demonstrate whether any act of redistribution would actually increase overall utility or happiness (after netting off any loss in terms of market efficiency), and if so by how much. It is this failure in both utilitarianism and economic theory to find any means of quantifying in utility terms the equity/efficiency trade-off which has been partly responsible for allowing the goal of efficiency to take precedence over the goal of maximising happiness.

It can be seen, therefore, that an undesirably unequal distribution of initial endowments is crucial in increasing the ethical distance between the goal of market efficiency and the utilitarian goal of the greatest happiness of the greatest number. It is this which many on the political right choose to forget when they champion the market as the true arbiter of people's preferences, and when they accord the status of near moral goal to the maximisation of market efficiency. They are often implicitly seeking to attach the attractiveness, such as it is, of utilitarianism as a moral doctrine to the concept of Pareto efficiency, which – by not allowing for even the richest of men to be made worse off for the greater good – is only an extremely watered-down variant of the utilitarian goal of maximising the satisfaction of desires of the greatest number.

The issue can perhaps be best understood by looking at the impact of inequality on the ability of individuals to express their true desires and preferences adequately in the market. As noted earlier, the free market is often very effective in ensuring that the huge variety of consumers' market-expressed preferences are efficiently met – that actual market demand for all the different types of car or music, for example, is matched by supply. It is not, however, efficient in giving market participants equal access to the wherewithal to express their preferences. On its own, the free market cannot usually correct for such initial disabilities as illiteracy or for initial inequalities of income and wealth. This is important because a genuinely free market can only achieve an optimal satisfaction of different preferences to the extent that they are revealed in the market. It cannot take account of the fact that the capacity to reveal preferences in the market is itself a function of income and wealth, and that, therefore, not everyone is an equal player in the market game of preference satisfaction. So, for example, the poor cannot generally express in the marketplace their desire (or absolute preference) for a clean and quiet environment, since they must use their limited resources to express relatively more crucial preferences for the bare essentials of food and shelter. This does not mean that a clean environment is any less desirable, in an absolute sense, to them than to the rich. Inequality of initial abilities, wealth, etc. ensures that the true preferences or desires of the poor are not given weight in the market equal to those of the rich. The 447 dollar billionaires in the world at present – whose combined wealth earned under the auspices of the free market is estimated to be worth more than the annual income of half the world's population[12] – will have a disproportionate market weight attached to the expression and satisfaction of their preferences.

When such inequalities of market clout persist, the goal of market efficiency – i.e., the optimal satisfaction of market-expressed (money-denominated) preferences – will fall far short of the utilitarian ideal of maximising the satisfaction of the true desires of the greatest number. To take a hypothetical example, suppose one of the world's 447 billionaires wishes to buy an island previously owned by someone who made it accessible to a large number of local residents for recreational purposes. Now, if all the potential users of the island were of equal financial muscle, the free-market mechanism could allocate the island efficiently to the person or group which desires to have it most keenly, and is therefore willing to pay the highest price for it; but if the local community has little money, or no mechanism for pooling resources to express a community preference, then the desires of the many will be as nothing before the desire of the billionaire for an island retreat. It is for this reason that, in the USA, many states have, on good utilitarian principles, taken so much of the shoreline out of the market arena and stipulated that it should be publicly accessible.

The limitations of Pareto or free-market efficiency as a valid goal of policy – in practical and ethical terms – and its shortcomings as a mechanism for generating human progress in fact run much deeper than this important question of equitable distribution. For one thing, the conditions required for a truly free-market Pareto-efficient equilibrium across the whole economy are very stringent, and bear little practical relationship to the real world, even in liberal economies; as we shall explore later in the book, market distortions arising from taxation *are* inevitable, returns *do* sometimes increase with economies of scale, market externalities *are* pervasive, the future *is* uncertain, and piecemeal individual decisions *can* lead to unforeseen, socially disastrous outcomes. Market failures, even in theory, are very hard to avoid, and market efficiency – even in the Pareto sense – is often impossible to achieve in practice. More crucially perhaps from a utilitarian point of view, the desires expressed and met through the marketplace are only a subset of all desires. There are many desired goods – e.g., community spirit, liberty and leisure time – which are not typically traded, but are important to happiness. The goal of maximising market efficiency may actually cause these non-traded goods to be compromised because the desire for them is not expressed in the market. Similarly, the market fails to take account of the desires of those not participating in the relevant market transaction, to avoid externalities such as pollution and resource depletion. It also, crucially, does not take account of the desires of future people – an issue of particular concern to environmentalists.

As an implicit ethical doctrine, the notion that the market knows best – that it is the most valuable mechanism, not only for meeting consumer preferences efficiently, but also for articulating and expressing the combined preferences of all market participants – ignores both the limitations of scope of the market and the existence of market failure. It also falls into the utilitarian trap of seeing all desires as essentially comparable on a one-dimensional continuum. The US consumer's desire for the cheapest beef imports from Brazil can, in this view, be directly measured against the desire of the Brazilian Indians for their ancestral rainforest (which is, against their wishes, being plundered for cattle-grazing land). Irrational desires, created desires (e.g., for fashion accessories) and even antisocial desires (e.g., the desire that someone else should not have something) are all treated as morally equivalent. The modern economy creates desires, both by raising expectations and by increasing dissatisfaction with current goods through advertising. We might ask, for example, whether the created desire for the latest fashion in designer clothes should be accorded the same moral weight as the desire for essential items of clothing. But the market mechanism can do nothing else but treat as equivalent all desires revealed through market choice. Furthermore, the modern economy also leads inadvertently to the creation of new desires for goods to counteract the bad side effects of growth – i.e., desires for regrettable necessities. It is questionable, for example, whether a desire, however strongly felt, for a regrettable necessity such as double-glazing to shut out the noise of traffic should be accorded the same positive weight in the utility calculation as a desire for something intrinsically pleasing like a piano or a TV. Satisfying the desire for regrettable necessities will leave someone no happier than before the desire was created, whereas, arguably, the satisfaction of the desire to possess a TV or a piano will leave people genuinely happier. An ethical system should look into the provenance and intrinsic moral quality of different desires, rather than accord the satisfaction of all types of desire the same ethical weight.

It is clear, therefore, that while market efficiency – in optimising the satisfaction of market-expressed desires – is a valid goal in itself, it should not be accorded the status of paramount moral and political goal. For this would not only be to side-step crucial ethical questions of distribution, but also to ignore the limitations of scope of the market, the existence of market failure and the incommensurable nature of complex human desires. It is for these reasons that no professional economist would argue that the goal of maximising economic efficiency represents in any exact way the utilitarian goal of maximising happiness: in other words, even if utilitarianism is accepted as the best moral system and with it a very limited definition of happiness as simply the satisfaction of desires, economists would have to acknowledge that the limitations of the market mechanism and the unequal ability of market participants to express their desires or preferences serve to limit dramatically the extent to which the free market can be regarded as maximising happiness. In fact, of course, many would not only quarrel with the utilitarian emphasis on the supreme moral value of maximising happiness, but would argue that there is, in any case, no simple equation between happiness, on the one hand, and the meeting of expressed desires by the provision of more money-denominated goods on the other. Economic goods have a value which can be compared in money terms; but happiness is a more elusive concept, including subjective and incommensurable aspects too complex to be susceptible to arithmetical precision or to being crudely compared, traded and maximised. Adam Smith himself certainly did not fall into the trap of equating greater efficiency in the creation of wealth with progress in happiness. Indeed, in *The Theory of Moral Sentiments*, he says of the poor:

> In what constitutes the real happiness of human life, they are in no respect inferior to those who would seem so much above them. In ease of body and peace of mind, all the different ranks of life are nearly upon a level, and the beggar, who suns himself by the side of the highway, possesses that security which kings are fighting for.[13]

It may seem, when baldly stated, to be an obvious truism that progress in happiness is not delivered with any precision by the free-market mechanism. However, it is also clear that in the political arena today, the pursuit of greater market efficiency is seen as a very high priority. If the pursuit of higher economic growth through greater free-market efficiency is understood by economists and philosophers *not* to guarantee progress in happiness, it is clearly assumed by politicians that the causal link is very strong. Most modern politicians have yet to acknowledge fully that limitations in the workings of the invisible hand challenge many of the central political assumptions of the 1980s and 1990s. In particular, they have yet to acknowledge that these limitations mean that even a free-market system capable of delivering exponentially rising prosperity is not as clear a guarantor of progress in welfare – let alone of the more elusive progress in happiness – as many assumed it would be a decade or two ago.

Before concluding our assessment of the pervasive influence of utilitarianism on economics, it is helpful to focus briefly on one branch of the discipline which appears to take account of some of the failures of scope of the market mechanism – namely, cost-benefit analysis. Cost-benefit analysis is a methodology designed to assess the social costs and benefits of projects carried out either by the public sector or by the private sector, where it is assumed that the projects will have effects not falling within the scope of the market mechanism. So, for example, the government will carry out a cost-benefit analysis of a project to build a new airport – trying to take into account all the significant social costs and benefits, and not just those accruing to the builders of the airport through the market mechanism. It will, among other things, assess the negative impact on the congestion of local roads, on the noise pollution levels suffered by nearby residents, or on the beauty of the local scenery. It will then try to balance these against, for example, the financial benefits flowing to commerce in the city concerned from having a new airport. To do this, it must attempt to reduce to a single unit of account all the values to be taken into consideration. That involves translating into monetary measures such incommensurable items as the negative value attached to the disutility of increased noise levels, and the value placed on lost scenery or tranquillity, and then comparing these with the value of faster journey times by air, more opportunities to take foreign holidays, etc. In this way, cost-benefit analysis shares many of the attractions and problems of utilitarianism. The aim – to maximise the social benefits of all concerned – is laudable. But in attempting to achieve this, cost-benefit analysis is forced to reduce all values and desires to a single commensurable unit of account, i.e., monetary value, which oversimplifies the complexity of the situation; in so doing, it comes up against the enormous theoretical and practical difficulties of establishing a meaningful monetary value for non-traded goods, difficulties which many people believe it fails to solve. Moreover, the central objective of maximising the social good may still allow scant regard for the rights of unfortunate individuals who happen to stand directly in the flight path of progress.

CHAPTER 7

The Measurement of Economic Growth

We have now explored some of the important theoretical limitations of the free-market mechanism as a motor for generating human progress. Before examining the main practical implications of these in the remainder of the book, this chapter analyses the closely linked problems inherent in *measures* of economic growth. For measures of economic growth suffer from essentially the same limitations – when used as gauges of total preference-satisfaction – as does the free-market mechanism, when relied on as the mechanism for satisfying everyone's genuine preferences. A discussion of the shortcomings in measures of economic growth can shed light on the growing disillusionment felt by many participants in the modern economic miracle, and explain why there is a growing divergence between economic growth as defined by economists and progress in welfare as experienced by people.

The Definition and Theory of Growth

Economic growth is an increase in the output of goods and services or in the income generated by an economy. The most common measure of economic growth is the gross domestic product (GDP), which quantifies the total value of goods and services produced in a year. Because the GDP series values the output of an economy at market prices which are, in the main, determined by people freely trading that output, it appears to weigh the various benefits in a commensurable unit of value (monetary price) which is objectively related to the subjective desirability of the benefits to those trading them in the market. Herein lies the chief attraction of GDP growth, not just for economists but for politicians and society at large. It is, to some extent at least, an objective measure of changes in the real value of an economy's production of benefits.

Before we can explore the ambiguities in the measure and in its relationship to progress in welfare, a few more definitions and explanations are in order. First, it should be noted that the GDP series only measures the value added of an economy, i.e., the net output of goods and services sold to the 'final' consumer or end user; it excludes intermediate products used in the production and reflected in the prices of 'final' goods and services. Secondly, because nominal GDP measures output at the prices prevailing at the time of sale, it would give a misleading impression of the growth in benefits enjoyed if these prices were subject to inflation; economists, therefore, deflate nominal GDP by the retail price index to give a 'real' (i.e. inflation-adjusted) measure of output. The figures quoted in this chapter are all 'real' or inflation-adjusted. Thirdly, real GDP can be divided by the total population of the country concerned to arrive at a real GDP per capita figure, in order to give a picture of the increase in the real benefits of people on average. Finally, we should note that there is an alternative measure of economic growth which is used frequently, called gross national product (GNP). GNP measures the total income earned by a country's citizens; this is equivalent to GDP (domestic output) plus the net income from abroad. The two measures can diverge considerably for a country with large overseas net assets or net debts: the standard of living of the Swiss or Dutch is considerably boosted by large earnings ('*rentier*' income) on overseas assets, while that of the Mexicans or Hungarians is reduced by large interest payments on foreign debt.

Economic growth is a powerful phenomenon which has intrigued economists since the time of Adam Smith. Classical theories of growth have concentrated on analysing four factors to explain an increase in an economy's potential output. The first of these is *capital accumulation*, which includes investment in machinery, equipment, etc. An increase in capital stock can only take place when part of current income is saved for investment; and a net increase in capital can only happen when the savings rate is high enough to finance additions of capital stock over and above that required to replace that which is worn out. High savings and investment are crucial conditions both for productivity gains (i.e., increased output per worker) and for economic growth. The second factor is *growth in the labour force*, as a result of either increasing population or the addition of a previously non-working element (e.g., women). This second factor is not, at least in the short term, essential so long as capital investment and technological progress allow for an increase in labour productivity; moreover, population growth does not necessarily ensure a high growth rate, and may instead reduce overall productivity if the economy cannot successfully absorb the new people into the workforce. The third factor in classical accounts is *growth in land area or an extension of the resource base* – for example, the opening up of the Midwest grain prairies or the discovery of oil. These can in some sense be seen as 'free inputs', but their exploitation normally requires considerable investment and is therefore, like capital accumulation, a product of the level of saving. Investments in improving the quality of existing land resources (e.g., irrigation projects, fertilisers, etc.) can be particularly important in boosting output. The fourth key factor is *technological progress*, the development and introduction of innovative techniques which can improve the productivity of labour, capital, land or resources. Without technological progress, diminishing marginal returns on new investment in capital would set in and increased savings and investment would eventually cease to lead to increased potential growth. There is no point in each peasant involved in the wheat harvest having three sickles instead of one, but there is great point in his having a reaper instead of a sickle, or a steel plough instead of an iron one. In most analyses, technological progress, and the investment required to make use of it, have been the key determinants of the long-term rate of economic growth. The amount of technological progress itself is obviously determined, in large part, by the amount of research and development. However, it should be noted that many more people than those who fund the research and development tend to benefit from it, unless the inventions are protected by patent; developing countries' growth rates are often boosted by their making use of innovations originally researched and developed elsewhere.

Economists have, at different points, stressed many other important elements which can help explain an increase in economic activity. As we saw, Adam Smith emphasised the importance of *the specialisation of labour*, or the division of labour, in increasing the economies of scale of production and enhancing productivity. Smith, and later Ricardo, also stressed the importance of *growth in international trade* which allows each country to specialise in those areas in which it has a comparative advantage, thereby greatly reducing the real costs of production. Modern economists such as Simon Kuznets have often emphasised the importance of *institutional and personal adaptability*, in particular the ability to adjust quickly and have a positive attitude towards embracing change. One aspect of this is the ability of a society to accommodate the casualties of change, either by helping them to re-skill, or by ensuring that those benefiting from change compensate the losers. If this does not or cannot happen, those threatened by growth-enhancing change may seek to halt it by political or violent means.

There is much academic debate about the relative merits of government intervention and of market liberalisation in helping to increase economic growth and facilitate a society's necessary adaptation to change. Free-market economists, when looking to boost the long-term growth rate of an economy, stress the importance of *deregulation*, which they argue will increase both economic efficiency and the flexibility of markets in changing circumstances. By contrast, the so-called 'new growth theory' places its main emphasis on the beneficial side effects for the economy as a whole of capital investment (whether public or private) in any one area of the economy. For example, infrastructure investments may improve efficiency in whole swaths of the economy. Similarly, *investment in 'human capital'*, by means of education, does not just benefit the people concerned but also enables industry to adopt new technology more quickly, fosters innovation, and can lead to a big increase in efficiency and productivity across the economy. So, for example, it is clear that the development of human capital through good education and training was one of the secrets of South Korea's stunning success in the 1980s and early 1990s. An important feature of the 'new growth theory' is that it counters the classical insistence on the diminishing marginal returns of new investment, and argues that investment can, at the level of a whole economy, be subject to constant or even increasing returns to scale. This helps explain how perpetual economic growth is possible. The theory also makes respectable once again some government interference in the economy to help boost investment, especially in areas such as education and infrastructure where much of the return is in the form of diffuse economic and social benefits which cannot easily provide a market return on private investments.

Further analysis of the causes and determinants of economic growth must lie outside the scope of this book. It is sufficient to observe here that these interacting factors – higher savings and investment, population growth, resource discovery, greater social and economic flexibility, improved education and infrastructure and, above all, technological progress – have together led to an exponential rise in economic growth and in the output of material goods; this modern phenomenon of exponential growth is quite without precedent in human history and has transformed the world we live in. Michael Todaro, in his book, *Economic Development*, estimates that since the time of Adam Smith (approximately 1770) the developed countries have shown an average annual growth rate of about 3 per cent for real GNP – representing a doubling of output every twenty-four years. This breaks down into an average 2 per cent increase in per capita output and a 1 per cent growth per annum in population, allowing real per capita output to double every thirty-five years. This rate of growth has brought about huge changes in material prosperity and lifestyles in just a few generations. Thanks to economic growth most of us have access to cars, TVs, mass-produced toys, all manner of labour-saving devices such as vacuum cleaners, toasters and electric washing machines, new services such as medical and property insurance, and annual holidays away from home; the list is almost infinite. It is no wonder that economic growth has come to be seen as the main motor of human progress, nor that the pursuit of ever higher GDP or GNP – the main measures of this growth – has become a principal object of policy almost across the globe. As Todaro puts it:

> Economists and politicians from all nations, rich and poor, cap-
> italist, socialist, and mixed, have worshipped at the shrine of
> economic growth. At the end of every year, statistics are com-
> piled for all countries of the world showing their relative rates
> of GNP growth. 'Growthmanship' has become a way of life.[1]

Mesmerised by the wonders of exponential growth in GDP, it is often possible for us to overlook ambiguities in the very concept of economic growth and limitations in the principal measures of it. An understanding of these ambiguities and limitations will demonstrate how complex is the relationship between GDP growth and progress in human welfare. It will also help explain why the quintupling of real income (GNP) or money-denominated output (GDP) in the UK since 1870 does not imply that our level of welfare, let alone happiness, is now five times higher than it was then.

The GNP or GDP measures of economic growth represent an aggre-gate of the real income available or output generated to satisfy market-expressed preferences. Now if all important desires were expressed in the market and met by way of measured economic output, then the GDP growth measure might seem genuinely to represent the growth of the total level of desire-satisfaction, with an aggregate valuation objectively derived from the prices willingly paid by the consumers of the desire-satisfying output. If, further, the simple meeting of desires represented the full definition of welfare – or even happiness – then this same GDP growth measure might serve as a measure of progress in welfare or happiness. Alas, it is not so simple. For one thing, as any economist would admit, GDP is an incomplete measure of economic output and, more importantly, many goods which are crucial to our welfare, and to our total level of desire-satisfaction, lie outside the scope of the market altogether. These non-traded goods – including leisure, housework, community spirit and externalities such as pollution and congestion – are often critical to our welfare and are not reflected in GDP. Just as crucially, the relationship between desire-satisfaction, on the one hand, and happiness or welfare, on the other, is very complex for the philosophical reasons discussed earlier in the book.

We have already established that happiness is an amorphous umbrella concept, including not just the satisfaction of desires but also a variety of subjective feelings of pleasure, attitudes of being pleased, etc. which do not admit of precise comparison between people, let alone across generations. We have also seen that there is no clear-cut and precisely measurable link between the subjective experience of happiness and progress towards meeting either objective welfare goals or market-expressed desires. Indeed, many argue that happiness is as dependent on the absence of strongly felt unfulfilled desires as it is on the satisfaction of desires; this view originated with the Greek philosopher Epicurus, who insisted that happiness involves the tranquillity arising from the absence of unfulfilled desires, and can therefore be more easily increased by removing desires than by trying to satisfy all those which have been created. The Epicureans, indeed, argued that the inflation of wants and desires can have a seriously negative impact on happiness. Since the modern economy has a propensity to create demand precisely by creating ever more of the unfulfilled desires which are a prerequisite of economic growth, such a view suggests a potentially radical break between economic growth and progress in happiness. For all these reasons, it seems clear that the nature of any correlation between GDP growth and progress in happiness must remain elusive – the preserve of imaginative poets and prescriptive theologians. Of more central importance to our story is the apparently less problematic correlation between GDP growth and progress in welfare (or progress in the realisation of the key elements of our notion of the good life). However, even this link – between the increased satisfaction of desires expressed in the market (as measured by rises in GDP) and progress in welfare – is complex and ambiguous.

Any particular definition of welfare or the good life will, of course, reflect those things which we judge will satisfy the important wants or desires of those concerned. But to do this it will inevitably include many non-traded goods (e.g., absence of pollution), which satisfy desires *not* expressed in the marketplace and which are therefore not measured by GDP; the definition of welfare will conversely tend to exclude the GDP-measured satisfaction of many desires which *are* expressed and met in the marketplace. So there are few definitions of welfare, or the good life, which include the meeting of fundamentally irrational or antisocial desires, even if expressed in the market; nor will they tend to equate the meeting of baser (e.g., pornographic) desires as of equal value with the meeting of desires for basic necessities or the meeting of higher wants (e.g., for education or music). In other words, definitions of welfare and the good life will tend to reflect value judgements about the quality of wants or desires which are quite independent from the quantitative assessment of the strength of their expression in the marketplace. Not all wants or desires are comparable on a one-dimensional continuum of quantitative value. So, in a definition of welfare, more value may, for example, be placed on the eradication of illiteracy than on the setting up of a national lottery, even if market demand for the latter is greater. Moreover, a definition of welfare will not allow the desires or wants considered important to be judged and weighted according to actual purchasing power. For as we have seen, the marketplace gives the rich much more clout in expressing and meeting their preferences than the poor. Measures of welfare need to be neutral between the interests of rich and poor.

With such a comprehensive theoretical breakdown between the definition of welfare and the measurement of the money-denominated satisfaction of market-expressed desires, monetary valuations can have little place in weighting the relative importance – from a welfare point of view – of different interests or wants. This leaves us with a considerable problem: if we cannot derive from the marketplace a commensurable unit of account (monetary value) with which to weight the different components of welfare, how can we hope to make a composite measure of progress in welfare? Tastes and values may not be entirely commensurable even for one individual – making a single composite indicator of value worthless. More important still, tastes and values vary from person to person, and from generation to generation, so that the definition of the good life or of welfare made by one group or in one period may be quite different from that belonging to another. Cut free from the weightings given by market values, changing values and tastes make it impossible for us to form a general assessment of progress in welfare or towards 'the good life', except by reference to one particular stipulated and essentially arbitrary definition. But before we consider this problem in more detail, it is useful now to turn from a purely theoretical and philosophical analysis of why we might expect GDP growth to be poorly correlated with progress in welfare to a discussion of practical examples of radical divergence.

The Limitations of GDP

The conceptual reasons for doubting the value of the GDP growth series as an indicator of welfare were not missed by the economists who designed the series. They would have argued that it was never designed to be a measure of progress in human wellbeing, but rather an indicator of the monetary value of annual flows of production. It was originally designed primarily as a tool to manage the economy in wartime; and, even today, the growth rate of money-based activity remains a key vari- able in the economists' armoury – one of particular importance for the short-term management of the economy. But over time the widespread consensus that the phenomenon of economic growth was leading to rapid material progress, and allowing for significant progress in welfare, led to the series being given a greater role in defining political goals than is warranted by its composition. There are a number of practical rea- sons why the GDP series is the wrong measuring rod for the welfare of society.

First, the GDP series omits many valuable activities, goods and ser- vices which are not traded; these may take the form of functions performed in the home (e.g., child rearing, housework or DIY) or, in undeveloped countries, of subsistence-level farming (where produce tends not to be commercially traded). This omission may be perfectly justified if one is interested purely in measuring monetary exchanges, but is of a scale which in itself suggests a radical divergence between the GDP series and measures of welfare. The UNDP's Human Development Report (1995) estimated that *household and community work* accounted for unrecorded output worth some $16 trillion in 1993, com- pared with the $23 trillion of recorded (GDP-measured) world output. (Of this 'invisible output' it was estimated that some $11 trillion was contributed by women.) The omission of this non-market work can result in any tendency towards greater commercialisation of activity leading to an overstatement, by the GDP series, of the increase in real output. So, for example, if a mother goes out to work, not only is her new work counted as additional output – so is the childcare she pays for in her absence. One net new productive activity has been registered as two net new activities. Similarly, the output increase of a move from subsistence-level existence to a specialised modern economy can be overstated by a GDP series, to the extent that the productive work of the earlier subsistence-level communities was not traded and went unrecorded. For this reason, some developing country growth rates can be deceptively high.

Secondly, the GDP series omits *leisure* that is not paid for. As a result, it does not include the welfare impact of the additional (or reduced) leisure opportunities generated by a modern economy: if a worker chooses voluntarily to forgo a week's income or output for a week's leisure, it is clear that he does not anticipate a lower level of enjoyment or welfare as a result of this choice; and yet the GDP and GNP series will only register the decline in output and income. In the early part of the twentieth century the omission of this item may have led to a considerable understatement of increases in welfare, as the average worker gradually earned the right to a shorter working week and to four weeks' holiday a year instead of the one week still usual in the nineteenth century. Over the last forty years, however, leisure time has almost certainly been growing much more slowly than GDP-measured economic activity, and may more recently have fallen for many groups, with the result that GDP growth has, in this respect at least, been overstating the improvement in welfare levels. It is, of course, difficult to assign an objectively meaningful value to leisure: if one values it by reference to the pay forgone, this would imply that the leisure of a teacher or nurse should be given a lower value than that of a bond-dealer. The problem of how to impute value accurately is one shared by many other non-money-denominated goods. The danger is that goods which are omitted from our key performance indicator, simply because they are not traded and because their value is hard even to impute accurately, may be undervalued or even ignored in the drive for efficiency. Many goods come into this category – the pleasure of sitting in the sun (now more dangerous thanks to CFCs), the pleasure of walking in unspoilt countryside (now harder to find the time or place for) or listening to birdsong (now harder to hear).

The third big problem with equating the GDP series with welfare is that it omits the non-traded direct costs (or benefits) of economic activity. These costs – called *externalities* by economists – are not borne primarily by the parties to the market exchange that cause them and hence are not reflected in market prices. They include, most importantly, environmental degradation in the form of pollution, resource depletion, and congestion. These general ill-effects of economic activity are not subtracted from the GDP growth series, as aggregate costs of growth to be set against aggregate benefits. The GDP series is a gross measure of monetary exchange – not a cost-benefit analysis of the impact of increased activity. This leads to the risk that a narrow focus on maximising GDP growth alone could result in our ignoring the non-traded costs of this growth. This would be particularly serious if the costs of growth started to rise much faster than the benefits – as many argue is now happening. The danger is that in our scientific age, costs which are not measured in the key target indicators may be problems which are not tackled. A redefinition of our central measures of economic growth to include and net off both the final costs and benefits of an increased level of activity would be likely to change our political priorities; it would lead us to focus on the costs of growth as much as on the benefits. The welfare of society will rise as a result of increased activity only if the marginal costs of that extra activity are less than the marginal benefits. Unless we measure the costs and compare them to the benefits, we cannot be sure that our policies are rational or that economic growth represents genuine progress. However, there are a number of practical and theoretical difficulties inherent in valuing environmental degradation, which make it far from easy to construct a rigorous comparison of the costs and benefits of growth; these difficulties will be discussed in the next chapter.

Another important ambiguity in the relationship between the GDP series and welfare arises from the treatment of *defensive expenditures* or *regrettable necessities*. For not only does the GDP series fail to subtract the value of the damage inflicted on the environment and on the quality of our lives by economic activity, it also includes as a positive addition defensive expenditures made to protect ourselves against such negative side effects of growth. So, for example, both the purchase of water filters to offset water pollution and the increased length of commuter journeys as cities sprawl outwards are counted as positive elements of GDP. Now, in one sense this is perfectly valid: the building of a water filter or a new long-distance commuter line is economic activity; it employs people, and it has a value to the purchaser or consumer who is better off, given the existence of congestion or pollution, than he would have been had the good not been produced. Nevertheless, by including defensive consumption undertaken to offset some of the negative consequences of growth which are not themselves subtracted, market GDP loses any reliability as a guide to the *net* increase in economic welfare. Another 'regrettable necessity' included in GDP is crime prevention expenditure. The fitting of burglar alarms, closed-circuit TV cameras and locks on every door and window may increase the feeling of security of those who purchase them, given the fear level induced by rising crime levels. But they are not valuable in themselves; they serve merely to protect (and only partially so) against the bad side effects (increased crime levels) of the rapid breakdown of communities and the erosion of opportunities for the unskilled, which are features of our post-industrial and increasingly unequal societies. The 'great car economy' has the same paradoxical impact on GDP data: the ever-increasing use of the motor car is reflected in the GDP series (more output of cars, tyres, petrol, etc.), but no subtraction is made to reflect the disutility of increased pollution and accidents. Instead, the spending on new roads to relieve congestion, on sound barriers to protect communities from the noise of these new roads, on catalytic converters to reduce pollution and on hospital care for the thousands maimed in accidents are all counted as positive additions to GDP.

There is a strong superficial attraction in attempting to correct the GDP series in order to offset the above limitations – by adding in the value of beneficial non-traded activities and goods, and by subtracting defensive expenditures and the current value of residual (i.e., uncorrected) environmental damage caused by increased levels of economic activity. But problems abound which threaten to make all attempts to convert the GDP series into an indicator of welfare look impossible in practice and implausible even in theory. First, while defensive expenditures do have a market value, it is not always possible for this value to be isolated, since it has often become embedded in the general cost of goods. Secondly, it is extremely difficult to see how to give leisure or residual environmental degradation an objective value; because they are not traded, we cannot rely on market prices, and any imputed value is bound to be somewhat subjective and open to challenge. Moreover, before an adjusted GDP figure could be a good measure of welfare, it would need to correct for some even deeper-rooted defects. In particular, it would need to distinguish fully between goods or activities as means to an end and goods or activities as ends in themselves; it would also need to allow for the impact of inequality; and, finally, in order to represent a welfare level which is sustainable into the future, it would have to include adjustments for resource depletion which take account of the interests of future generations. It is to the analysis of these defects and challenges that we turn now.

While it is perfectly legitimate to try to subtract from GDP only some of the more obvious defensive expenditures which are required purely because of the negative environmental impact of growth, and thereby to focus on the dynamic environmental cost-benefit equation of growth, it should be noticed that the logic of such an exercise could – by extension – commit us to making complex adjustments in many if not most areas of the economy. For the GDP series does not distinguish in any field between goods which are bought by consumers for their intrinsic satisfaction value and those which are bought as a means to facilitate, secure or protect satisfaction derived from other goods. The GDP series does exclude intermediate goods used during the production process, since it includes only goods sold to the final consumer; but it takes no account of the fact that many goods purchased by final consumers are in effect *intermediate goods* purchased for their value as 'means' to securing the 'end' of higher welfare. So, for example, time and money spent on gaining a qualification is a means to the end of getting the desired job, itself perhaps a means to being able to afford a house, holidays, etc. Many goods are wanted solely as a means of satisfying the desire for other goods. Fred Hirsch, in his book, *Social Limits to Growth*, argues that we should see consumers as themselves performing a processing role, purchasing inputs to be converted into desired output. When we do this and realise that GDP data do not distinguish between intermediate and final consumer goods, then it is clear that changes in the efficiency of conversion of intermediate into final goods would change the welfare content of a given level of GDP. Hirsch gives the following examples:

> Suppose that the process becomes less efficient in the technical sense of requiring a larger input to produce a given output – because, for example, additional heating is required to maintain a given temperature in a cold winter, or because additional years of full-time education are required to attain the credentials necessary for entry to a given job. In such cases increased expenditures on the intermediate good that serves as an input appear in the conventional measure of national accounting as adding to consumption, but actually will leave the consumer no better off in terms of the object of his or her consumption.[2]

If we imagine first trying to assess the combined impact of the rising and falling height of a myriad different hurdles to the attainment of a given level of welfare, and then trying to adjust for the consequent change in the efficiency of use of intermediate inputs in producing desired ends, it becomes quickly clear that the scale and complexity of adjustment required to make the GDP series an accurate measure of welfare is awesome.

If the GDP series is to have any hope of reflecting changes in the total welfare of the average person, it will also need to take account of *changes in inequalities of income*. To the extent that we are interested in the welfare of the majority or of the average citizen, we need to adjust for any increase in the concentration of income in the hands of the few. Furthermore, even if we accord no value to equality in itself, and profess a total lack of interest in whether increases in welfare accrue to the already rich or to the poor, there remains another reason for making adjustments to the GDP output series to take account of changes in income inequalities, if we are to gauge rises in *total* welfare. For there will normally be a diminishing marginal benefit from extra income or goods; the second Ferrari purchased by the same rich pop star is likely to yield less extra utility to him than the same £100,000 spent on food would yield to the hungry; but the market mechanism and the GDP series will accord them both the same value. The weighting accorded to different desire-satisfactions in GDP is not a function simply of anticipated utility, but also of the financial muscle of the respective participants in the market. GDP data are therefore a poor indicator of changes in total or average welfare levels.

This limitation is becoming more important as inequalities increase in the brave new world of global free markets. It has been estimated that between 1979 and 1993, the poorest 10 per cent in the UK saw their real income fall by nearly 20 per cent, while the richest 10 per cent enjoyed a rise in real income of over 60 per cent.[3] The UNDP's Human Development Report (1996) reveals that the poorest fifth of the world's people have seen their share of global income fall from 2.3 per cent to 1.4 per cent over the last thirty years, while the share of the richest fifth has climbed from 70 per cent to 85 per cent. The poorest one billion people in the world saw their real incomes actually decline between 1980 and 1993. Todaro, in his book, *Economic Development*, shows that while the 'gini coefficient' – a measure of income inequality ranging from 0 (perfect equality) to 1 (perfect inequality) – has been rising in most developing countries over the last thirty years, the same has also been true in the

USA; between 1977 and 1989, the richest 1 per cent of US citizens cap-tured 60 per cent of the real growth in post-tax income. In many countries, the top 20 per cent enjoy as much as 50 per cent of the income; in the UK, the richest 20 per cent have incomes roughly ten times those of the poorest 20 per cent.[3] Given these unequal income distribution weightings, there is a very real sense in which the growth of the GNP series reflects principally the growth in the incomes and desire-satisfac-tions of the rich. If, in addition, the principal means of boosting GNP is to take efficiency measures which put further pressure on the incomes of the least skilled and fortunate, increases in GNP may not only largely reflect increases in the welfare of the rich but may also be at the expense of the poor. Some economists have therefore suggested constructing an 'equal weights' GDP index, which measures the growth rate of the income of each quintile (or fifth) of the population and weights it by the equal population weight of each quintile instead of by its unequal income weighting. This adjusted index accords the same weight to a 1 per cent rise in the income of the poor as to a 1 per cent rise in the income of the rich. Others have suggested a 'poverty weighted' index which gives a higher weight to percentage rises in the incomes of the poor. These indices have recently tended to yield significantly lower growth rates than the unadjusted GDP series, particularly in highly polarised countries such as Brazil. The problem with such adjustments, of course, is that it is impossible to measure objectively the rate at which the marginal utility of extra income diminishes, and thus it is impossible to apply an income dis-tribution weighting which is objectively valid in terms of welfare. Adjustments for income inequality will therefore always be controversial and have a large subjective value element.

Finally, we should note that the GDP series takes no account of the *welfare of future people*. Environmental degradation often has its principal impact not on the welfare of contemporary people but on that of future generations; this is particularly true of irrevocable damage to resources which would otherwise be renewable (e.g., deforestation or the extinction of whale species) and of the depletion of non-renewable resources. Many environmentalists therefore argue that it is important to distinguish between the sustainable use of renewable natural inputs and the once-and-for-all squandering of 'geological' or 'natural capital'. They point out that companies must, according to accounting convention, allow for depreciation of physical capital (i.e., make an allowance for the fall in value of their machinery, etc. as a result of wear and tear) in calculating their profitability, in order to give an accurate picture of sustainable profits; this enables them to show that profits are not coming simply from the squandering of capital and the reduction of potential output in the future. In the same way, national accounts subtract capital depreciation from GNP to give an economy's net national product (NNP); NNP measures the income generated by an economy after it has set aside sufficient money to maintain its capital equipment intact. Green economists argue that we should similarly allow for the depreciation of natural capital, by allowing for the future cost of any feasible replacement or repair of environmental resources, and by deducting an estimate of the value of the welfare permanently lost to future generations as a result of current consumption of irreplaceable resources. They argue that it is totally inappropriate to treat resources as free inputs into the economic system – as traditional economic theory implies – and that we should adjust fully for the effects of resource depletion and environmental degradation. Adjustments of this sort can be very significant. The World Resources Institute in Washington, for example, has estimated that if the depreciation of oil and forestry resources is subtracted from Indonesia's GNP, and if allowance is made for the costs of soil erosion, the growth rate between 1971 and 1984 would have been 4 per cent per annum rather than the official figure of 7 per cent.[4] However, as we shall explore in more detail in the next chapter, it is often far from easy to assess the value of resources in the future or to estimate repair or replacement costs into the next century. In particular, it is difficult to decide whether it is appropriate to apply a 'discount rate' to future costs.

It should be very clear from this discussion that the GDP series is fatally flawed as an indicator of changing welfare levels. However useful as a tool for the short-term management of the economy, it is simply inappropriate as a measure of human wellbeing. This helps explain how it is possible to have continued economic growth, as measured by GDP, co-existing with an increasingly anxious society, weighed down by the 'feel-bad factor'. This is in no way to argue that economic growth is irrelevant to progress in human welfare, or totally uncorrelated with it. The widespread misunderstanding among non-economists of the significance of GDP growth comes about precisely because the correlation between growth and human progress was undeniably positive, if inexact, during much of the nineteenth and twentieth centuries, and remains so in many developing countries (where basic material needs have yet to be fully catered for). However, the current mood of anxiety gripping much of the developed world despite respectable GDP growth, and the growing conscious and unconscious disillusionment with growth as the principal motor of progress, almost certainly reflects the fact that the marginal welfare benefits of extra growth are declining in rich countries (and becoming less evenly spread), while the marginal costs of pursuing even more growth are rising. In particular, there is mounting evidence that largely unmeasured social and environmental costs – such as social dislocation, stress levels and environmental degradation – are becoming more prevalent and important. Before considering these costs in more detail, it is useful to consider some brave attempts to construct alternative indicators of progress in welfare or human development which try to pin down the exact state we are in.

Alternative Measures of Progress in Welfare

The task of adjusting the GDP series to make it a more accurate indicator of changes in welfare, and a better measure of the success of policies designed to help ensure that economic growth is translated more effectively into genuine human development, is – as we have seen – problematic for both practical and theoretical reasons. Nevertheless, several serious attempts have been made. Perhaps the best known of these is the Measure of Economic Welfare (MEW) constructed by William Nordhaus and James Tobin in 1972.[5] The most important adjustments they made were to assign positive values for leisure and non-paid employment, and to subtract the monetary value of some regrettable necessities like the costs of commuting and police protection. They largely ignored environmental costs, and many would quarrel with their particular choice of which regrettable necessities should be subtracted (and which ignored). There is also, as we have noted, much disagreement about how to value leisure – which was the biggest adjustment in the MEW index. Nevertheless, the results of their project were interesting. MEW was larger in absolute terms than GNP (i.e., there were more previously excluded benefits than costs) but over a long period it grew considerably more slowly than the GNP series. Herman E. Daly and John B. Cobb Jr, in their book, *For the Common Good*, note that, in per capita terms, the annual growth rate from 1929 to 1965 of the 'sustainable' variant of MEW was 1.1 per cent compared with 1.7 per cent for NNP (i.e., GNP less depreciation), while in the post-war period (1947–65) sustainable MEW grew by a mere 0.4 per cent per annum, compared with GNP growth of 2.2 per cent per annum.

Daly and Cobb invented their own indicator, the Index of Sustainable

Economic Welfare (ISEW), in 1989. This measure also suggested that, when the costs of increased economic activity are netted off against the benefits, the real growth rate is over the long term still positive, but significantly lower than GDP statistics would suggest. From 1951 to 1986, ISEW showed a per capita growth rate in the USA of just 0.53 per cent per annum, as compared with 1.9 per cent per capita GNP growth. The ISEW index actually indicated a small drop in economic welfare between 1970 and 1986, which was particularly marked in the early 1980s. ISEW makes a large adjustment for changes in the inequalities of income distribution, and this is the principal factor making the ISEW growth rate negative in the 1980s. It also subtracts the estimated nuisance value of noise pollution, and adjusts for the costs of environmental degradation; at the same time, it adds in the imputed value of household labour, but omits adjustments for the value of leisure as too speculative. There are many contentious elements in the adjustments made, not least the chosen method for weighting consumption growth by changes in an inequality index, and the subtraction of much of the cost of education (seen as a regrettable necessity). Daly and Cobb have also taken the contentious step, with respect to the depletion of non-renewable resources, of deducting 100 per cent of the value of mineral extraction-based production (i.e., using a zero discount rate). As they themselves admit, 'Closer examination of decisions that must be made in any such index shows how large the arbitrary element is.'[6]

It is this arbitrariness which is the Achilles' heel of all attempts to adjust the GDP series, and the reason why broader measures of welfare have failed to gain general acceptance in economic or political circles. It is to a considerable extent a matter of subjective judgement and normative values how one defines and ascribes value to costs and benefits – how, for example, one decides the weight which should be given to the imputed costs and benefits of future generations, and what value should be placed on income gains amongst the poor as against those of the rich. The more ambitious and sophisticated the adjusted index is, the more its conclusions will be dependent on the value judgements embedded in the adjustments and weightings chosen. For this reason many countries are now choosing to issue separate 'satellite' accounts which give complementary information analysed on the basis of clearly articulated assumptions, but which do not attempt to construct a fully integrated series (which would mask the often contentious normative assumptions made). The UK issued such satellite 'green accounts' for the first time in 1996; they estimated, for example, the cost of the depletion of UK oil and gas reserves at some £2.2 billion in 1993, equivalent to a little under 0.5 per cent of GDP.[7]

Some recent attempts to establish alternative measures have taken a different route, and, rather than trying to adjust the GDP series, have given most weight to objective non-money-denominated indicators of welfare. One such alternative measure is The New Economy Well-Being Index (NEWBI), devised by D. Corry et al. This index does include growth in real income per head, but only as one of seven indicators. The others reflect levels or changes in inequality, unemployment, inflation and interest rates. The seven indicators are equally weighted to give a composite index of wellbeing; this index indicates among other things that we have never again had it so good in the UK as we did in 1973, and that since then the level of wellbeing has fluctuated wildly, rising sharply in the mid 1980s but still not quite back to 1973 levels. The extent to which this and any similar index is dependent for its results on subjective decisions about the weightings to be used to combine the different factors is shown by the effect of increasing the weight attached in NEWBI to unemployment as a negative wellbeing factor. If unemployment is given three times the weighting of the other six factors individually, the index suggests a significant decline in wellbeing since 1973, with only a modest recovery in the 1980s.[8]

A very different welfare measure is the Human Development Index (HDI), published annually in the UNDP's Human Development Report. The HDI is based on three indicators: life expectancy at birth, educational attainment (a combination of adult literacy and school enrolment ratios) and the standard of living as measured by real GDP per capita (at purchasing-power parity). The index is a simple average of these three factors, and is used to rank all countries on a single scale. Some of the results are very interesting. Spain, Holland, Greece, Costa Rica and Vietnam all have rankings on this composite human development indicator which are far higher than their respective GDP-per-capita rankings. By contrast, Singapore, Hong Kong and Gulf states like Kuwait and the UAE all have substantially lower human-development rankings than GDP rankings, suggesting among other things that these countries have seen a less equitable distribution of the development benefits of economic growth. The Human Development Report has also spawned a number of different measures of welfare – a 'capability poverty measure' and a 'gender empowerment measure' (measuring gender inequality).

Fascinating though these alternative indicators are, they are all plagued by an essential arbitrariness in the weightings chosen for the different welfare factors. Classical economic statistical series like GDP maintain their hold on our attention precisely because they omit the areas where only contentious subjective measurement is possible, and because they make use of the seemingly 'objective' weightings provided by monetary valuation; this gives the statistics an air of precision and accuracy which is appealing in this scientific age, but which depends, as we have seen, on their largely ignoring the limitations of scope of the market, the effects of inequalities of income, and the many complexities of the human predicament. Indices such as the HDI and NEWBI do avoid the problems associated with assigning monetary value to such factors as literacy levels, life expectancy and unemployment, but are left with no commensurable unit of account with which to weight the relative importance of different factors. However crucial it may be to assess the quality as well as the quantity of economic growth, and however much we may yearn to establish definitively whether or not there has been progress in welfare in a particular period, any attempt to construct a single reliable indicator seems doomed to be arbitrary and inadequate. Instead we are better advised to make flexible use of a whole range of 'complementary indicators' of the quality of life. Michael Jacobs, in his book *The Green Economy*, sums up the matter well:

> The problem here surely lies in the desire to have a single indicator which can measure welfare. Such a desire is understandable . . . But the attractiveness of the idea cannot hide the meaninglessness of its execution. Welfare is not a unitary concept, and cannot be expressed in one indicator. Economic performance must be assessed using a variety of indicators, each showing in its own terms one aspect of what is considered important. It is true that in many cases these will move in opposite directions, making it difficult to say whether, 'overall', society is getting better or worse off. But this problem is not erased by the use of a single indicator, it is simply hidden within its calculations. It is much better that the changes in the different indicators are out in the open, where they can be seen. We can all then make our own judgements on whether any given change from one year to another represents progress or not; and economic policy can be decided accordingly.[9]

Human progress is a complex phenomenon not easily amenable to

quantifiable and scientific certainties. It is as much a subjective and evaluative concept as it is a question of fact. It is necessary to establish what
value yardstick we are using to measure whether or not there has been
progress and from whose point of view the judgement is being made.
Different yardsticks and different standpoints will yield conflicting
judgements. That is the essence of humanity.

Governments are likely to continue to ignore the important theoretical and practical shortcomings of the use of the GDP series as an indicator
of welfare; they will continue to take comfort from the impossibility of
constructing a single alternative composite indicator of welfare which
can command widespread respect as an objective measure. For politicians, like the modern media, prefer to have straightforward and
measurable goals, which the pursuit of economic growth and the GDP
series seem to provide. Subjective judgements on the basis of a variety of
different yardsticks smack of woolly thinking in this harsh age of efficiency. Governments also often have a vested interest in downplaying the
focus upon the costs of growth. Any admission of the futility of some
forms of economic growth might reduce the apparent attractiveness of
growth policies, and give legitimacy to the current 'feel-bad factor'.
Furthermore, any serious doubt about our ability to grow welfare exponentially, even by pursuing free-market policies, might make it harder to
fend off demands from poorer sections of the community for redistribution of existing levels of wealth and income.

CHAPTER 8

Environmental Limits to Growth

We all live under the haunting fear that something may corrupt the environment to the point where man joins the dinosaurs as an obsolete form of life ... our fate could perhaps be sealed twenty or more years before the development of symptoms.

David E. Price, 'Is Man Becoming Obsolete?'[1]

As the burgeoning environmental problems facing the modern world impinge more and more on our collective consciousness, there is a growing scepticism that the unbridled pursuit of economic growth and technological progress can remain the principal engine of human progress. We are gradually being forced to acknowledge the existence of important physical constraints on the scale of human ambition, and to recognise limits to our ability to control our destiny. From a psychological perspective, it is possible to see today a re-emergence of conceptions of man's relationship to the world which are more akin to ancient views than to those of the confident nineteenth and early twentieth centuries. Once again, we seem to be faced with insecurity in the human predicament, as the enormous expansion of our activities multiplies the instances of dangerous and unpredictable friction with our natural habitat. There is increasing awareness of the complexity of the natural systems we are disrupting, and of the associated danger of chaotic environmental reactions which are beyond our ability to predict or perhaps even control. Furthermore, as mankind has moved from a respectful harnessing of nature to attempting boldly to re-engineer and conquer it, many people feel a renewed sense of unease that we may be tempting fate by overstepping the proper limits to man's ambitions. The brilliance of scientific and technological discoveries and applications has led, it is felt, to a dangerous arrogance, bred of ignoring the limitations of the compartmentalised knowledge of specialists. At the same time as these fears have been growing, there has also been a rising nostalgia for a past of pristine nature and rural beauty, breeding an almost ancient belief in a lost paradise. The local environments of our childhood – still extant patches of wilderness and the carefully husbanded countryside of generations of rural peasants – have succumbed to the relentless pressure for space and modern farming techniques. Water meadows, bluebell woods, streams, ponds and hedgerows are vanishing. As Aldous Huxley once put it, 'we are losing half the subject matter of English poetry'.[2]

This chapter examines the rising environmental costs of economic growth, and the importance of these costs in reducing the correlation between economic growth and human progress. The first section analyses both the increasing scale of our activities and the complexity of the ecosystems we are disrupting, and assesses the combined impact of these two factors on our ability to manage a controlled, harmonious and sustainable relationship with our natural environment. The second section examines the important contribution made to the prevalence of environmental degradation by the failure of the invisible hand of the free market either to deal with externalities such as pollution, or to cater for the interests of future generations. The chapter concludes by focusing on some of the important ways in which modern man might try to circumvent these kinds of market failure by cooperating to safeguard our common environmental heritage. For it is upon the efficacy of such attempts that our hopes for sustainable human progress into the future must rest.

A Problem of Scale and Complexity

To a considerable extent, the environmental crisis is a product of the unprecedented scale of human activity, and of the ever more rapid speed of the associated changes in man's relationship with the natural world. Money and money-based activity can grow exponentially, and so can human populations, but the earth is finite and there are limits to the carrying capacity of the earth's natural ecosystems. The world population has grown from 1.2 billion people in 1850 to 2.6 billion people in 1950 and to 5.3 billion in 1990, as a result of death rates falling far more rapidly than birth rates. With some 40 per cent of the Third World population now under 15 years of age, a huge further increase in world population – to perhaps 8.5 billion by 2025 – is virtually assured as the number of potential parents swells faster than the birth rate per person falls. However, this

staggering increase in the number of human beings is only partly responsible for the unprecedented global impact of human activity upon the
environment. For the biggest absolute increases in demand have continued, at least until recently, to come from the rich developed countries,
even though their populations are in many cases not growing. The enormous rise in the material prosperity and resource consumption of these
rich countries has ensured that they have remained the biggest users of
the earth's resources. The developed countries (excluding the CIS and
Eastern Europe), with 16 per cent of the world's population, consume
over half of the world's fuel and a third of the world's cereal production.
The average North American consumes five times as much grain and
sixty times as much fuel as the average citizen of India.[3]

Continued economic growth in the developed world and population
growth elsewhere, together with the desire among poorer countries to
emulate the West's economic expansion, promise further enormous
increases in environmental pressures. In the Worldwatch Institute report,
State of the World 1996, Lester Brown notes that since 1950 the demand
for grain has nearly tripled, while the consumption of fossil fuels, and
hence carbon emissions, has risen approximately fourfold. His opening
essay argues:

> These spiraling human demands for resources are beginning
> to outgrow the capacity of the earth's natural systems. As this
> happens, the global economy is damaging the foundation on
> which it rests. Evidence of the damage to the earth's ecologi-
> cal infrastructure takes the form of collapsing fisheries, falling
> water tables, shrinking forests, eroding soils, dying lakes, crop-
> withering heatwaves and disappearing species.[4]

He goes on to highlight the combined impact of these many forms of
environmental degradation on the ability to grow world food supplies fast
enough to feed the additional 90 million people on the planet each year.
Ever since Malthus, in the first edition of his famous *Essay on the Principle
of Population*, wrongly predicted at the end of the eighteenth century that
population growth would soon outpace the growth in food supplies,
thereby leading to mass starvation and an end to human progress, the
ability to grow food supplies by opening up new lands and by technological progress has been one of the triumphs of mankind. The most
important physical constraint on improved wellbeing for greater numbers
of people has been pushed back with astonishing success. Whereas the

American farmer produced four times his own consumption in 1820, he was able to produce eighty times his own consumption by 1987.[5] This rise in agricultural productivity had continued apace in the 1970s thanks to the 'green revolution' – new higher-yielding crops and more effective fertilisers – but Brown points out that in the late 1980s the growth in land yields started to dwindle; indeed, between 1984 and 1992 there was actually a 6 per cent decline in grain output per person. Over the three years 1992 to 1995, the world produced less grain than it consumed, with the result that world grain stocks, which stood at 104 days' worth of consumption in 1987, were by early 1996 standing at only 49 days' worth – below what is generally considered a minimum safety level.[6] Even if Europe and the USA's 'set-aside' land had been put back in production, grain stocks would still have fallen in these years. Brown and other commentators blame this deterioration in grain supplies upon the effects of soil erosion, depleted aquifers (essential for irrigation) and the diminishing marginal returns of using extra fertilisers, as well as on the damaging effects of air pollution and of extra UV radiation resulting from the depletion of the ozone layer. The UNDP's Human Development Report (1996) estimates that the costs of desertification now run to some $42 billion a year globally. At the same time, water tables in many key agricultural regions are dropping fast because of over-exploitation. The enormous Ogallala aquifer which lies beneath the US Midwest grain prairies is seeing water levels drop by four feet a year, which could threaten the viability of the great plains within twenty years.[7]

The absolute necessity of finding ways to counter this apparent constraint on grain supplies is made all the more urgent by the limits on other food sources. Over-grazing in most of the world's grasslands means that a rise in grain production is necessary if there is to be any increase in animal livestock. At the same time, all of the world's major fishing grounds are being exploited close to or above their sustainable yields. Fish-farming can only be a substitute if there is enough grain to feed the fish. Moreover, if this need for increased grain yields is not solved in a sustainable manner then this will in turn cause the relentless pressure on the world's dwindling forests to increase still further. Some 20 million hectares (an area larger than the UK) of rainforests are felled every year, with the total area remaining globally having nearly halved since World War II.[8] This has profound implications not only in terms of the lost sustainable production from such forests, but also in terms of the loss of the carbon-dioxide-absorbing capacity of the trees, a loss which contributes to global warming. Even more crucially, perhaps, deforestation leads to

increased soil erosion and contributes to lower water tables and more surface flooding. The land cleared is itself usually almost infertile within
only five to ten years. The impact of deforestation on soil erosion and
land fertility is further compounded if farmers, lacking adequate firewood, have no choice but to burn manure instead of feeding the ground
they farm.

The dangers inherent in the sheer scale of our activities are not, of
course, limited to the over-exploitation of land, forest and sea and to the
risk of our breaching the limits of sustainable food production.
Technology may once again push back the frontiers of food scarcity, but
other problems would still remain, since the environment is the source of
much more that is vital to us than just food, wood and water, and is also
the sink for all our waste.

When looking at the environment's role as source, environmentalists
argue that if human progress is to be maintained in the future, the use of
all vital resources must be sustainable. Resources are broadly speaking of
three kinds. First, there are the *eternal resources* – sunlight, the winds and
the tides; these can be harnessed directly (solar heating, windmills or tidal
power stations) or indirectly (chiefly through the photosynthesis of solar
energy by plants). Herman E. Daly, the environmental economist, refers
to sunlight as 'solar income' and argues, in his book, *Steady-State Economics*,
that the economic growth of the last two hundred years has only been
made possible 'because man broke the budget constraint of living on solar
income and began to live on geological capital'.[9] This 'geological capital'
constitutes the second type of resources, known as *non-renewable resources*,
which include most importantly oil, coal and gas and also metals such as
copper, nickel, iron, etc. Whereas solar income can never be used up, this
geological capital can be depleted, necessitating the discovery either of
new previously unknown reserves or of substitutes. The third type of
resource is the *renewable resource* – fish, timber, grain, clean air, fresh water,
etc. If sunlight is the equivalent of perpetual income, and non-renewable
resources of non-interest-bearing capital (used once and then gone forever), renewable resources can be seen as behaving like interest-bearing
capital. They naturally regenerate and can produce a perpetual income or
yield, but only if the capital is left intact. If these resources are consumed
at less than their regeneration rate, they can last forever; but once the
regeneration threshold is crossed, the renewable resource becomes over-
exploited and the recurrent yield will fall. The yield of the renewable
resource may, of course, be increased by better management and technological advance; so grain yields can be increased considerably by use of

better crop strains and fertilisers. But it is important to distinguish between genuine sustainable productivity improvements and better short-term exploitation. So, for example, the use of sonar to detect fish shoals does not expand the fertility of the fish stocks themselves; it merely makes exploitation of them easier and over-exploitation more likely.

Long-term sustainable human progress is dependent on man's activities being largely reliant on the eternal resources and on the sustainable yield of renewable resources; all other resource consumption is based on the once-and-for-all consumption of resources which will as a result not be available to future generations. As the scale of our activity increases, it becomes increasingly difficult to live within the regeneration constraints of our renewable resources. The same is also true of the assimilation of waste products by the environment. While some waste products cannot be absorbed at all, and will always constitute a pollution legacy for future generations, others – both organic and inorganic – can be absorbed, treated or destroyed on a sustainable basis by natural processes in soil, air or water. If, however, the waste dumped exceeds the natural absorption rate of the relevant environmental medium, these natural processes become swamped and are often destroyed. Rivers and seas, for example, which can absorb so much of our waste indefinitely if it is dumped at below the absorption rate, can become lifeless and inert if the rate is exceeded.

The natural world, and the ecosystems within it, are remarkably good at adapting, evolving and adjusting to changing situations and to an increasingly hostile environment, but adaptation takes time. As the biologist Rachel Carson put it in her influential book, *Silent Spring*:

> . . . time is the essential ingredient; but in the modern world there is no time. The rapidity of change and the speed with which new situations are created follow the impetuous and heedless pace of man rather than the deliberate pace of nature.[10]

This ever-greater speed of change not only threatens to overcome the regenerative and adaptive power of the natural world; it also threatens to exceed mankind's own ability to adapt to a changing environment by swamping the capacity of human institutions to manage the implications of change – both environmental and social. To understand the dangers in this regard, it is necessary to go beyond consideration of the increasing scale of human activity relative to the finite earth, and focus on the importance of thresholds and the complexity of ecosystems and the biosphere in making the risks we face unpredictable and sometimes chaotic. Only then can we understand the enormity of the challenge presented by environmental degradation to human reason and to its claim to be able to control the natural world.

Perhaps the best example of the importance of environmental thresholds is the behaviour of fish stocks subject to over-fishing. For thousands of years fish from the seas, rivers and lakes has formed a vital part of man's diet. This century alone it is estimated that the world's fish catch may have risen a staggering twenty-fold. Brown notes that the world fish catch grew from 22 million tons in 1950 to 101 million in 1994 – expanding at a rate of 4 per cent per annum. But in the last few years, ominous signs of over-exploitation have multiplied. The total fish catch has remained nearly static since 1988 worldwide, but it has collapsed in some of the best-known fisheries in the world. According to the UN Food and Agriculture Organisation, the catch in every one of the world's fifteen oceanic fisheries has either reached or exceeded its sustainable level; thirteen of them are now in decline.[11] Moreover, two-thirds of the principal fish species traditionally caught are under threat. Atlantic stocks of blue-fish tuna have already fallen by 94 per cent. In the North Sea, the fishing industry now catches more than half the cod and haddock remaining each year, and close to three-quarters of young cod are caught before they are mature.[12] Boats equipped with sonar, with nets many miles long and hundreds of metres wide, are catching remaining stocks with industrial efficiency. The catastrophic decline in whale numbers as a result of industrial hunting looks like being repeated in the case of fish stocks. As the Canadian fishing industry has found to its cost in what were formerly the richest fishing grounds in the world – off Newfoundland – there can be a sudden disastrous drop in numbers when the population of spawning mothers falls below a certain threshold. There is not a slow linear decline, giving a second chance for adequate conservation measures; the mistake, once made, is close to irreversible, and a sustainable industry can be destroyed by a rate of over-fishing of perhaps only 20 per cent above perfectly safe levels. In Newfoundland some 35,000 fishermen have been put out of work by the collapse of the fishery in 1992.[13] If the European Union and its quarrelsome member states fail to agree huge cuts in fish catches, the same fate will befall many of Europe's fishermen. If they continue to catch fish above the regeneration threshold, and hence catch those fish which must spawn if there is to be another generation, they will be squandering a high-yielding asset that might have persisted undiminished for ever if the catch was just slightly lower and below the key threshold. As any saver knows, once you begin to live on the interest-bearing capital itself, rather than on the interest income it provides, the decline in interest payments is exponential and cata-strophic. If fish stocks collapse, another precious renewable resource will have been destroyed, and the food constraint on human progress will have tightened further.

In the case of many other environmental issues, the non-linear impact of crossing sustainable thresholds is rendered still more dangerous by the enormous complexity of the natural systems being disrupted. In *Silent Spring* Rachel Carson brought the world's attention to the destabilising and cumulative effects of the poisonous sprays unleashed on the world on a military scale after 1945. Many of these sprays – like DDT – have left a legacy of toxic residues, resistant super-pests and destroyed ecological balance. She pointed out that the belief in the efficacy of spraying was the result of a gross underestimation of the complexity of ecosystems, as well as of the importance of threshold effects. Pests have natural predators, but sprays kill the predators as often as the pests themselves. Furthermore, the sprays can dramatically speed up the evolution of new resistant strains of super-pests and these, free of their natural predators, multiply expo-nentially to form a new and larger plague. This was an early example of the potentially chaotic impact of tampering with complex ecosystems. While in many ways nature is irrepressible, a balance in nature is fragile; external shocks to this balance can destroy it, and the new natural equi-librium which evolves may not be that which was predicted or desired.

Perhaps the most frightening example of the dangers inherent in the complexity of the ecosystems we disrupt is that of global warming. So far, global warming appears to have led to only a slow rise in temperatures (0.6°C this century) and in sea levels. However, the Intergovernmental Panel on Climate Change (IPCC) which met in 1995 predicted a further rise of between 0.8 and 3.5°C in global average temperatures by 2100. It has been estimated that this might lead to as much as a 1.2-metre rise in sea levels, although recent IPCC estimates suggest a somewhat smaller rise. The enormous complexity of the processes involved in determining global warming makes it very difficult to predict with any accuracy how much warming will occur. It is known that greenhouse gases like carbon dioxide and methane prevent some of the outgoing radiation from escap-ing into space and hence tend to raise temperatures. It is also known that carbon dioxide concentrations are rising due to fuel consumption and deforestation. But there are many other feedback mechanisms; global warming will increase water evaporation (helping to cool the oceans) and may increase cloud cover – which may reduce the warming impact of sunlight but also trap heat. Warming may affect the ability of the oceans to absorb carbon dioxide and so on.

Faced with such uncertainties, and with predictions of at worst a 1.2-metre rise in sea levels, some have argued – like Wilfred Beckerman, in his book, *Small is Stupid* – that it would be irresponsible to put a brake on economic growth by sharply cutting fuel use, given that the extent of the risk is so unclear, and that the possible damage to low-lying countries like Bangladesh and certain Pacific islands would in any case be a small price to pay, in financial terms at least, for the enormous benefits of rapid world economic growth. The dangers in this way of thinking lie in the fact that it ignores the complexity and potentially chaotic nature of many of the forces and factors involved in the global warming process, and therefore overlooks the danger of non-linear chaotic reactions. As we know from the work done by Edward Lorenz and others on chaos in weather patterns (the famous butterfly-wing effect), the feedback mech-anisms involved in weather systems, or in ocean currents, tend to have effects which are anything but linear, and which are impossible to predict with accuracy ahead of time. It is a feature of chaotic systems that even if they can be modelled using quite simple equations, tiny differences in initial conditions can lead to catastrophic changes. Many scientists there-fore expect that even relatively small changes in global temperature may spark off considerable instability in the world's weather.

A sinister example of the sensitivity of these complex systems to small changes is suggested by recent evidence that global warming may be destabilising the world's ocean currents. Oceanographers have drawn attention to the key role played in powering the world's ocean currents by the sinking in just a few places worldwide of vast quantities of heavy, highly salinated water caused by ice creation. One of these 'pumps' is in the Greenland Sea, associated with a tongue of ice known as the Odden Feature. During the 1980s and early 1990s, perhaps as a result of global warming, the Odden Feature declined rapidly and then all but disap-peared, reducing very sharply the quantity of North Atlantic Deep Water formed in this area. Scientists fear that this disruption could cause a weakening of the Gulf Stream, which alone is responsible for the benign winter climate of north-west Europe, and might also trigger other sharp and unpredictable changes in the global climate.[14] Indications are that sudden 'flips' from one weather state to another were common in the last inter-glacial period, and the fear is that by altering ocean currents global warming could potentially return us to unstable weather patterns that would create havoc with food supplies in many parts of our crowded planet. It may even be that such relatively small changes could be enough to herald a new ice age. Our relentless growth is causing us to tamper with mechanisms of central importance to us, with effects which we cannot predict or control. We are left, despite all our scientific sophistication, with a naked battle between hope and fear – optimism that things will work out and pessimism that we may finally have overreached ourselves.

The unpredictability of the impact of environmental degradation lies at the heart of the challenge it presents to the march of human progress. Human reason, wonderfully adept at creating new activities and solving problems when they are apparent, can often neither predict nor pre-empt dangerous threats arising from our tampering with the complex systems of the natural world. In addition, human nature is not well adapted to dealing with differing levels of risk. We are not good at weighing the likelihood of short-term disadvantage against a small risk of long-term catastrophe. In this scientific age, we like hard facts and certain proof. And since the burden of proof is on those who wish to stem the tide of economic growth, or interfere in free-market mechanisms, we tend to accept massive environmental degradation unless we can all see for certain that it will lead to disaster. As Carson says, quoting the ecologist Paul Shepard, 'Such thinking . . . "idealises life with only its head out of water, inches above the limits of toleration of the corruption of its own environment . . . Who would want to live in a world which is just not quite fatal?"'[15]

The problems of uncertainty and of our tendency not to act until the risks are clear for all to see (which may be too late) are compounded by the global or international nature of many of the threats which face us. Acid rain, for example, which is eating away the forests of Europe and poisoning many of its lakes and rivers, is often caused by polluters hundreds of miles away from where the damage is inflicted and in many cases living under different jurisdictions. The UNDP's Human Development Report (1996) estimates that acid rain is affecting 60 per cent of Europe's commercial forests, inflicting economic losses of perhaps US$35 billion per annum, as well as doing important aesthetic damage to the formerly pristine wilderness of mountain and tundra regions. This damage can be only limited or reversed by international agreement, which may involve countries such as the UK making sacrifices in order to preserve woods and lakes in Germany and Scandinavia. One such agreement was the 1988 Large Combustion Plant Directive in the European

Union which set targets for the reduction of the sulphur dioxide and nitrogen oxide emissions responsible for acid rain.

Perhaps the most successful international environmental agreement to date was the 1987 Montreal Protocol which set targets for the elimination of CFCs to prevent a massive deterioration in the ozone layer. But in this case the agreement was made easier by the fact that most CFCs were produced by a few chemical giants who stood to gain from introducing more costly alternatives. By contrast, the outlook for meaningful agreement to limit greenhouse gas emissions looks much more doubtful. For not only are the risks less clear cut, but the culprit – the burning of fossil fuels and oil – is engaged in by much of the world's population. Moreover, those whose consumption is growing fastest – the developing countries – currently consume only a small fraction of the resources concerned. If a global limit on greenhouse gases is to be applied, rich countries will need to make big cuts to allow poor countries to raise consumption. The differences in starting points mean that awkward questions about the redistribution between countries of their respective share of the sustainable level of emissions will need to be tackled. The differences relate not only to different levels of income, but also to different levels of fuel efficiency. In the mid-1990s per capita incomes were higher in Japan, Switzerland and France than in the USA, but fuel efficiency in these countries was far higher and the level of emissions per capita less than half that of the USA. Should their greater levels of efficiency exempt such countries from further cuts? In practice, of course, it is the USA which has been least keen on adopting any mandatory cuts in carbon emissions.

The need for international agreement to tackle many of the most pressing environmental issues is a function of the paramount need for cooperation among competing individuals, companies and countries to tackle these issues together, so as to create a level playing field and avoid the problem of some 'free-riding' on the restraint of others. In a completely free-market, free-trade environment, those who take voluntary restraining measures to prevent environmental degradation will often lose out to competition from those not undertaking restraint. The pursuit of individual self-interest alone is not enough to ensure that unnecessary environmental degradation is avoided.

One way to characterise both the difficulty of avoiding many forms of environmental degradation and the need for cooperation in doing so is by using the analogy of commons (i.e., the common land where villagers were allowed to graze their animals before such land was generally enclosed in the eighteenth century). Such commons belong to no one in particular, and the use of them is free. In this respect, they represent a useful analogy to such common environmental amenities as the oceans, the forests (in many cases) and the air we breathe. The key feature of a common is that it is open to many consumers, often without any requirement on them to contribute to its upkeep or help safeguard its future. Indeed, it is impossible in a genuine common to exclude people from it. As a result, it will be in each individual's self-interest to continue to increase his use of the free good, or common, up to the point where it no longer provides him, and hence anyone else, with additional net benefit. The maximisation of individual self-interest can in this way lead to over-exploitation of the common, with disastrous consequences. It is quite possible that each individual using a particular common may genuinely want to avoid its degradation, but in the absence of cooperation feel unable to help prevent it. For, unless there is a strong social ethic or law (and in the case of global commons, international agreement) to ensure cooperation, there will actually be an incentive for rational self-interested individuals to rush to exploit the common as quickly as possible before it is destroyed, and to 'free-ride' on any voluntary restraint shown by others using the common. Such self-interested behaviour can then destroy the common, an effect referred to by economists and philosophers as the 'tragedy of the commons'. We can see a graphic illustration of this analogy in the case of the present fishing dispute in the European Union. The EU has a quota system which attempts to regulate the 'common' and prevent over-fishing, but short-term self-interest on the part of individual fishing communities, and the individual governments who represent them, ensures that unsustainable quotas are set, as each country refuses to accept big cuts in its own area and for its own fleets. The blame for falling fish stocks is placed on scapegoats like supposed 'quota-hoppers' – in the UK case, Spanish boats who were legally sold permits by UK fishermen. Rivalry and distrust undermine the necessary cooperation. Worse still, of course, the quotas which are set are difficult to enforce and are frequently evaded by black-market landings. Self-interested short-term competition and a lack of genuine cooperation ensure that the commons will be squandered for all.

The Failure of the Invisible Hand

Environmental degradation associated with pollution, resource depletion and the disruption of ecosystems is responsible for some of the most important costs of technological progress and economic growth. To understand the prevalence of these costs, we need to go beyond analysing the failures of science, technology and international cooperation to cope fully with the increasing scale and velocity of human endeavour and with the unpredictable consequences of tampering with complex ecosystems. For the ubiquity of environmental problems is also the result of important failures in the workings of the invisible hand of the free market, and it is these which are the subject of this section.

Despite the fact that we increasingly attach importance to environmental disruption, our preferences in this regard are not fully met by free-market mechanisms. To a large extent, this is because environmental costs and the expression of our environmental preferences lie outside the market mechanism. All too often, pollution and environmental degradation are, in the economic jargon, 'externalities'; the essence of externalities is that they entail costs (or benefits) which are not reflected in market prices. The agents causing the unwanted pollution or environmental degradation do not see the ill-effects reflected either in their actual costs or in the prices paid to them for their goods. As a result, the market mechanism does not force them to take the environmental costs into account. Suppose, for example, that the owners of a factory continue to employ a highly polluting method of production (which blackens the sky and corrodes the lungs of the surrounding area), because the costs to them of doing so are significantly lower than those of switching to a less polluting method. If the factory's owners and clients are not the people primarily affected by the pollution, but instead the costs are felt largely by third parties, then these 'external' costs will not, in a pure and unregulated free market, be reflected in the factory's own private costs. As a result, there will be no incentive for the factory to stop polluting. In such a case, there is no market in the pollution and no price attached to it, and the free market provides no mechanism for discouraging the pollution.

The invisible hand of a perfect free market can, even in theory, only lead to the efficient optimisation of those preferences which are expressed in the market; individual decisions are dependent on the signals given by market prices, and where these prices fail fully to reflect all the relevant preferences and costs – as in the case of externalities – the individual decisions of self-interested market participants can no longer add up to an outcome which provides the maximum benefits to society as a whole. The pursuit of rational self-interest implies that individuals weigh the private marginal benefits accruing to them from a market transaction against their own private marginal costs, and then seek to maximise their private net gain. Where there are externalities, the full social costs – which include both the external and the market-expressed costs of society as a whole – are not fully reflected in the private costs (or benefits) of the participants in the relevant market transaction; in such cases, the rational pursuit of self-interest by individual people and companies will not, contrary to Adam Smith's intuition, maximise the social good. So, in our example, where most of the costs of the air pollution fall on those other than the polluters themselves and their clients (e.g., in the form of increased incidence of lung cancer in the surrounding population), the full social costs may dramatically exceed the social benefits resulting from the polluting activity; but it may still be quite rational, from a self-interest point of view, for the polluters to continue to pollute, so long as their private benefit exceeds their private costs. Indeed, unless the external costs (and benefits) can somehow become reflected in their own private costs (and benefits) through taxation, legal liability, etc., the polluters may actually be forced to ignore the external element of social costs. For in an unregulated and competitive environment, the polluter who takes external costs into account and opts in an altruistic manner for a cleaner but more expensive mode of operation may be strongly disadvantaged and even forced out of business by competition from those with fewer scruples.

As the scale of our activities grows and our planet becomes more congested, the maximum absorption thresholds and regeneration capacity of the environment are more and more frequently breached. Extra activity is more likely to cause congestion; pollution is more likely to be at a level which causes damage; and the depletion of renewable resources is more likely to be unsustainable. Many activities which on a smaller scale have no ill side effects begin crucially to affect the welfare of others when their scale grows larger. By exacerbating the environmental crisis economic growth actually serves to increase the interconnected nature of human activities and the interdependence of economic agents by multiplying the number of instances where market activities have important consequences which are felt beyond those directly involved in the transactions. In this way, economic growth has a tendency to increase the prevalence and importance of environmental externalities, and to widen the gap between the full social costs and the aggregate of the market-reflected private costs of economic transactions. As a result, after decades of high growth, market prices have become a less good reflection of aggregate social preferences than they were, and it has become increasingly common for the satisfaction of the market-expressed preferences of individuals in the free market to be incompatible with meeting the preferences of society as a whole. In our ever more environmentally degraded world, the invisible hand of the free market will increasingly fail to be the motor of human progress. Piecemeal individual economic decisions, all made without reference to external costs, will more and more frequently lead to a tragic explosion of aggregate external costs which no one in the society would have desired. This is the so-called 'tragedy of piecemeal decisions'.

Externalities take many different forms, and their different characteristics influence how easy or otherwise it might be to find ways to reduce them. At their simplest, externalities can be just the local spill-over effects of an individual's actions. If I choose to build a house extension in my garden, this may shade my neighbour's garden; this negative side effect of my actions need not, in a *laissez-faire* regime, be taken into account by me in my calculations. Such local externalities are not, however, very difficult to incorporate into the market mechanism by the ascription of 'property rights'; so, if my neighbour has a right not to be shaded, I will only be able to do so if I can compensate him by enough to make him want to be shaded. In this way, the external costs of my action will have become fully part of my private costs; the externality will – in the economists' jargon – have been 'internalised'. It is, however, much more difficult to set up such property rights as a means of facilitating the internalising of external costs within the market mechanism in the case of more diffuse or pervasive externalities. So, for example, when farmers decide to use a particular pesticide which may boost their own crop yields but which will have the cumulative effect of destabilising the local ecology and encouraging a new super-pest, or when farmers over-apply fertilisers and boost their own production somewhat but with the result that the water table becomes polluted with nitrates, they are not – in an unregulated framework – forced to take account of the wide divergence between the social costs of their activities and their own private costs. But in such cases it is far from easy to see how to use property rights to enable all those affected to avoid these externalities. The same is true of the noise pollution generated by aircraft. This externality is also not generally reflected in the airlines' own costs, but it would be wholly unworkable to attempt to achieve this by relying on 'amenity rights' to avoid such noise. How would the airline in practice go about meeting the compensation claims of every individual affected, even if it were legally required to do so?

Externalities are most prevalent in exactly these sorts of cases. Indeed, as Michael Jacobs points out in his book, *The Green Economy*, they are most frequently associated with 'commons' (like the oceans), where property rights are by definition not present, or with 'public goods' (like clean air), where they are meaningless. An important feature of common and public goods is that it is very difficult to exclude people from using them. Moreover, in the case of a pure public good, it can, unlike other goods, be consumed by one person without the amount available to someone else being reduced. So I cannot be excluded from enjoying clean air, or from seeing a lighthouse (another public good) when out at sea, nor need my use of either affect anyone else's enjoyment of them. As a consequence, public goods and commons are very vulnerable to the free-rider problem. If someone tries to get me to pay for the air to be made cleaner, or the lighthouse to be maintained, or fish stocks to be preserved, I am likely to refuse to pay, since I can make use of them whether I pay or not. I cannot be excluded from them, and can hope to free-ride on the payments of others. Since everyone will reason in this way, the free market tends to be a poor provider of pure public goods and a poor steward of commons. These functions therefore have generally been provided by government rather than by the private sector.

The nature of public goods and commons is crucial to understanding the important role for government intervention in any effort to reduce the externalities which affect them, such as pollution, congestion or resource depletion. When, for example, a fisherman fishes in an already over-exploited fishery, he inflicts an external cost on all its other users; because most of the depletion cost of his over-fishing will be suffered by others than himself, while he alone will enjoy all the benefit derived from his catching the fish now, self-interest will dictate that he carry on fishing even if the full social costs of doing so far outweigh the private benefits to him. The temptation to free-ride on the voluntary restraint of others, and the tendency to mistrust the motives of others, means that only government-enforced quotas, regulations or taxes will have any chance of averting such a tragedy of the commons. In a common, there is no way to set up a market mechanism which could coordinate the actions of all concerned to avoid depletion, and which could determine the optimal total level of the fish catch; because no one owns the fish, prices will reflect only the demand for fish and the cost of catching them, neither of which will necessarily be linked to the sustainability of supply. Where over-fishing is a danger, the depletion of fish stocks can only be avoided if the general right to free access to the commons is somehow revoked, and if a maximum catch is determined by government decree, enforceable collective action or a monopoly owner.

In the case of public goods such as clean air, since no one can be excluded from them and since they are indivisible, it is impossible to privatise them; it is not possible for parcels of clean air to be hired out, and it is therefore impossible to allow the free market itself to decide how much should be charged for the right to pollute the air, or how much should be charged to those who use it in order to pay to keep it clean. The upkeep of such pure public goods has ultimately to be the responsibility of government, who alone may be in a position to prevent free-riding. It was for these reasons that Adam Smith himself believed that public goods had to be the province of government, although he could not have foreseen, back in the eighteenth century, how many public goods would need to be defended against the external costs of market activity. The free market increasingly needs government intervention to set a sustainable environmental framework within which it can operate safely if it is to avoid environmentally disastrous outcomes. But if pure public goods can only be safeguarded by government action, governments can employ a number of 'market' tools to help them manage them. For example, they may ask private companies to help maintain them on their behalf, and they may dissuade companies and individuals from generating external environmental costs, not just by regulation, but by mimicking the market – for example, by levying pollution taxes which try to reflect the true social costs of pollution.

Policy-makers, particularly in more interventionist countries, do employ several such methods to ensure that the social costs of environmental degradation are taken into account by those causing it. Governments sometimes regulate or even prohibit pollution or resource depletion by law; for example, in the 1956 Clean Air Act, the then Conservative government prohibited the burning of coal in London and other big cities, and this led to a dramatic reduction in smogs and particle pollution. Some governments also set quotas, by deciding the maximum acceptable level of pollution and then allocating quotas to the polluters. Prohibitions and quotas do, of course, represent a considerable regulatory distortion of the free market and can, as a result, lead to some sub-optimal and inefficient solutions, even if the overall goal of reducing pollution (or depletion) is met. For example, there may be a polluter who derives a particularly high benefit for society and himself from engaging in a polluting activity. So long as the total acceptable level of pollution is not breached, it will be advantageous for society as a whole if this polluter carries on his polluting activity while another polluter, who derives much less benefit from doing the polluting, refrains completely. To engineer this, various government-sponsored schemes have been evolved which seek, in economists' jargon, to 'internalise the externality' and thereby allow the market to decide which is the most efficient way to reduce environmental degradation to acceptable levels. One type of scheme seeks to reflect the full social cost of pollution or depletion in the market mechanism by levying taxes (e.g., a carbon tax) on environmentally damaging activities; if these taxes reflect the true external costs of the given environmentally degrading activity, then the individuals or companies concerned will see their private costs converge with the full social costs; they will therefore be strongly incentivised to reduce the level of activity to the optimal level, i.e., to continue to pollute or deplete resources only where the benefits of doing so exceed the full social costs. Another method is to allow quotas allocated to firms to be traded, so that the market can efficiently allocate them to the producer for whom they are most useful. This has the advantage over the tax system that the government is able to ensure that a precise target is met. Like taxes, tradable quotas also provide the correct incentives to limit environmental degradation in a relatively efficient manner; those who can do so cheaply can profit by then selling their quotas to those for whom it would be very expensive to limit environmental degradation.

Such methods can go a long way to helping to reduce the overproduction of pollution and other external costs, but there are often important practical and theoretical limitations to our ability to correct market mechanisms in these ways. For one thing, the regulations (or taxes or quotas) necessary to do so are often very complex to administer and enforce, and may swamp industry in red tape. This becomes particularly important in the traded goods sector. For if companies so regulated (or taxed) are competing with companies from other countries who are not regulated, they will be facing unfair competition and may lose market share. To be fair as well as effective, such regulations or taxes therefore need, in many cases, to be international. But the problems in reaching such international agreements are manifest. In addition, it is often very difficult to set a value on the environmental costs being incurred, or to decide what are the rational environmental limits to be imposed on economic activity. We can explore some of these difficulties by looking at one of the key examples of environmentally degrading economic activity – our use of the motor car.

The environmental economist, E. J. Mishan, described the invention of the car as 'possibly the greatest calamity to have befallen the human race'. More dispassionate observers would quarrel with this and point to the huge increase in mobility, freedom and privacy which the car has bestowed. But it is undoubtedly the case that those who purchase and drive cars and lorries inflict many external costs on society as a whole which are not reflected in their own private costs. The European Commission's green paper, *Towards Fair and Efficient Pricing in Transport* (1995), includes various estimates of the scale of these costs. In the European Union each year, road transport claims roughly 50,000 lives, and injures over three million people; the paper estimates that the 'external' costs of this accident toll (i.e., those not included in insurance premiums, etc.) amount to 1.5 per cent of EU GDP. In addition, congestion – another important externality – is also a growing problem, as the number of journeys increases faster than the available road space. When an extra individual decides to use a congested road which is already close to saturation point, he will often have a disproportionately negative effect on the traffic speed of all other users of the road; but the individual will only take account of his own time loss, and will still use the road so long as the overall benefit to him is greater than the cost to him of doing so; he will have no regard to whether or not the full social benefit of his taking the journey exceeds the full cost to society. The aggregate external cost of road congestion has been estimated to amount to some 2 per cent of EU GDP. Other important externalities of road transport include air pollution and noise pollution. One estimate suggests that air pollution from road transport kills more than 6,000 people in the UK alone each year, and entails an external cost of nearly £20 billion.[16] The EU paper does not even attempt to place a value on many other externalities, such as the damage to scenery from the expanding road network, or the damage to the social cohesion of towns and villages dominated by motor traffic; it would be even more difficult to place an objectively satisfactory monetary valuation on these than on the variables already considered.

The importance of these external costs of car transport for our story lies in the fact that the free market cannot limit them without government intervention. The problems of road transport reflect many of the features of the tragedy of the commons and the tragedy of piecemeal decisions which we have already discussed. No one has specifically chosen that our lives should be so dominated by traffic congestion, noise pollution and accidents. Because these costs are largely external to the market and to the prices paid by motorists, and because they represent the cumulative impact of many individual decisions, it cannot be argued that they have been deliberately chosen. But nor is voluntary self-restraint in anyone's self-interest; unless particular road-users can be sure that others will refrain from making journeys where the social cost exceeds the benefit, then it is in their own self-interest to abuse the common space of road and air as well.

Recently, governments have sought to limit the external costs of car usage directly by regulations, and have also begun to look seriously at ways to ensure that motorists pay more of the full costs of using their cars by levying various pollution and congestion taxes. New regulations have required the fitting of catalytic converters and have placed noise limits on motorbike engines. In the area of taxation, various studies have looked into road pricing to try to reduce congestion. The problem, however, is not only how to assess accurately what congestion costs are, but also how to charge road-users when congestion is great but not to charge them when there is no congestion. Similarly, it is technologically unfeasible to tax cars with reference to the actual amount of pollution they produce, which depends, among other things, on how well the engine is serviced, how the car is driven, the ambient temperature, etc. Perhaps the most effective use of taxes to reduce external costs so far has been the differential levels of taxation placed on different types of fuel. One study suggests that the marginal external health costs per litre of fuel vary enormously – standing at 84 pence per litre for diesel (the main producer of deadly particulate matter), 43 pence per litre for leaded petrol and 9 pence per litre for unleaded petrol.[17] So far, diesel has escaped extra pollution taxes, but only a small differential in taxation has been very successful in engineering a switch from leaded to unleaded fuel. Differential taxes do not need to reflect very accurate assessments of relative external costs; they need only be big enough to induce drivers to switch from the more polluting to the less polluting fuel. In many cases, some of the tax revenue produced can be used very effectively to raise the efficiency of the tax differential by subsidising the capital costs of switching from one fuel to another.

For all the enthusiasm of many economists for sophisticated schemes to internalise externalities, and reduce the gap between full social costs and those reflected in market prices, the technical and theoretical difficulties remain a serious obstacle. It is often very difficult to decide what is an acceptable level of pollution or resource depletion; not only will this be partly an ethical and political question but the decisions are in practice always subject to huge uncertainties. We do not know what the precise impact of carbon dioxide emissions will be, or how damaging nitrates in water supplies are. We do not know whether artificial hormones used in cows will affect human health. In addition, even where it is possible to forecast the effects of our activities, it remains very difficult to value them.

By their very nature external costs do not come with a ready market valuation or price. Market values can be imputed to them by a variety of methods, such as surveys which assess the 'willingness to pay', or studies which seek to estimate relevant preferences as actually revealed in market transactions. So, for example, economists try to estimate how much people value the absence of aircraft noise by comparing the value of the same sort of home in an area which suffers from noise pollution and an area which does not. But all such techniques have their limitations. In particular, it is very difficult to assess the value placed on environmental amenities by people who are far removed either in place or time from the decision-making process. Many environmental problems cross borders and many have implications for generations to come. So, for example, in assessing the external cost of sulphur emissions from UK power stations, we have to take into account the value the people of Germany and Sweden place on their forests and trees, and not only the Germans and Swedes of today but also of as many future generations as will suffer from the ill-effects of our pollution. Moreover, many will argue that some forms of environmental degradation, like the loss of animal species, the reduction of biodiversity or the loss of aesthetically important scenery, are not even in theory reducible to monetary equations. There is a clash, they will argue, between aesthetic or intrinsic values, on the one hand, and instrumental utilitarian values, on the other, and this clash makes the calculus of costs and benefits even harder to assess. This has particularly exercised the US Congress, which has had to arbitrate between the intrinsic value of certain owl species in a special forest habitat and the instrumental value of that forest as virgin timber. It is the frustrations caused by the incommensurability of values which so often lead to the absolutist rhetoric either of free-marketeers or of environmentalists. In an age which likes quantitative and precise answers, all or nothing is too often the only language heard.

Perhaps the single most important failure of scope of the market mechanism is its inability to take full account of the interests of future generations, or even the interests of the present generation beyond the current market horizon. Markets have a strong short-term bias; while the price mechanism may ensure equilibrium between demand and supply today, it does not necessarily maximise the chances of such an equilibrium in the future. In part, this is because people tend to have a pure time preference for jam today over jam tomorrow; in part, too, it is because future generations are not present to bid in the market. Even if current generations claim to care about the fate of their children, they are unlikely to care as much as the children themselves will in due course. But this is not the whole story. If market operators could predict future supply and demand accurately, then some of them would be willing to pay now for profit tomorrow, and the price mechanism would start to crowd out today's consumers. In practice, though, the future is inherently uncertain. Not only is the future supply/demand situation in physical terms uncertain, so too is the future behaviour or fortunes of all the individual market participants.

This can be illustrated by taking the example of oil prices. The price of oil only partly reflects the likely future supply/demand situation. Oil does have a futures market which allows the market to reflect expected future supply/demand in the price. But there are limits to the scope of this futures market. It does not operate beyond the next few years, because beyond that point uncertainty is so great that no market participant is willing to commit to a particular price. Even the oil companies which own the assets do not attach great value to production beyond the next ten years. There might, after all, be a massive change in the market, such as the availability at some point in the future of unlimited fission power or cheap solar energy, which would completely change the demand for oil. The price mechanism on its own is therefore unlikely to go far in safeguarding the interests of future consumers and producers. In a modern market economy, uncertainty is the enemy of husbandry.

Even in cases where there is little uncertainty and where society is willing to consider the interests of future generations, there is another limitation placed on the extent to which the market will wish to set costs or benefits tomorrow against costs or benefits today. This is the mechanism of 'discounting' future costs or benefits to arrive at what economists call their 'net present value'. In order to decide between the utility of incurring a cost today over incurring a cost tomorrow, market participants (including governments) seek to make them comparable by converting the future costs into equivalent present values. To do this they use a discount rate, for example, the assumed average rate of return on cash in the intervening period. Suppose we are deciding between incurring a cost of £1 million for pollution clean-up now and incurring double the cost, inflation adjusted, in fifty years' time; and suppose the real rate of interest over that period is assumed to be 5 per cent. Discounted by 5 per cent per annum, the value today of the £2 million cost in fifty years' time is only £174,000 (the amount of money which if invested at 5 per cent would be £2 million in fifty years' time). Now, in one sense, this discounting is totally rational and mimics the decision-making strategy of anyone making a sensible long-term market investment. However, the assumption in this example of a high real rate of return of 5 per cent presupposes that a high rate of economic growth and generally high investment returns will persist over the next fifty years; we then deduce from this assumption that an inflation-adjusted cost of £2 million will be much easier to meet then than a £1 million cost now, given the high real growth in the intervening period and given that society will then be much richer. Such a methodology may, in the words of economist Herman E. Daly, confuse current trend with destiny. The assumption that continued high growth will persist is the very assumption questioned by environmentalists worried about environmental constraints; but this assumption is held to prove logically that the decision to conserve resources for tomorrow, or to pre-empt higher costs for tomorrow, is expensive in today's values, and hence is unlikely to be rational. The mathematical discounting methodology built into market mechanisms and into government cost-benefit analyses, combined with the inherent market dislike of future uncertainty and the very human preference for jam today, militates strongly against our meeting fully the requirements of intergenerational justice.

There are two further reasons for disliking the use of discount rates in assessing the value of environmental degradation. First, the presumption that future generations will be richer, even if true, may be completely irrelevant when considering assets we are squandering for which there are no likely substitutes. Scenery, wilderness and rainforests, for example, are next to impossible to re-create or find substitutes for. In the case of such irreplaceable assets, even if future generations are financially richer, they will be unlikely, for this reason, to be less concerned than we would be that these assets have disappeared. Indeed, there is every reason to suppose that as societies become richer they value the qualitative aspects of the environment more rather than less. Instead of discounting the loss to future generations, we should in such cases be magnifying it. Secondly, the discounting methodology assumes that the fruits of future growth will flow to those who will suffer the environmental degradation. This is patently untrue in many cases. For these reasons, many environmentalists argue that, rather than trying to value the damage we are doing to future generations by making unwarranted assumptions about their values, interests or predicament, we should instead endeavour to preserve as much as possible of our legacy. Only then can we be sure that we are not squandering an environmental asset which may be key to progress in a future generation.

One useful way to visualise the problem of ensuring that future generations have their fair share of environmental resources is, as we saw earlier, to look at our non-renewable resource base as being like geological capital – assets bequeathed to us which we can either use up or pass on to future generations. Regarding non-renewable resources like this can be helpful in two ways: first, it suggests a basis for correcting GDP statistics by netting off estimates of environmental depletion costs against economic growth. Instead of seeing resource exploitation as output in the GDP statistics, we can count it as the depreciation of geological capital – as a cost which leaves us with a lower asset base. Secondly, it can suggest a numerical basis for internalising the externality of resource depletion – i.e., for imposing a change in the price of resources to reflect the costs which depletion implies for future generations. We can set taxes or quotas at the level we estimate is required to ensure that the current price of resources reflects the 'replacement' cost of the assets being used up. For example, in the case of oil, the government would need to set the tax or quota at a level which reflects the expected cost to future generations of replacing depleted oil assets with, say, windmill or solar-cell power stations.

There are, of course, numerous significant practical difficulties involved in such a project. These include the problems of assessing the likely future replacement cost of resource assets – given that the price of new technologies often falls dramatically over time – as well as the near impossibility of getting international agreement on the need to raise prices now in order to provide for future generations, at the expense of today's voters. Furthermore, the methodology does not help in the case of irreplaceable assets. But there is another major reason why such policies of repricing non-renewable resources are rarely espoused by those outside environmentalist circles. This is the fact that the 'ecodoomsters' have cried wolf a number of times. When the famous report entitled *The Limits to Growth* was published in 1972 on behalf of the environmental association known as the Club of Rome, it predicted, on the basis of known reserves and projections of demand, that we would run out of many basic minerals by the year 2000. The oil crisis of 1973, although politically inspired, added emotional weight to the argument. Petrol ration coupons were issued to every household in the UK, and Western material prosperity seemed threatened. Mankind had, it seemed, become totally dependent on scarce and rapidly vanishing resources. But in the case of nearly every one of the minerals highlighted in the 1972 report, known reserves are now greater than they were twenty years ago. In the case of oil, this is despite consumption since 1970 higher than the known level of reserves then. The ecodoomsters misunderstood the nature of reserves and the interaction of consumption, reserves and the price mechanism. High prices in the face of scarcity lead, *ceteris paribus*, to lower consumption or substitution and, at the same time and most critically, to more exploration. No company will bother to explore for reserves not needed for more than a generation or in areas where production costs are higher than current prices. It is wrong, in short, to underestimate the power of shortage and of the price mechanism to ensure that remedial action is taken to preserve or increase reserves.

Despite this and other examples of environmentalists overstating the extent of market failures, we can say in conclusion that there are very important limitations of scope of the market system which help cause excessive environmental degradation. The free-market mechanism cannot, without wholesale government intervention, fully reflect the costs to society of externalities like pollution, congestion and resource depletion; nor can it fully reflect the interests of future generations. Moreover, measures designed to correct the free-market mechanism can be fiendishly difficult to set up, in theory and in practice. This is particularly true where complexity and threshold effects make predictions of the future ecological or supply/demand situation uncertain – as in the case of global warming. These environmental examples of market failure underline the importance of maintaining a strong social ethic, and of having robust mechanisms for international cooperation. When it comes to externalities like pollution, no man or country is an island, and there *is* such a thing as society. The maximisation of the market-expressed preferences of today's individuals will not, on its own, lead to the socially preferred outcome for all time. The invisible hand is not a sufficient mechanism for ensuring sustainable human progress.

Reconciling Growth and the Environment

As economic activity grows, the environmental constraints on the pursuit of progress in welfare seem to tighten remorselessly. Our planet is of finite size, and as we consume ever more non-renewable resources and cross ever more of the sustainability thresholds of renewable resources, our economic growth is increasingly being financed at the expense of future generations. It can be argued that, if the benefits of economic growth are subject to the law of diminishing marginal returns (i.e., extra wealth makes less and less difference to our welfare the richer we get), and if the marginal environmental costs (both to us and to future generations) of economic growth are rising, then it makes sense to down-grade the central importance hitherto accorded to the pursuit of economic growth. Economic growth is less strongly correlated with increases in welfare than before, and may – if the marginal costs of it start to exceed the marginal benefits – soon become inversely correlated. On this argument economic growth may not only cease to be one of the motors of human progress, but may come fatally to undermine it. Sustainable human progress may indeed require the abandonment of growth policies.

However, there are powerful arguments against the 'no-growth poli-cies' advocated by some elements of the Green movement. For one thing, pollution tends to be most damaging and prevalent in countries which are poor. It is wealthy countries that can afford to cut air pollution and clean up their rivers. As we have seen, Britain's cities are cleaner now than they were in the 1950s because of the Clean Air Act, banning coal fires. Germany and Switzerland, among the richest countries on earth, have some of the very best environmental protection. From a pollution point of view, zero growth might be totally counterproductive. After all, Russia has had low or negative growth for decades and suffers terrible pollution; it desperately needs growth to help pay for the clean-up. Moreover, there is an important question of distributional justice. It is clearly verging on the obscene for Western commentators to suggest that growth is suddenly a bad idea for the whole world because of rising envi-ronmental degradation, unless they are proposing a redistribution of current wealth and living standards from developed to developing coun-tries to help those who have not yet enjoyed so many of the benefits of growth. These benefits include the ability to clean up local environ-ments. It is estimated that as many as 700 million people in developing countries suffer from dangerous levels of indoor pollution from poorly ventilated stoves, that over one billion have no access to safe drinking water, and that in a number of major cities in developing countries as much as half the population lives in shantytowns with next to no envi-ronmental infrastructure.[18] It is ethically inconsistent to be concerned about intergenerational inequality (i.e., whether we are leaving a fair share of resources to future generations) yet at the same time to be unconcerned about intra generational inequality (i.e., whether the poor of today have their fair share). It is ethically wrong to argue that the requirements of intergenerational justice should be met at the expense of efforts to reduce inequality in the world today.

It is an often repeated truism that the lion's share of environmental degradation can be ascribed to the richest fifth and the poorest fifth of the world's population. It is the developed countries which still consume the majority of the world's non-renewable resources, and have been doing so for a very long time, while it is in the poorest developing countries that deforestation and soil erosion are taking their heaviest toll. Out of necessity, hungry peasants are squandering their inheritance by over-exploiting marginal land and felling virgin forests, thereby further reducing their chances of sustainable growth and progress in the future. In such cases, poverty is directly contributing to environmental degradation. If economic growth in developing countries were to be equitably enough distributed that it served to eliminate poverty, there is little question that such economic growth would be hugely beneficial from both a welfare and an environmental point of view. Human progress clearly depends on economic growth in these areas. The marginal benefits of economic growth are far higher in poor countries than in the rich ones, and in some cases the marginal environmental costs may even be negative. Given global environmental constraints, it might therefore seem legitimate to argue that since the rich West has less need to grow than the poor Third World, it should consider slowing down its rate of growth and its rate of resource consumption to allow room for higher growth in the Third World. This would, needless to say, be a difficult course for any democratic Western government to agree upon, when so many of its voters are still desirous of the perceived benefits of future growth. It is only the promise of more tomorrow for everyone which keeps the lid on internal demand in Western countries for redistribution from the affluent few to the less affluent many. Moreover, it would be very difficult in practice for the West to adopt a consciously low-growth policy in a free-trade environment where it is competing with fast-growing low-cost producers.

It is clear, then, that the pursuit of economic growth remains a political necessity in the West, and a welfare necessity in the Third World. It is also clearly essential, though, that mankind should find new ways to improve the environmental efficiency of growth. For we cannot continue to enjoy the current pace of world economic growth unless we can reduce the environmental costs associated with it. Two simple statistics can make the scale of the problem clear. The USA has 6 per cent of the world's population and currently consumes nearly one third of the world's annual production of non-renewable resources.[19] This entails that, in the happy event that the rest of the world were able to enjoy US consumption levels, the earth would need – unless the environmental efficiency of growth is improved – to support six times the current level of resource depletion. One does not need to be a hard-core environmentalist to doubt that this is feasible. Similarly, only 8 per cent of the world's population currently has a car; if Western dependence on the car is to be matched in India, China and Africa, the environmental toll could become intolerable. To some extent, technological advance will come to our rescue again, as in the past. So, for example, big advances in the technology of photovoltaic cells and wind turbines mean that it may soon be possible to generate electricity as cheaply from the eternal sources of sunlight and wind as from the polluting and non-renewable resources of oil and coal. With bountiful supplies of electricity, we might also eventually be able to electrolyse water economically to create portable hydrogen, which could power quiet and pollution-free cars, and so on. However, being freed from the energy constraint might be a mixed blessing; it would make the recycling of some non-renewable resources (e.g., metals) sustainable indefinitely into the future; but it would also free us to increase the scale of our activities still further, and more quickly, with perhaps disastrous consequences in relation to other environmental constraints. Even limitless energy would not solve all the problems of waste pollution, congestion and food shortages.

Much can, of course, also be done in the ways outlined above to improve the environmental efficiency of growth by correcting some of the failures inherent in free-market economics; we can try to ensure that the true costs of pollution are charged to polluters; we can encourage less resource-intensive consumption by charging a price for resources that tries to reflect their value to future generations; and we can develop ways of measuring economic growth that take into account the costs of growth, thereby encouraging the development of economic policies which are genuinely conducive to sustainable progress in welfare. The rich West could also try to reduce the burden of debt on Third World countries, since often it is the desperate need for foreign exchange to make interest payments which encourages the felling of rainforests and the over-exploitation of farmland for export crops. The West, too, could transfer environmental-control technology to developing countries cheaply, by way of aid in some cases, rather than protecting it with patents. At the same time, there need to be more global agreements on environmental standards. In a free-trading environment, polluting and resource-depleting industries will move to wherever the environmental standards are lowest; a level playing field would stop poor countries being exploited as dumping grounds for waste, and as cheap sources of irreplaceable resources, and it would stop those exercising beneficial environmental restraint from being penalised by unfair competition.

All these measures would no doubt help to improve the environmental efficiency of economic growth, but they are also very difficult to set up and operate on the necessary global scale. By contrast, the current, largely unregulated, global free-market system has the apparent advantage of being simple and requiring relatively little global cooperation, but only because it fails to take account of a central truth – that our planet is a global public good; your rainforests are my oxygen; my non-renewable resource consumption is your children's future compromised. Like all public goods, our planet can only be saved by cooperative behaviour, and by the creation of a regulatory framework. As with all public goods, the fate of our planet is at the mercy of those who would free-ride on the restraint and contribution of others. No one wants to pay their full share of costs. If we are to tackle the environmental crisis and raise the sustainable welfare content of economic growth, we will need to develop new ways of advancing cooperation in the global village in which we live. But there is plenty of room for pessimism about whether we can learn to cooperate better in safeguarding our future, rather than competing to destroy it as quickly as possible.

CHAPTER 9

The Futility of the Rat Race

I confess I am not charmed with the ideal of life held out by those who think that the normal state of human beings is that of struggling to get on; that the trampling, crushing, elbowing and treading on each other's heels, which form the existing type of social life, are the most desirable lot of human kind, or anything but the disagreeable symptoms of one of the phases of industrial progress . . . But the best state for human nature is that in which, while no one is poor, no one desires to be richer, nor has any reason to fear being thrust back by the efforts of others to push themselves forward.

J. S. Mill, *Principles of Political Economy*

Rather than trinkets, the distinctive appurtenances of the rich then become squirrels' wheels for those below: objects of desire that the most intensive effort cannot reach.

F. Hirsch, *Social Limits to Growth*

In our effort to understand the increasing failure of economic growth to deliver unambiguous progress in welfare, let alone happiness, we need to go beyond analysis of the failure of the invisible hand of the free market to cope fully with the rising environmental costs of growth, and the failure of scientific reason fully to control complex ecosystems and predict the side effects of ever faster technological change. In this chapter, we will touch first on some of the traditional religious and philosophical reasons for believing that there is an inherent futility to the competitive pursuit of wealth, before analysing some important explanations of why there should now be a growing feeling of disillusionment with the material and social rewards of economic growth. We will try to explain why greater wealth is not allowing for more leisure and is not leading to a more relaxed and contented society, but is instead causing us to be yet more grasping, selfish and antisocial. We will analyse some of the reasons why the social costs of growth are burgeoning.

Many of these social costs represent a deterioration in some of the key non-economic elements of the good life, such as leisure time, solitude, peace and quiet, good parent–child relationships, community spirit and freedom from stress and anxiety. Because these elements of the good life lie outside the formal domain of the market and the normal ambit of economic analysis, they tend to be compromised by the hurried pursuit of economic growth; for in our scientific and numerical age, costs and benefits which are not formally measured and entered into the calculus of market mechanisms tend to be costs and benefits which are not seriously considered. If it is indeed the case that the unmeasured non-market social costs of growth are starting to rise faster in marginal terms than the benefits, then the pursuit of economic growth may at some point become self-defeating in welfare terms. Moreover, even within the class of marketable goods and market-expressed preferences, the modern economy often appears to be more efficient at creating new desires than fulfilling them. In particular, in our increasingly congested world, the desires of the citizens of affluent countries are more and more often for goods that only superior *relative* wealth can buy. In this sense, at least, there is a growing futility to economic activity at an aggregate level; for one person's gain in relative wealth is someone else's loss. As we shall explore in this chapter, the rising importance of increases in relative rather than absolute wealth ensures that the pursuit by individuals of their own self-interest fails, at the aggregate level, to add up to an advance in the welfare of society as a whole. Indeed, more and more economic activity is accounted for by the provision of goods and services designed simply to offset the bad side effects of ever fiercer competition for relative advance.

There have, of course, always been many people who have believed that the pursuit of ever greater material wealth is futile, distasteful or even wrong. Christian doctrine exhorts us to place spiritual and moral requirements before bodily needs or material progress ('Ye cannot serve God and mammon'), and has traditionally argued that the desire for material wealth inevitably crowds out higher moral and spiritual aspirations. The pursuit of wealth, in this view, is incompatible with moral progress and the pursuit of eternal salvation. The well-known passage from the Gospel According to St Matthew (chapter 19) reads:

> Jesus said unto him, If thou wilt be perfect, go and sell that thou hast, and give to the poor, and thou shalt have treasure in

heaven: and come and follow me./ But when the young man heard that saying, he went away sorrowful; for he had great possessions./ Then said Jesus unto his disciples, Verily I say unto you, That a rich man shall hardly enter into the kingdom of heaven./ And again I say unto you, It is easier for a camel to go through the eye of a needle, than for a rich man to enter into the kingdom of God.

In the pagan classical world, many thinkers also espoused an ascetic doctrine, but often based on the rather different grounds that the pursuit of material wealth would lead only to frustration and unhappiness. So, for example, Epicurus and his disciples held that tranquillity and freedom from anxiety – which could be achieved partly by reducing the number of desires – was the key to happiness. Theirs was not a maximising creed; they believed that happiness came from knowing the limits of life, not from pursuing the maximum number of pleasures. The Epicureans eschewed activities which involved competition, and believed that it was unwise to attempt to secure a position of great wealth, because of the considerable anxiety involved both in earning it and in striving to keep it; for them, ambition for wealth or political power would bring only disappointment and frustration. The Epicureans believed that the simple pleasures of the stomach and of friendship alone vouchsafed sustainable happiness. As Lucretius wrote in the first century BC:

> And yet, if a man would guide his life by true philosophy, he will find ample riches in a modest livelihood enjoyed with a tranquil mind. Of that little he need never be beggared. Men craved for fame and power so that their fortune might rest on a firm foundation and they might live out a peaceful life in the enjoyment of plenty. An idle dream. In struggling to gain the pinnacle of power they beset their own road with perils. And then from the very peak, as though by a thunderbolt, they are cast down by envy into a foul abyss of ignominy. For envy, like the thunderbolt, most often strikes the highest, and all that stands out above the common level.[1]

The extreme moral asceticism of early Christianity, and the somewhat ignoble Epicurean doctrine that one should avoid all attempts to rise above other people in wealth and influence for fear of disturbing one's tranquillity or exciting the jealousy of others, have both found gentler echoes through the ages in a nostalgia for a simple, more morally virtuous and less grasping life of tight-knit families and communities. The Augustan poets of Imperial Rome continually evoked images in their poetry of the simple rustic life, of peasants tilling the peaceful countryside 'at a strict mother's bidding'[2] – images placed in stark contrast to the opulent and morally decadent society of the metropolis. Many poets have since combined this nostalgic tone, and the theory that material progress goes hand in hand with moral regress, with the incontrovertible truth that death treats rich and poor indiscriminately; for many people, our common fate makes a mockery of worldly ambitions, and shows the ultimate futility of all material acquisitiveness and competition. Thomas Gray, in his eighteenth-century poem *Elegy written in a Country Church-Yard*, paints an arcadian picture – in a manner reminiscent of the Latin poets – of the simple and austere life of the rural peasant, and then adds:

> *Let not Ambition mock their useful toil,*
> *Their homely joys and destiny obscure;*
> *Nor Grandeur hear, with a disdainful smile,*
> *The short and simple annals of the poor.*

> *The boast of heraldry, the pomp of power,*
> *And all that beauty, all that wealth e'er gave,*
> *Awaits alike the inevitable hour.*
> *The paths of glory lead but to the grave.*

And later in the poem come the immortal lines:

> *Far from the madding crowd's ignoble strife*
> *Their sober wishes never learned to stray;*
> *Along the cool sequestered vale of life*
> *They kept the noiseless tenor of their way.*

A century later, the utilitarian philosopher John Stuart Mill, many of whose writings reveal a deep interest in the philosophy and economics of progress, included in his *Principles of Political Economy* a chapter entitled 'Of the Stationary State'. In this he looks forward to a time when economic progress will eventually give way to a pleasing 'stationary state'. He disagrees with Adam Smith and others who argue that such a state must be wretched for the poor, and instead maintains that, in rich states, redistribution of wealth is more important than growth, and that population control is a better way to achieve and maintain the eradication of poverty than the pursuit of further economic growth. After deploring the unpleasantness of the competitive behaviour required to sustain economic growth (in the passage quoted at the beginning of this chapter), Mill writes:

> A population may be too crowded, though all be amply supplied with food and raiment. It is not good for man to be kept perforce at all times in the presence of his species. A world from which solitude is extirpated, is a very poor ideal. Solitude, in the sense of being often alone, is essential to any depth of meditation or of character; and solitude in the presence of natural beauty and grandeur, is the cradle of thoughts and aspirations which are not only good for the individual, but which society could ill do without. Nor is there much satisfaction in contemplating the world with nothing left to the spontaneous activity of nature; with . . . every hedgerow or superfluous tree rooted out, and scarcely a place left where a wild shrub or flower could grow without being eradicated as a weed in the name of improved agriculture. If the earth must lose that great portion of its pleasantness which it owes to things that the unlimited increase of wealth and population would extirpate from it, for the mere purpose of enabling it to support a larger, but not a better or a happier population, I sincerely hope, for the sake of posterity, that they will be content to be stationary, long before necessity compels them to it.[3]

In Mill's romantic vision of the ultimate 'stationary state', he envisages that all efforts could then be directed to mental culture, to the pursuit of social and moral progress, and to the increase of leisure, rather than being used up in a competitive struggle for greater material prosperity.

Written some 150 years ago, in 1848, Mill's prophecy of a stationary state is as far from coming true as ever. While many poets, philosophers and clergymen have continued to scoff at the futility of the rat race, and to denounce as evil the single-minded pursuit of wealth, the goal of increased material prosperity has nonetheless continued to engage men's efforts and to employ their dreams. Moreover, there is no reason to doubt that, for much of the last 150 years, the great increases in material wealth, and the workings of the invisible hand of the free market, have indeed led to genuine progress in welfare. Although there may be an ultimate futility to all our activities, and no direct link between moral and spiritual progress and material advance, apologists for growth have had no trouble in pointing to the social benefits it has brought – hospital care and education for all, sewers, running water, indoor toilets, refrigerators, washing machines, shorter working hours for ordinary people and an end to child labour. A combination of rising real wages for all sections of society and technological advance has made available even to the poor (of developed countries, at least) material comforts that were formerly the preserve of the rich. As the economist Joseph Schumpeter famously put it, economic progress has ensured that the silk stockings once available only to queens are now (thanks to nylon) available to every factory girl. In this context, radical redistribution of wealth has increasingly seemed to most commentators to be a poor substitute for vibrant wealth creation, since exponential growth has apparently ensured that, although the poor never catch up with the rich of their own time, they can achieve the material standard of living enjoyed by the rich only a generation or two earlier; surely, the argument has gone, it must be better to level up than down. The assumption has continued to be that eventually everyone would be able to live in comfort, free from the anxieties of poor housing and inadequate medicine, and be able to enjoy increased leisure time and previously undreamed-of freedom of choice; surely such benefits would be worth both the loss of the solitude of an empty landscape, and the passing away of the social continuity and moral conformity of harsh rustic village life; and surely such material improvements to the lot of ordinary men and women could not be evil, nor at odds with the dictates of a Christian God. Thanks to the invisible hand of the free market, individual acquisitiveness has been harnessed to everyone's benefit.

It has often been assumed – and this was no doubt behind Mill's vision – that there is a diminishing marginal utility to extra wealth, and that – as a society becomes richer and most of the population becomes provided with the key comforts of life – there will be an increasing tendency for people to wish to forgo extra income in return for more leisure, so as to be able to devote more time to their families, their hobbies and community activities. Western society, in this view, should long have ceased to consist of grasping Victorian sweatshops and should have become gentler, kinder and more cultured; as ordinary people have acquired the material accoutrements of past nobility, they should also have acquired an aristocratic love of leisure and the means to indulge it. In practice this has only come true to a certain extent. Indeed, more recently, it again appears that the world of the free market is becoming a meaner, more frenetic and unsatisfying place. The poorest elements of society are getting poorer again, as disparities of income widen sharply; and average working hours in the USA and the UK have started to rise again over the last twenty years, reversing the downward trend seen since Victorian times. Roughly a quarter of all full-time workers in the USA now work more than 49 hours a week, and in the UK a quarter of all fathers work more than 50 hours a week. At the same time, an increasing number of workers are employed on short-term contracts with no paid holidays.

At the end of the twentieth century, labour-saving technology is no longer allowing workers to work shorter hours and have more leisure, but is instead resulting in the reduction of the number of secure jobs to the bare minimum, with those lucky enough still to have permanent jobs working longer hours; their efforts are supplemented where necessary by the just-in-time employment of temporary workers. In this way, labour-saving advances are leading to a maldistribution of the productivity gains which result from them – with some people getting more money than they need but no leisure, others getting an excess of leisure (in the form of unemployment) but very little money, while still others get too little of either. The increasingly frenetic pace of activity and the relentless drive for efficiency have led to many individuals being stretched to the limit of their endurance, spurred on to compete vigorously with their colleagues by the fear of losing their jobs. Workers of all sorts increasingly suffer from burnout, stress and anxiety. The sheer rapidity of technological change has also caused stress and anxiety, as people struggle to stop their skills becoming out of date. The workplace is no longer normally a stable balance of power between a united workforce and entrepreneurial capital owners, nor is it a collective and paternalistic enterprise. Instead, it can all too often be characterised as an engine of wealth creation, fuelled by the internal competition for survival of each and every member of the enterprise, who must prove that he or she contributes more than his or her equivalent, or face unemployment.

Technological advance often promises to allow workers and consumers more flexibility and choice and a better quality of life, but in practice it frequently leads only to rising expectations on the part of both employers and consumers. So, for example, modems and the virtual office have led not so much to the flexibility to work at home instead of in the office, and in the evening instead of the morning, but to a requirement to work in both places at any time. Similarly, the mobile phone has not just made easier the occasional necessary phone call while travelling, but has necessitated that the employee of the modern age must always be contactable and available to think about his or her work. What remains of leisure time is, for many modern workers, used up in increasingly long and arduous commuter journeys, in juggling a dazzling array of consumer opportunities, and in hours on exercise machines and in gyms getting the exercise which our mechanical convenience age has ensured they cannot get in more natural ways.

Many reasons have been advanced as to why the citizens of some of the richest nations on earth appear to be sinking back into a Darwinian competitive struggle for survival, and why acquisitiveness seems to increase rather than decrease with greater material wealth. One of the most interesting theories is that suggested by Francis Fukuyama in his book, *The End of History and the Last Man*. Following Nietzsche, he argues that much of the motive for work comes not from the satiable desire for material goods in themselves, but from the insatiable desire for recognition that comes from status and competitive success. Many people simply do not want to be contented, undifferentiated drones, but wish to excel and earn glory; the simplest way to do this in our materialistic societies is through entrepreneurial success and competition. Indeed, Fukuyama argues that in times of peace, this is an essential outlet for aggressive ambition which might otherwise be turned to more destructive ends. According to this thesis, man is a restless, striving animal, unlikely ever to be content even with plenty. The more pampered his existence, the more desperate he will become for differentiating glory, and for success in competitive struggle.

Another plausible explanation for the insatiability of desire in a modern economy takes a different tack. In this view, motivation remains predominantly material, but because much of the energy of industry is directed to marketing and advertising, new desires are created as fast or even faster than the old ones are satisfied. Jeremy Rifkin, in his book, *The End of Work*, quotes one Charles Kettering of General Motors in the 1920s as saying: 'The key to economic prosperity is the organized creation of dissatisfaction.' General Motors was an early pioneer of yearly model changes designed to make people discontented with the model they already had. Any parent can see the rawest examples of the power of advertising in this regard, with children who desperately want to have the latest version of the latest toy, or the latest design of training shoe, not so much for the intrinsic utility or pleasure they will get from them as compared with what they have already, but because it appears to be part of human nature to want to be at the cutting edge of fashion. Children and adults can often be made genuinely unhappy if such created desires are not met. Human nature may always have been thus, but modern fashions change monthly instead of over decades, and advertising ensures that everyone is fully appraised of how backward they are in the race to keep up. Goods have a built-in obsolescence which is further emphasised by advertising and fashion. The wheel of material desire turns faster, but the rat gets no further.

Other explanations for the intensification of the rat race cite economic factors. Thus it may be argued that, although organised dissatisfaction helped to drive a genuine surge of prosperity and progress in welfare in the first thirty years after World War II, the economy has more recently ceased, for various reasons, to adjust quickly and smoothly enough to ever-present change and to the long-standing requirement for productivity increases, thereby causing a higher number of casualties of change. Some economists blame labour rigidities for impeding the efficient operation of the labour market, and for preventing those displaced by change from finding alternative employment quickly. Others place the blame instead on an accelerating speed of change or on the severity of economic shocks induced by such factors as oil embargoes, macho monetary policy and the recent huge extension of the free-trade zone. Those who see the rat race as primarily the result of economic conditions may also argue that, in an increasingly competitive and open global economy, there is no longer much room for any one country to pursue social agreements designed to avoid competing away higher social and environmental standards. They may consider that competitive advantage is ephemeral, and that it is necessary to be ever ready to take the ruthless decisions required to be in a position to innovate, adapt and lower costs faster than other nations. In this view, it is dangerous folly in a free-trade world to preach standing still – a stationary state of material contentment and moral virtue, standing serenely apart from the maelstrom of base competition.

A final, and most compelling explanation for the quickening pace of the rat race and for the apparently increasing futility of modern economic growth is the growing importance of relative wants and relative rather than absolute wealth. It has been noted by a number of economists and philosophers that economic goods and wants can be divided into two broad classes. On the one hand, there are absolute needs, chiefly for material goods, which can in theory be increasingly satisfied for everyone. It is possible logically – so long as one ignores the impact of advertising in creating perpetual dissatisfaction – for everyone to have their requirements for, say, food and video recorders satisfied, and economic growth can progressively deliver this end. On the other hand, there are also relative needs or wants – for example, for status goods or positions – which are, by definition, not satiable for everyone, and which even unlimited growth could not deliver to all. Keynes, among others, pointed to this important distinction. His contemporary, R. F. Harrod, coined the phrase 'oligarchic wealth' to describe, for example, homes in the best areas, tables in the best restaurants, or membership of the most exclusive golf clubs. The point of this oligarchic wealth is that it can, by definition, never be available to everyone. Therefore if greater numbers attempt to procure it, as tends to happen when more in society have succeeded in satisfying their absolute needs, there will be one of two outcomes: either the relative price of the status goods in question will rise to preserve their élite character, or the goods in question will lose their élite status and be devalued by congestion.

Looked at from the perspective of society as a whole, increased economic activity specifically orientated to securing improvements in the relative positions of individuals has an inherent and inevitable tendency to increase the level of frustrated aspirations. For it is, of course, impossible for *everyone* to have, on average, a higher relative status than they had the year before. This suggests that, while such relative competition might have positive economic side effects, there is an essential social futility to much of the motivation for wealth creation. In this way, the distinction between status goods and basic material goods may help explain some of the frustrated expectations of a society which has increasingly widespread middle-class aspirations, and may go some way to explaining the persistence of the so-called feel-bad factor in today's increasingly affluent societies. As J. S. Mill once said: 'Men do not desire to be rich, but to be richer than other men.' We might add: 'And the man of average wealth cannot be richer than the average of other men.'

In his important book, *Social Limits to Growth*, Fred Hirsch pointed out that exponentially rising material wealth is making the socially futile and frustrating pursuit of relative wealth increasingly prevalent and obligatory. As economic growth allows more people to fulfil their requirements and desires for essential and reproducible material goods, it increases the scramble for what Harrod called 'oligarchic wealth' and Hirsch calls 'positional goods', i.e., those goods which are inherently finite in number, and which beyond some limit cannot be made available in their original form to all who want them. Economic growth not only enables more people to bid for these scarce positional goods; it also extends the number of goods that come into this category, as rising demand for certain goods (e.g., antique furniture) reaches supply constraints for the first time.

There is, thus, an ever fiercer competition for a wider range of increasingly scarce goods, and hence an ever fiercer pursuit of the relative wealth necessary to be successful in the competition. In this competitive struggle, some positional goods become rationed by ever higher prices (e.g., old houses). Others are damaged and devalued by congestion (e.g., unspoiled beaches): although the increase in numbers of people making use of such positional goods may lead to a significant rise in average enjoyment at an early stage of rising prosperity, beyond a certain point the increasing extent of demand leads to congestion which damages the positional good itself so that it is devalued for all. More growth is then required to pay for the defensive spending needed to offset the ill-effects of this congestion.

Hirsch noticed that this effect of increased competition and congestion was relevant to many kinds of goods which are desired for their intrinsic properties, and not in any direct sense for their status or recognition value; most of the individuals who desire, for example, antiques or holidays in Majorca may believe themselves indifferent as to how many other people enjoy the same goods, so long as it does not lead to congestion, and hence either rising relative prices or a deterioration of quality. But rising material prosperity and economic growth is precisely leading to such congestion and deterioration of quality in more and more areas of our lives. Take, for example, the enjoyment of visiting local areas of mountain wilderness, or of having a deserted cove within cycling distance. It is not that those enjoying them desire exclusiveness of access in itself. It is that, as more and more are in a position to visit them, the inherent value to those who previously enjoyed them declines. Silence is replaced by noise, and tranquillity by traffic jams and exhaust fumes. The congestion only stops increasing when the mountain area or cove is so spoilt that people prefer to stay at home. Those still seeking silence and tranquillity will now need to earn more money in order to spend more on either travelling further afield or paying an entrance fee to secure exclusive access to a protected area. In this way, economic growth often forces us to turn previously free goods into economic goods with a price attached.

Now, of course, the very turning of a free good into a traded one increases the recorded level of GDP or economic activity. This is another example of GDP statistics overstating the actual increase in welfare. It is true that more people are now visiting mountain areas and beaches, and that – until serious congestion sets in – this represents an increase in net welfare; it also represents a wider distribution of welfare. But once the congestion threshold has been reached, some of the increased spending in the economy represents increased defensive expenditure by people trying to secure the same level of welfare they already enjoyed before the increase in congestion. The defensive expenditure includes, in this example, buying exclusive access or purchasing air tickets to secure the same good (e.g., clean air and tranquillity) in some remote foreign country, which was previously available free on our doorstep. In this case, as in so many, a rise in GDP may indicate not so much a rise in the standard of living as the need for increased efforts to keep the standard of living of those competing for scarce goods from falling.

Positional goods which are inherently restricted in size or number, but are not prone to congestion because they can physically only be made available to a few, will tend to be competitively rationed by an increase in the price that must be paid to secure them (relative to the prices paid for material goods whose supply can be increased). So, for example, authentic Georgian country manor houses with paddocks near London are rationed by rising relative prices, as demand increasingly outstrips finite supply. So, too, country houses in the Dordogne or Tuscany, which were once cheap, are now considerably more expensive relative to non-positional goods. In some cases, a finite class of positional goods, instead of being rationed by price, is subject to other kinds of hurdle. This can be seen most clearly by looking at the example of jobs.

The job market intersects with the theory of positional goods at a number of points. In some senses, all jobs with more prestige, interest, status or income than average could be regarded as positional goods: to secure them, it is essential not just to have an absolute level of qualification, but to be *relatively* more qualified for the job than other applicants. If more people become qualified in an absolute sense for a particular finite class of positional job, one of several effects may happen. Sometimes, there may be a Dutch auction in salaries for these jobs (i.e., salaries will be bid down to a low enough level to clear the market). In such a case, the positional job is devalued in terms of financial reward by increased competition; so, for example, publishers are not normally paid well partly because there are large numbers of qualified arts graduates able to do their job, and the profession is perceived to be sufficiently interesting that many are willing to do it for comparatively low pay. Very often, though, particularly for prestigious jobs in lucrative professions, this Dutch auction effect does not occur, even when there are plenty of suitable aspiring applicants. In part this is because of the importance of high earnings in the race to secure other positional goods. As a result, those currently in prestigious jobs have a very significant vested interest in maintaining, or attempting to improve, their salary differentials by raising hurdles or barriers to entry to their profession. In some professions – like law and accountancy – this takes the form of what are effectively quotas for new entrants (by way of restrictions on the number who can be successful in the professional examinations, whatever the absolute standard); such quotas ensure a high income (and long working hours) for current practitioners. In other professions, where quotas are not applied – or have been dismantled by deregulation – the profession can attempt to avoid the Dutch auction in salaries by adopting as standard progressively higher qualification hurdles. Qualifications serve not just to raise productivity but also to differentiate applicants; for example, as more people get a first degree, it becomes necessary to have an MBA or a doctorate in addition to achieve the differentiation previously conferred by a degree, and this higher qualification may have only marginal relevance to the content of the job being competed for. Another new hurdle is also sometimes erected – for example, in some City of London and Wall Street financial institutions – namely the requirement to demonstrate complete commitment to a job, in the form of willingness to work a more insane number of hours than the competition, and to put work more fully ahead of family and other interests.

It is a feature of all these methods of resolving increased competition for positional jobs that they tend to involve working longer hours; if a Dutch auction occurs, and the positional job is devalued in financial terms by competition, the process is likely to be accentuated by individuals seeking to maintain their earlier income advantage by working longer hours – a decision which will only increase the downward pressure on incomes per hour; if to prevent a Dutch auction an official or unofficial quota system is used to maintain or create an artificial shortage of professionals (as in accountancy or law), there will frequently be times of strong activity when those professionals will have to work very long hours; if, on the other hand, the qualification hurdle keeps rising for entry to a type of job or profession, people must invest more time in becoming trained; and finally, if hours worked are themselves used as the differentiating mechanism, there may be no reasonable limit to the commitment in hours which the most ambitious and least family-orientated will be willing to demonstrate. In conclusion, those lucky enough to have the better jobs must now spend longer training, and longer working, to keep the same position on the prestige and income ladder that they might have held in much easier conditions before the advent of such strong competition. This is an important element of the rat race.

Hirsch's perceptive theory of positional goods can go a long way to explaining the prevalence of disappointed expectations and the feel-bad factor in our society. For it explains the growing extent to which welfare in a society cannot in aggregate be subject to improvement because, for individuals, welfare is increasingly a relative concept. The absolute level of income, wealth and qualifications may be rising for the average person and for society as a whole, but access to the finite class of positional goods is still determined by each individual's relative position or ranking in terms of income, wealth and qualifications. This is true of positional goods which are rationed by price and of goods whose quality deteriorates through congestion, thereby necessitating increased defensive expenditure or work to preserve a given level of positional advantage. In both cases, because of more competition and congestion, greater and greater absolute expenditure of money or effort is required to maintain a given level of welfare. Furthermore, the same *relative* position on the wealth or qualification ladder is required from year to year to secure the same *absolute* level of welfare in respect of positional goods. It is not possible to opt out of this rat race without having a lower relative position and hence a reduced ability to secure a given level of absolute welfare. For example, those who did not opt for high-stress, highly paid jobs in the 1980s, but chose to work in less stressful or more socially useful, and less well-paid jobs, now find that they cannot afford the sort of house which someone doing the same job with the same real income could have bought ten years earlier. In the area of positional goods, relative position dictates the absolute level of welfare one can obtain. The rat race may be collective madness, but it is wise for any individual to join in unless he or she is oblivious to the charms of positional goods.

The theory of positional goods may also explain why dissatisfaction persists in more affluent countries, and why it may be less prevalent in somewhat less well-developed countries. Obviously nothing equates to the feel-bad factor present in really poor countries where the population is struggling to feed, clothe and house itself. But once most people in a society achieve a level of affluence above the basic subsistence level, there is a period of development when most of their new desires are for material goods which can be reproduced in nearly endless quantities – refrigerators, TVs, washing machines, video recorders, etc. At this stage, growth can deliver more desired goods to all; the poor gain, as their income rises and the price of new goods falls, and the rich do not suffer from the gains of the poor. However, when these standard material wants have been met for a large section of the population, the ratio of positional goods desired relative to material goods may start to rise significantly. In crowded countries, like the UK or Japan, where scarcity of land makes attractive living space a positional good, this is particularly true. The more people who try to buy the limited number of attractive homes, the harder everyone has to work if they are to afford them. In such affluent but congested societies, relative gains in income become key, and aggregate increases in satisfaction or welfare may be increasingly difficult to achieve.

It is important to stress that many of the negative aspects of additional pressure on the positional goods sector are caused by desirable upward mobility in society. No discussion of positional goods can ignore the central question of fair distribution. At one extreme, fine period houses and domestic servants were naturally cheaper when few could aspire to them, and when labourers were very poorly paid. Not many will mourn the passing of those days. But in the same way, more everyday goods, such as the beaches of the south coast of England and the hills of the Lake District, were inherently more attractive when fewer could afford to go to them; for they were not covered in litter nor surrounded by five-mile traffic jams. Herein lies the central problem for any society wishing to avoid the worst excesses of the rat race: they are caused largely by the extension – the laudable extension – of middle-class aspirations, opportunities and freedoms to a larger fraction of the population. Society has not faced up to the distinction between those aspirations which can be fully satisfied for ever greater numbers of people, and those which, given congestion, cannot. As a result, many of those with increased aspirations will necessarily find them unmet while, at the same time, others who *can* meet them have to expend more and more effort, time and money on doing so. In this way, the laudable aim of widening aspirations may increase frustration and alienation among those who still cannot meet their aspirations, while at the same time making those who remain able to meet them feel yet more harassed. Of course, in a mobile society, those who can meet their aspirations for positional goods are more likely to do so on the basis of merit, or through hard work, than as a result of privilege or birth, and this is socially and economically desirable. At the same time, though, the requirement for ever more money to purchase or defend the same level of positional advantage makes it ever harder to attract talented people into the lower paid socially useful professions, like teaching or nursing. Increasing the pay for such essential public-sector jobs would require more taxes; but taxes are not popular, since even those who are theoretically better off than they were do not always *feel* richer, because so much of their higher income goes on defensive goods to protect a current level of welfare from increased positional competition.

Redistributive taxes are becoming particularly unpopular with the middle classes because, in a society increasingly dominated by aspirations for positional goods, competitive advantage in relative income is all the more desperately guarded. But at the same time, the impossibility of positional goods being available in uncongested form to all in society – whatever the level of aggregate wealth – undercuts some of the practical and moral arguments for maintaining economic growth as a higher priority than redistribution. Increasing growth rather than redistribution is held out by free-market economists as the preferred mechanism for meeting the aspirations of the have-nots. The wonders of exponential growth suggest that the trickle-down effects of growth will serve the interests of the poor far more than would the incentive-reducing and growth-sapping redistribution so resisted by the rich. In the free-market view of the trickle-down effect, the poor can gain from their share of new growth, while the rich are still incentivised to speed the creation of wealth because they will also gain. But as we have seen, growth actually seems to be failing the interests of rich and middle-income groups in some respects – increasing the price to them of competing for positional goods – while at the same time *not* making positional goods any more available to the poor. Of course, the composition of who is rich and who is poor may change; but so far as positional sectors of the economy are concerned, it is as though we are back in the pre-growth era, when a finite amount of wealth belonged either to the rich or to the poor, but could not belong to both. There is no hope that the poor will soon be able to enjoy the positional advantage of the rich, unless the latter lose out.

It is important to remember, of course, that this argument only applies to positional goods, and not to the vast material sector of the economy. While the poorest 50 per cent are as far away as ever from many positional goods and from the comforts such goods would provide, they do indeed have much greater access to washing machines, telephones and video recorders than ever before. Rapid growth may lead to an increasingly futile and costly competition for positional goods and jobs, but it does also increase quickly the availability of cheaper material goods for all. In deciding the balance of economic, social and redistribution policy, it is essential therefore to assess how far welfare is dependent on positional goods – extra demand for which will lead merely to extra frustration – and how far it is still dependent on reproducible material goods; only to the extent that welfare is dependent on the latter will everyone be in a position to benefit from incentives to greater economic growth.

The increasing importance of relative gains in wealth is another example of the economic activity of citizens of modern societies becoming more interconnected, with the market decisions of individuals more frequently having important consequences for the welfare of others which are felt beyond those directly involved in the decisions. In the same way that the growing scale of our activities is expanding the prevalence of environmental externalities – i.e., unwelcome environmental side effects of economic activity which are not reflected in market prices – so it is also increasing the incidence of what might be called 'social externalities', i.e., where the decision by individuals to compete for positional goods heightens the congestion or competition costs for all others in contention for them. For example, my decision to compete for ownership of a country cottage, or for a particular management position, or for road space in central London, all have important spill-over effects on other people desiring the same things. Since none of these goods (beyond a certain point) is expandable in size or number, supply cannot expand to meet latent or expressed demand; if I get the job or the thatched cottage, someone else does not; if I am joined by half of London in my attempt to use the roads at five p.m. on Friday (all of us now being rich enough to afford a car), we will all sit in traffic gridlock.

The beauty of the invisible hand of the free market is that it appears to be able to harness the freely expressed competitive self-interest of individual market participants, and provide for the greater good by means of mutually advantageous cooperative trading; the price mechanism serves to match supply and demand according to supplier costs and consumer preferences, allowing for the optimisation of market-expressed preferences and an optimal use of resources; and an increase in demand and greater competition can be expected to lead to an increase in supply and greater efficiency. And so it does, normally, when the demand is for material goods. However, when competition for positional goods is put into the equation, the invisible hand loses much of its allure: where positional goods are concerned, the freedom for one individual successfully to pursue his own self-interest will always be to the detriment of someone else. One person's gain will be someone else's loss. Fiercer competition for positional goods cannot expand supply and will not increase efficiency; indeed, it is likely to lead to considerable inefficiencies resulting from congestion, higher hurdles to success (in the form of rising prices or qualification requirements) and increased expenditure on the defensive goods needed to maintain positional advantage. Any individual may be making a rational choice by trying to secure positional advantage – but in aggregate, when the interactions of all such decisions are taken into account, the social outcome is likely to be negative.

In theory, everyone in society could decide to cooperate to limit the futile competition for positional goods, agreeing collectively to suppress their individual freedom to compete with one another in this area, and instead to share the limited access to positional goods available, without suffering the ill-effects of competition. In this way, society as a whole would be wresting control back from the incremental impact of the piece-meal decisions of self-interested free-market participants which now decide our fate. So, to give a small-scale example, some cities, like Athens and Mexico City, make use of a rota system for vehicles (based on odd and even number plates) to limit traffic congestion, while Singapore uses more sophisticated measures to achieve the same end. Individual liberty is curtailed for the general benefit. So, too, in the area of employment, it is possible to place constraints on personal freedom, and to restrict an individual's ability to compete for more and better work, or more income, by working ever longer hours; this might allow the jobs to be shared among more aspiring applicants, and would limit damage to health and safety caused by positional competition based on excessive working hours. In such cases, mutual agreement to be bound by rules, which no one is given the freedom to break, might lead to a social outcome which, in the eyes of the majority in society, would be preferable to the outcome which would be entailed by the aggregate of individual self-interested decisions.

In societies with a strong and pervasive social ethic and moral princi-ples, there may be a willing compliance by almost all in society with such mutually agreed rules, and this may obviate the need for them to be encapsulated in law. No one in a strongly puritan country, for instance, would ever have competed by working on the Sabbath. But as tradi-tional social ethics have broken down in Western democracies, and enforcement has come to rely on the law, rather than on the social pres-sure for conformity to agreed codes of practice, the scope for such collective agreements designed to avoid futile competition for positional goods has come to be limited by three factors: first, laws aimed at social engineering of this sort involve a significant diminution of individual liberty with which few liberal democracies feel entirely comfortable; freedom of choice is still seen as a guarantor of human progress rather than a threat to it. Secondly, such agreements tend to be difficult to enforce, since – in the absence of a pervasive social code – individuals have a strong incentive to free-ride on the restraint shown by others in the area of competition and congestion. Thirdly, to the extent that such agreements or legislation only treat the symptoms of positional competition rather than its cause, they are likely merely to replace one mode of competition with another.

If we take, for example, the question of hours worked, it is possible – as the EU Social Chapter does to a certain extent – legally to set a limit on the number of hours anyone can be obliged to work; in theory, a limit could also be set (though the EU Social Chapter does *not* do this) on the number of hours anyone would be allowed to work, even on a voluntary basis. This might remove hours worked as a mechanism for job competition or relative income gains, and this might be socially desirable – helping to preserve more marriages and possibly helping to create more jobs as overtime is limited. However, particularly in Anglo-Saxon cultures, such an agreement tends to be seen not as a civilised attempt to stop competition from leading to socially damaging excesses, but as an unacceptable infringement of individual liberty. At the same time, such agreements are notoriously difficult to enforce: how does one, for example, prove whether work has been taken home in the evenings or not, and if so, whether this represents a voluntary decision to polish the day's work, or results from undue pressure by employers? Moreover, if such provisions were to be extended to management positions, then to the limited extent that commitment to working very long hours had previously been used either directly or indirectly (as a result of professional quotas) as a hurdle to reduce the large demand for prestigious jobs to the smaller level of supply, the removal of this hurdle would mean that another hurdle would be likely to be found in order to prevent a Dutch auction in salaries. Such a bidding down of salary levels (in the City of London, for example) would, of course, have the benefit of allowing the numbers employed to be increased without raising the price of goods and services to the consumer, but it would tend to be resisted by the profession concerned in order to protect their high salaries; to protect their positional income advantage in the face of a limit on the number of hours that might be worked, they might instead raise new educational qualification hurdles to create an artificial shortage of applicants.

Clearly, educational qualifications have advantages over most other job hurdles, in that both those who clear, and those who just fail to clear, the hurdle will receive a better training as a result of the new hurdle, and society as a whole may benefit considerably from this. Some hurdles – particularly educational qualifications – are more socially useful and more personally rewarding in themselves than others. However, many kinds of positional goods or jobs are unlikely ever to be rationed in such socially useful ways. Applicants for some positional jobs, for example, are still screened by accent or breeding, and – in the absence of a sea change in social aspirations and values which can limit both the desire for positional goods and the willingness of individuals to compete aggressively for them – most other forms of positional good will continue to be either congested and devalued by the extra numbers able to access them or rationed by relative price inflation and other socially wasteful hurdles.

So long as middle-class aspirations for positional goods continue to increase, therefore, the rat race looks set to remain as intense as it is futile. The growing importance of relative gains in income is leading to an increasingly commercialised society, where time is becoming more precious, and people are less and less likely to engage in socially useful but poorly paid or unpaid activity. As time becomes a more valuable commodity, there is also an increasing incentive to sacrifice leisure time spent, for example, on hobbies or with friends and family. The rat-race society is a selfish, unsociable and harassed one. Moreover, since in the rat race relative gain is key, an often destructive rivalry and competition looks set to become the social norm – pitting colleague against colleague, and neighbour against neighbour. Adam Smith emphasised in his first major work, *The Theory of Moral Sentiments*, the role in forming a cohesive society of sympathy, imagination, desire for approval and benevolence; but he was also convinced that the motive of self-interest, which occupied centre stage in his later work, *The Wealth of Nations*, would help lead to the development of a cooperative and mutually dependent society; for, thanks to the division of labour, it was in everyone's self-interest to engage in mutually advantageous cooperative transactions. Unfortunately, as we have seen, the self-interested pursuit of positional goods does not fit into this pleasing analysis. Where positional goods are concerned, other market participants become the enemy to be defeated in the struggle to succeed. This results in the irony that as our destinies become ever more interconnected, and as our collective salvation depends ever more obviously on cooperation, we increasingly tend to see other people not as fellow citizens but as obstacles in our way. This economic and social reality must take much of the blame for the breakdown of social behaviour across the whole spectrum, from poor driving manners to violent crime.

CHAPTER 10

The Challenge of Uncertainty and Complexity

Out of the ferment of optimistic thought in the Enlightenment, there emerged a dominant view in Western liberal democracies that the twin engines of human progress were the power of human reason to control our predicament, and the power of the invisible hand of the economic free market to harness self-interest to promote the greater good. Since 1914, however, optimistic faith that progress in the use of reason would itself ensure genuine and durable progress in the moral and political sphere has struggled to survive in the face of the horrors of modern warfare, rabid nationalism, sectarian violence and civil wars. More recently, even faith that human reason can progressively extend our control over our physical predicament through progress in scientific knowledge has been called into question by the burgeoning scale and complexity of our interface with the natural environment, and by the increasingly compartmentalised, ever more specialised, and less totally comprehensible nature of human discovery. In the arena of economic activity, though, the beauty of Adam Smith's invisible hand of the free market was that it appeared to explain how liberty and the pursuit of self-interest could help maximise social welfare, without the need either for moral motives or for comprehensive rational planning in our complex modern world. Here was a mechanism that appeared to provide for material and social progress, through economic growth, without the need to assume away either the frailty of human morality or the limits to human reason.

We have already discussed over the last four chapters three pervasive shortcomings of the free-market mechanism which must limit faith in it as an unambiguous generator of progress in welfare; these are the lack of a connection between market efficiency and distributive justice, the failure of the free-market price mechanism to include within its scope environmental externalities (such as pollution and congestion) and, finally, the inability of the invisible hand to ensure that the self-interested pursuit by individuals of relative wealth and positional advantage will lead to an advance in the interests of society as a whole. We have also noted that many of the social and environmental costs of economic growth, which flow from these failures of scope or competence of the invisible hand, are not netted off against the benefits of growth in the GDP statistics, with the result that the GDP growth series is fatally flawed as an indicator of progress in welfare; economic growth represents no guarantee of progress in welfare. These observations are not hugely controversial amongst professional economists themselves; their importance lies principally in the failure – all too often – of politicians, policy-makers and public opinion to take due notice of their implications.

There are also, however, some very controversial areas of disagreement amongst professional economists themselves about the efficiency of the free-market mechanism even within its traditional area of scope, and it is some of these which are the subject of this chapter. In particular, there is a strong disagreement about how far – in our uncertain and complex world – there is a need for a rational policy of intervention to improve the basic workings of the free market. This debate, at the very centre of economics as an intellectual discipline, is crucial to our story. For if one believes that, regardless of externalities and distribution questions, the free market sometimes requires government intervention to make it work efficiently, and also that intervention for other reasons does not always in practice reduce efficiency, then the whole presumption in favour of relying on the unfettered workings of the free market to produce progress in welfare would be severely weakened; without, of course, wishing to return to a fully planned economy, it would be respectable again to seek to channel, control and direct the activities of the free market to ensure progress in welfare for all, now and in the future. But if, on the contrary, one believes that – beyond establishing a framework of law and a monetary system – there is no workable role for government initiatives actually to improve the operation of the free market, and that intervention itself is almost always intrinsically damaging to efficiency, then there may be little choice but to accept as a package the imperfect workings of the invisible hand as the best hope for sustained human progress; in this second view, human reason would then be confined to the service of individual self-interest, and we might be forced to accept, at least in the field of economic policy, the impotence of the collective exercise of human reason in the service of the democratic will.

The arguments which rage in the political arena in relation to economic questions often represent a confusion between two different aspects: (i) normative or moral questions about what the aims of policy should be and what yardsticks we should use to measure their success; and (ii) practical economic questions about how to bring about these aims most efficiently. The normative or ethical aspects of the economic debate are essentially arguments based on different sets of value judgements. Those arguing may agree on a single analysis of how the economy works but differ as to whether particular outcomes are actually morally acceptable. So, for example, while many people in 1990s France do not dispute that a lower minimum wage would lead to lower unemployment, they nevertheless hold that it would be morally wrong to tackle unemployment by increasing income differentials. This is a normative view about how society ought to be organised and what distribution of income is acceptable. In a normative approach to economics, the most efficient outcome is not necessarily the most desirable; one may need to sacrifice some efficiency and growth for greater fairness. Similarly, of course, there may be two equally efficient outcomes which differ markedly in terms of equity of distribution. By definition, judgements about economic progress from normative standpoints are ultimately subjective; they may depend on the different values placed on liberty versus fair distribution, or on the interests of future generations versus the interests of today's poor, or on environmental quality versus rising material prosperity. These are the central ethical and normative debates relating to economic questions, to which we will return in the final chapter.

Whatever one's moral standpoint and moral goal, however, there is a separate political debate centring on underlying differences in beliefs about how the economic interactions between people actually work and operate in practice in any given situation. This is the area of positive economic debate. Economics is usually seen as the objective study of the way an economy works; it seeks to give scientific explanations and attempts to make rational predictions. But there are many schools of economics – from classical free-market monetarism to Keynesianism – which differ markedly in their analysis of how the economy works in practice. These competing analyses underpin many of the differences between the policies adopted by various political parties or countries. Even given an underlying agreement on values, there can be vigorous political debate about which of the different economic blueprints will in fact best sustain human progress. Indeed, the different answers to the objective questions raised in this and the next chapter themselves imply very different political attitudes. So, for example, the contrasting assessments of how prevalent instances of genuine market failure actually are can imply radically different views about whether the agreed goal of maximising progress in welfare is best achieved by free-market reforms (designed to boost economic efficiency) or, alternatively, by seeking to manage and reduce the costs of economic growth through greater government intervention. Similarly, the decision about how seriously to take the challenges presented by the new 'science' of complexity must affect the amount of faith we can have in the ability of the free market accurately to reflect people's true preferences. The different answers to such questions not only help determine political attitudes to the free market, but also influence how optimistic one can be – in the increasingly deregulated and complex world of today – about the likelihood of sustained human progress.

Keynes and the Prevalence of Market Failure

Classical free-market economics assumes that an economy will – if left to operate freely – quickly find a competitive equilibrium, i.e., a set of prices for all goods in the economy which will ensure that demand in every market is equal to supply. This set of prices is said to 'clear' the markets, while achieving an efficient (though not necessarily fairly distributed) allocation of goods across all market participants. This view of the market mechanism does indeed seem to hold true in most ordinary circumstances. In general, the free market has proved itself admirably capable of achieving an efficient allocation of the resources required for production, and of ensuring the efficient production of the goods and services which consumers actually want. Moreover, the price system achieves this in a decentralised manner. One only has to consider the failures of the centrally planned economies of the Soviet Union and Eastern Europe in the forty years after World War II to see how enormously complex and important is the process of allocation of resources; central planning has shown itself incapable, no matter how big the civil service, of allocating most resources with anything like the efficiency of Adam Smith's invisible hand, and it is this central truth which underpins the theoretical framework of free-market economics. However, it is also apparent that, in practice, important elements of the markets sometimes do *not* clear efficiently or quickly. The classic example of such a market failure is, of course, the depression of the 1930s when, for a long period, the economy appeared to settle in an equilibrium which failed to clear the market in labour, leaving a huge imbalance between the supply and demand for labour. It was this depression which gave rise to the famous Keynesian critique of free markets.

John Maynard Keynes is generally acknowledged to have been the most influential economist of the twentieth century. While accepting much of the framework of classical economics developed since Adam Smith, he mounted a sustained challenge to certain of its central tenets. In his most famous work, *The General Theory of Employment, Interest and Money*, Keynes's central target was the assumption in classical economics from the time of David Ricardo that – in a competitive equilibrium – demand is always equal to supply (or, as Jean-Baptiste Say famously put it: supply creates its own demand); this classical assumption implied, for example, that in a genuinely free market there could never be any truly involuntary unemployment. All that was required to reach such a happy equilibrium was to remove all impediments to the operation of a free market. In chapter 3 of *The General Theory*, Keynes wrote of this classical consensus:

> The completeness of the Ricardian victory is something of a curiosity and a mystery. It must have been due to a complex of suitabilities in the doctrine to the environment into which it was projected. That it reached conclusions quite different from what the ordinary uninstructed person would expect, added, I suppose, to its intellectual prestige. That its teaching, translated into practice, was austere and often unpalatable, lent it virtue. That it was adapted to carry a vast and consistent logical superstructure, gave it beauty. That it could explain much social injustice and apparent cruelty as an inevitable incident in the scheme of progress, and the attempt to change such things as likely on the whole to do more harm than good, commended it to authority. That it afforded a measure of justification to the free activities of the individual capitalist, attracted to it the support of the dominant social force behind authority.[1]

The core of *The General Theory* is an analysis of how economies can become stuck in a long period of suppressed demand, subnormal activity and high unemployment. Keynes highlights the importance of uncertainty in causing recessions – stressing its tendency both to reduce consumption by increasing the desire to hoard savings and to decrease the propensity to invest. Analysing the nature of the long-term expectations upon which investment decisions are based, Keynes writes in chapter 12:

> The outstanding fact is the extreme precariousness of the basis of knowledge on which our estimates of prospective yield have to be made. Our knowledge of the factors which will govern the yield of an investment some years hence is usually very slight and often negligible.[2]

Following a brilliant critique of the herd instincts of stock-market speculators, Keynes concludes that most investment is the product of 'animal spirits' and 'spontaneous optimism', rather than carefully worked-out mathematical predictions; indeed, the limited nature of our existing knowledge of the future 'does not provide a sufficient basis for a calculated mathematical expectation'. As a result, investments are liable to sudden collapses of confidence: 'In estimating the prospects of investment, we must have regard, therefore, to the nerves and hysteria and even the digestions and reactions to the weather of those upon whose spontaneous activity it largely depends.'[3]

Crucial to Keynes's argument is the observation that, with the onset of recession, a perceived reduction in the incentives to invest (given uncertainty about the future) will often coincide with a higher propensity to save on the part of worried consumers. While by definition the value of savings (including net capital inflows from abroad) in any time period can be assumed to equal the value of actual investment, there is no automatic link between the level of planned saving and that of planned investment. If planned savings (i.e., the amount of liquidity people wish to hold) are higher than the planned level of investment, there will be a contraction in actual aggregate demand for goods and services. Furthermore, the shortfall in actual demand is often made more significant by being extrapolated forward by businesses to an expectation of a prolonged period of low demand, thereby causing further cuts in planned investment and employment. As Keynes himself argues in chapter 16 of *The General Theory*:

> If saving consisted not merely in abstaining from present

consumption but in placing simultaneously a specific order for future consumption, the effect might indeed be different. For in that case the expectation of some future yield from investment would be improved, and the resources released from preparing for present consumption could be turned over to preparing for the future consumption . . . In any case, however, an individual decision to save does not, in actual fact, involve the placing of any specific forward order for consumption, but merely the cancellation of a present order.[4]

Now, by definition, if the money supply (i.e., the amount of cash in circulation, plus the level of bank deposits) remains fixed, it is impossible for *everyone* to increase their holdings of cash (and cash equivalents); if everyone vainly attempts to do so, consumption expenditure, and hence incomes, will fall – thereby ensuring that income losses prevent any increase, on average, in liquid savings. These income losses, and falling demand, will – Keynes argued – lead to higher unemployment which will, in turn, result in actual demand being even further below potential demand. Moreover, the market system has no mechanism for reflecting how much demand there would be if unemployment were eliminated, and if the propensity to save returned to normal. Instead, actual demand in a depression reflects the demand existing at prevailing slump levels of income and employment, given the prevailing heightened propensity to save for precautionary reasons. To close the gap between actual and potential demand, and thus re-create a full employment equilibrium, Keynes advocated that the authorities should seek to boost the money supply in order to satisfy the desire for increased holdings of liquid savings, while at the same time increasing spending on public works in order to generate more investment and employment and hence stimulate more spending. He argued that this sort of intervention was greatly preferable to the classical free-market prescription – namely, waiting for a drop in wages and prices to lead to a positive rise in the real value (i.e., inflation-adjusted) of existing savings sufficient to generate an increased propensity to spend and invest. Such a *laissez-faire* free-market approach would, Keynes argued, take an unacceptably long time to work, even if measures were taken to increase wage and price flexibility. Moreover, he argued that the classical assumption that interest-rate falls in a recession would bring the desire to save back into equilibrium with the desire to invest was sometimes false. In some cases, at least, interest rates might not be able to fall sufficiently under a *laissez-faire* approach to generate dis-saving and encourage investment. This is the so-called 'liquidity trap' where, in uncertain slump conditions, long-term interest rates cannot fall low enough to encourage sufficient investment, because below a certain level yields would not adequately compensate potential investors for giving up the perceived benefits of liquidity and for taking on the perceived risk of credit default or future inflation.

In the sixty years since Keynes wrote his famous work, economic fashions have come and gone. Much of the debate between free-market monetarists and Keynesians focuses on the central issue of how important and frequent are instances of Keynesian sub-optimal market equilibria (or prolonged economic disequilibria), how long they last and how one should tackle them. Opponents of Keynes, from the 1930s onwards, have argued that many of the conditions Keynes built into his theory (e.g., the liquidity trap) are very special cases. Free-market economists have argued that if market imperfections, trade union agreements, etc. are removed to allow greater flexibility in wages and prices, the economy can be relied on to adjust quickly back to a perfect equilibrium, thereby eliminating involuntary unemployment and 'clearing' the labour market. They have dismissed Keynes's argument that sharply falling nominal wages and prices (in an unregulated economy) will tend to increase uncertainty and thus further dampen the propensity to spend and invest (at least in the short term). In general, right-wing free-market economists tend to assume that markets would always quickly reach a healthy equilibrium if so-called 'supply-side' measures were taken to remove major distortions and, in particular, to increase labour-market flexibility. They argue that, at best, the Keynesian analysis provides the right answer only in highly unusual slump conditions, where the speed and scale of adjustment required is very high, and that in all other cases, the Keynesian prescription simply leads to inflation in the long run. Free-market economists' optimism about the efficiency of free markets and the speed with which they clear leads them, in general, to champion free competition, deregulation and the removal of as many market distortions as possible: trade barriers should be removed to foster free trade; employment protection should be scrapped to allow wages to adjust and thereby prevent unemployment; intrusive environmental legislation and red tape should be kept to a minimum. They also tend to argue that most attempts to intervene in the market to reduce the costs of growth are misguided and will only serve to reduce market efficiency; it is better to focus on deregulation, which will have the overriding benefit of improving the efficiency of markets and thereby boosting economic growth.

By contrast, present-day followers of Keynes still tend to emphasise the insuperable nature of many of the obstacles to a truly free market, and therefore to stress the positive role of intervention to manage demand as well as to improve the supply side. These new Keynesians have added more general reasons why there is a strong likelihood of market failure, from time to time, leading to prolonged periods of sub-optimal growth or employment. They stress, for example, as Paul Krugman does in his book *Peddling Prosperity*, the importance – even in highly unregulated economies – of *imperfectly* competitive markets (e.g., as a result of information failures, or natural oligopolies) and of slightly irrational behaviour by individuals. One of the theoretical conditions for an optimal equilibrium in a free competitive market is that individual market participants always behave in a fully rational manner and with perfect foresight (and hence always give the correct signals of where their true interests lie); but this is clearly not the case in real life. Krugman uses the example of the housing market, and points out that when the number of unsold houses starts to rise (i.e., there are more people desiring to sell their houses than there are people wishing to buy them) prices are frequently very slow to fall. This is often not due to reg-ulations or market distortions, but is merely the result of individuals making the free decision not to cut the price of their houses. This deci-sion may not be totally irrational from an individual point of view, and may not simply be the result of a failure on the part of most market par-ticipants to recognise that there is a general slump in the housing market. Some of the individuals concerned may be justified in deciding that their houses are sufficiently unusual and differentiated from the others that, despite the slump, they will be able to find willing buyers at the old price if they wait. However, if too many people make this sort of understand-able decision, there will be a collectively irrational and serious glut of unsold houses, which – at the level of the market as a whole – will only clear when there has been a large downward adjustment of prices. Moreover, many market participants will be wary of being the first to cut prices in case they lose out. In the housing market, as in the labour market, the behaviour of individuals depends for its success on what other market participants do; but individual decisions on how to behave are based upon uncertain expectations about the unknowable future behaviour of other market participants and of the economy as a whole. An optimal equilibrium, even in free and unregulated competitive markets, can often be absent for long periods, given that people are not blessed with perfect foresight and cannot work out what their fellow market operators, in aggregate, will do in an uncertain environment. In such cases, prices may for a long time fail to adjust to the level required to clear the market and may fail to give the correct signals about the extent of under-utilised supply.

The importance of the Keynesian critique of the workings of the free market for our story is not just that it calls further into question the ability of the invisible hand to maximise the social good in all situations, but also that it appears to justify some rational government intervention designed to ensure the smooth operation of the market. Moreover, those who see some market failures as inevitable, no matter how much deregulation there is, are less likely to make deregulation a priority over the correction of the social and environmental ill-effects of economic growth. Analysis by Professors R. Lipsey and K. Lancaster is particularly relevant to this debate about the relative merits of deregulation and intervention. For they have shown that unless a market can be truly free of *all* distortions, it is not possible to demonstrate theoretically that removing one of several distortions will necessarily lead to the market behaving in a more efficient manner.[5] These findings cast doubt on the wisdom of the political obsession in Britain and the USA in the 1980s with removing as many of the distortions in an economy as possible. For significant distortions will always remain in any actual economy; even in the most free of actual free markets, some taxation and regulation is required in order to pay for common defence and to uphold the rule of law. On these grounds, many economists, while agreeing that distortions which perform no useful function – or a negative function – should be removed, think it is altogether more questionable to insist on removing distortions which have a useful social impact, in the name of promoting greater market efficiency and higher economic growth. These economists, and their followers, are much more likely to see it as worthwhile to maintain or adopt environmental and social protection legislation, designed to lower the costs of economic growth. They will argue that the extra distortions such measures produce may not in fact lead to any more disequilibria than markets are already prone to and may not damage growth; there may indeed be less of a trade-off than right-wing economists and policy-makers would have us believe between economic efficiency, on the one hand, and the reduction of inequality or environmental damage, on the other.

Not surprisingly, there is little consensus in these vexed areas of economic debate. It is clear that the Keynesian revolution did lead for a while to an exaggerated view of the scope for successful government intervention, and of the need for such intervention – which in many cases went far beyond the special cases envisaged in Keynes's own work. In particular, in the post-World War II period, there was an exaggerated belief in the efficacy of wholesale management of demand in the economy. For while governments may have some informational advantages over individual market participants – particularly relating to aggregate behaviour – it is crucial to remember that they, too, are faced with uncertainty as to the impact of their actions in a constantly evolving environment. So, for example, as Milton Friedman has argued, Keynesian economics sometimes makes the mistake of ignoring the 'long and variable lags' before active monetary intervention can have any impact on the real economy. More often than not, intervention designed to deal with subdued demand will only have an impact when demand has already recovered, and as a result will merely lead to unintended inflationary price rises.

Many observers agree that governments do have a necessary role in organising cooperative behaviour in situations where the individual piecemeal decisions of self-interested market participants acting on their own would lead to collective folly; governments are, for example, often best placed to organise arrangements for sharing common assets and for using common space in an efficient manner; they can also help promote joint efforts to conserve resources or reduce congestion and pollution, by policing agreements and organising a penalty system to punish those who would free-ride on the restraint shown by others. Most would agree, too, that governments have some role in producing a coordinated response to extreme market disequilibrium in times of depression, war or serious political and environmental shocks. But where intervention strays into the area of second-guessing the detailed market allocation of capital resources or labour, outside these special cases, it is likely to be counter-productive. The level of unemployment or pollution can be the legitimate subject of democratic government decisions as to what constitutes the public interest; but state planning is very unlikely to be able to match the awesome power of the decentralised free market either in deciding what is the optimal level of provision of detailed marketable services, or in catering for the full variety of market-expressed consumer preferences.

During the 1980s, disillusionment with the competence of government, and doubts about governments' ability to get the answers right even as regards the large macro-economic issues, became widespread – partly because of the failure of most governments' response to the 'stagflation' (recession with high inflation) of the 1970s. There was, as a result, a sharp swing back towards *laissez-faire* reliance on the virtues of the unimpeded invisible hand of the free market. But by the 1990s, the score card between Keynesians and free-market monetarists has become more evenly balanced than many suppose. The worst excesses of Keynesianism did have a hand in producing the stagflation of the 1970s, and did cause many countries to undervalue the importance of labour-market flexibility in the battle to maintain full employment. The wholesale nationalisation of industrial sectors of the economy prescribed by some Keynesians of socialist orientation also led to manifest inefficiency. But on the other side of the argument, the experience of the 1980s and the 1990s has demonstrated that deregulation has led to greater volatility in both asset prices and economic growth than was seen in the twenty-five years after 1947, and has contributed to a series of financial catastrophes (e.g., the savings and loans crisis in the USA in the late 1980s). Deregulation was also partly responsible for the BSE crisis in Britain, where regulations on the manufacture of livestock feed were relaxed in the early 1980s, with disastrous results for the beef industry and consumers. Supply-side reforms enacted in the USA and the UK during the 1980s, such as reduced marginal rates of tax and lower social welfare payments, quickly led to much greater income inequality, while not producing until the late 1990s any convincing evidence of a measurable increase in long-term growth rates. At the same time, increases in labour-market flexibility (admittedly rather limited) have not prevented Continental European unemployment from soaring to significantly higher levels than were seen in the highly regulated Keynesian 1960s. It is not surprising that in many countries in the late 1990s electorates are becoming increasingly disillusioned with the ideological certainties of both old Keynesians and classical free-marketeers, and appear intent on electing pragmatic governments which have a commitment to balancing some necessary increases in labour-market flexibility with a willingness to curb the excesses of the free market, while showing due humility about their ability to achieve too much. Electorates may be right to doubt whether either the invisible hand of the free market, or the intervention of governments, has the power to generate sustained and unambiguous progress in welfare.

The Impact of Shocks and Complexity

The impact of rapid change is central to modern doubts about progress. Belief in the possibility of positive change, and in the ability of mankind to control and engineer change, are psychological prerequisites for a confident belief in progress; but if change is particularly rapid, and represents a shock, it may instead undermine belief in progress, by increasing the feeling of insecurity and disorientation amongst those sections of society where people are required to adapt to new circumstances more quickly than their emotional make-up and skill-sets allow. At the same time, very rapid change can limit the ability of the environment to adapt quickly enough to avoid significant negative consequences, and can often lead to chaotic and unpredictable results in complex ecosystems. Furthermore, some economists are now beginning to argue that sharp economic shocks can have a negative impact, not just on the environment and on people's feeling of security, but also on the rate of economic growth itself, and on the ability of an economy – even in the long term – to remain in a benign equilibrium; shocks create uncertainty, damage confidence and make economies behave in unpredictable ways. In this view, economies, like the people who inhabit them and the environment in which they operate, adjust more efficiently and more predictably to slow and deliberate change.

Since the early 1980s, a number of new Keynesian economists have placed considerable emphasis on the economic theory of 'hysteresis' in an attempt to explain the impact of shocks. Hysteresis is the name given to situations in which the behaviour of an economy in the short term determines which of many possible long-run equilibria it will eventually settle into. According to the theory of hysteresis, a shock which pushes an economy into recession, for example, will not only have a number of short-term negative consequences, but these short-term effects will themselves also have a long-term impact on which equilibrium position the economy will reach when the recovery comes. So, a sharp recession may have the effect of destroying capital, since below a certain financial threshold companies will be forced to close down plants that otherwise could have been productive again later. At the same time, the recession may have a semi-permanent effect on the demand for, and supply of, trained labour in two ways: first, those who remain 'insiders' in the labour market (i.e., still have jobs) will, when demand picks up, be more interested in getting real wage increases for themselves than in seeing those who lost their jobs return; the companies, too, may be quite happy to have a smaller, better-paid workforce, whose members are motivated to achieve higher productivity by the fear that if they do not exert themselves they will lose their scarce, highly paid jobs. Secondly, those unemployed for a long time may become discouraged from looking for work, and lose the up-to-date skills required to compete for jobs. As a result of such hysteresis effects, recessionary shocks may have a negative long-term impact on the potential growth rate and on the natural level of unemployment of an economy.

Those who believe that hysteresis effects are important will attach great significance to avoiding economic shocks. They may, indeed, place the blame for many recent economic problems, such as high unemployment, on financial and market shocks, and may, in turn, blame some of these shocks on sudden moves to deregulate markets (e.g., the complete abolition of capital controls or the rapid liberalisation of trade). They may argue that sudden deregulation and liberalisation, together with the use of sharp interest-rate rises as a policy tool to combat the threat of inflation, have led to deeper cyclical slowdowns since the 1970s than were necessary, thereby destroying more jobs, in some cases, than will be created even in the long run by the introduction of more flexible markets and the attainment of lower inflation. Classical free-market economists, by contrast, are sceptical of hysteresis effects; holding to their belief in the ability of genuinely free markets to clear quickly and return naturally to an optimal equilibrium position, they do not shy away from inducing those recessions or shocks which are sometimes the inevitable consequence of quickly removing undesirable market distortions. Free-market economists argue that the removal of distortions, such as employment protection legislation and other red tape, will over the long term reduce the negative consequences of shocks, by allowing the market to clear more efficiently and return to an optimal equilibrium more quickly. Furthermore, recessions may, in their eyes, have the long-term benefits of reducing inflationary expectations and producing leaner and fitter industry.

The jury is still out on this debate about the importance of hysteresis effects. Unemployment has risen sharply since the mid 1970s in most European countries, particularly during the sharp recessions induced in the early 1980s and early 1990s by the very tight monetary policy response to the oil price and German reunification shocks. Moreover, in many countries, once the unemployment rate has risen, it has remained stubbornly high, despite free-market reforms. But free-market economists maintain that this is because deregulation has been too little, too late to prevent European labour pricing itself out of world markets. They argue that efforts to deregulate should be redoubled; for otherwise – shocks or no shocks – there will inevitably be a further rise in the natural rate of unemployment.

The theory of hysteresis is an attempt to build into classical theory the often negative and inherently unpredictable long-term effects of shocks. Like Keynes, those who believe in hysteresis think that an economy can settle into many different equilibria – only one of which is optimal; which equilibrium state the economy gravitates to, after a shock, depends on the particular short-term circumstances pertaining at the time. Moreover, according to the theory, the exact nature and extent of the shifts from one equilibrium state to another are often essentially unpredictable in advance, even if fully explicable after the event. A number of economists have noted that, in this sense, hysteresis shifts resemble the non-linear reactions seen in many other complex systems when key thresholds are crossed, and resemble the chaotic reactions to even small changes in initial conditions highlighted by chaos theory.

This analogy between hysteresis and chaos theory suggests the need for a yet more radical rethinking of the classical equilibrium model in economic theory; and, over the last decade, some academics have indeed begun to stress the general importance of complexity and chaos theory to economics. As M. Mitchell Waldrop makes clear in his book, *Complexity*, there are for many scientists and economists fascinating parallels between the study of human economic behaviour and that of complex biological or physical systems. They argue, for example, that macro-economic systems are like the weather; both are highly complex adaptive systems, and in both cases their complexity renders accurate predictions beyond the short term almost impossible. Waldrop's book includes a quotation from J. H. Holland of the University of Michigan which makes the analogy clear:

> 'Look at meteorology,' he told them. 'The weather never settles down. It never repeats itself exactly. It's essentially unpredictable more than a week or so in advance. And yet we can comprehend and explain almost everything that we see up there. We can identify important features such as weather fronts, jet streams, and high pressure systems. We can understand their dynamics.'[6]

The analogy between the study of weather systems and the discipline of economics is appealing to any operator in the financial markets, who is faced with many conflicting and inaccurate economic predictions, but is also furnished with backward-looking economic analysis of great insight and explanatory power. As Waldrop explains, scientists centred around the Sante Fe Institute in New Mexico in the late 1980s began to argue that many complex systems, including economies, display what appears to be 'spontaneous self-organisation' 'at the edge of chaos' – that is, they appear to be in a twilight zone between stable equilibrium and complete chaos; these systems rely for their dynamism on positive feedback mechanisms, increasing returns and non-linear relationships. The complexity theorists argue that the old certainties of equilibrium states, diminishing returns and predictable linear equations do not enable one to build a good model of real-life dynamic complex systems. The reassuring picture portrayed by Adam Smith's theory of the invisible hand, where a free economy is seen to settle into a stable and harmonious equilibrium, maximising the social good, gives way to a more uncertain, unpredictable world – where even small unforeseen events can change the course of history, where changes can be explained after the event but not predicted, and where the economy's remarkable decentralised power of organisation and resource allocation is dynamic, evolving, inherently unstable and never settles down into an equilibrium.

Complexity is important to an understanding of economics in several ways. First, the very complexity of our economic interactions underlines the dubious nature of the assumption in classical economic theory that people and firms make their choices with rational foresight. Many of our economic choices depend for their success or failure in welfare terms on the unknowable future behaviour of other market participants. Our choices are interdependent with the choices of others, and are made in an uncertain environment where we cannot be sure what the behaviour of others will be. We must continually adapt our behaviour to the dynamic and ultimately unpredictable environment in which we live. In Waldrop's book, Stanford University professor W. B. Arthur argues that people are faced with a situation analogous to a game of chess. It is not just that the possible permutations are effectively endless, but also that any move has uncertain effects, because the reactions of the other player are unpredictable; a player must in fact operate with a set of scenarios or a plan in his mind, and a guesstimate of the likely outcome, but he can only fully analyse the situation *after* the event. In the real world, of course, there are more than two players. Such fundamental uncertainty, and the impossibility of making fully informed choices in complex situations, undermines the whole logical edifice of the invisible hand, and calls into question the assumption that a genuinely free market will ever reach an optimal equilibrium. To quote Waldrop again:

'And by the same token,' said Holland, 'there's no point in imagining that the agents in the system can ever "optimise" their fitness, or their utility, or whatever. The space of possibilities is too vast; they have no practical way of finding the optimum. The most they can ever do is to change and improve themselves relative to what the other agents are doing. In short, complex adaptive systems are characterised by perpetual novelty.'[7]

Economic operators can never be perfectly rational or have perfect foresight in complex situations; they can never know precisely the outcomes they are choosing, since the outcomes will depend on the unpredictable permutations of large numbers of individuals acting on imperfect information. We have seen in earlier chapters how the piecemeal decisions of individuals in a free market may not always lead to the desired social outcome – particularly in the case of public goods and environmental externalities. This is not entirely because individuals predict that others will free-ride on any restraint they show, and because there is no mechanism in a free market to allow individuals to arrive at collective decisions to share scarce public goods or refrain from exacerbating pollution or congestion. It is also because individuals influence each other and interact with one another, often in unpredictable ways, and because their combined behaviour sometimes has important non-linear threshold effects which are not analysable by any individual who is ignorant of the aggregate position. To take a trivial example, I cannot know what the impact on my own welfare, or that of others, will be if I decide to use the M40 motorway at 10.30 a.m. on a particular Saturday; it will depend on the decisions of countless others, as well as on chance events such as accidents. My decision might cause no congestion, or it might be the one which tips the road over its capacity threshold, leading to bottlenecks for all. Wherever complex systems and non-linear reactions are at stake, there is clearly good reason to doubt the frequent political assumption that people's behaviour in markets is a reliable expression of their true preferences, and that in this sense the 'market knows best'. Individual consumers can be safely assumed to be the best arbiters of their own preferences; but they may accidentally misrepresent this preference through inadequate knowledge of the environment in which they express their preference in the marketplace; they may inadvertently contribute – in complex situations – to an outcome they detest.

While some forms of market failure resulting from such information and coordination problems may lend themselves to correction by government intervention, there is need for humility in this quarter too; in many cases, the results of implementing government intervention will also not be knowable in advance. Moreover, since, as we have seen, there is room for genuine scepticism in our complex world about the efficacy of economics as a predictive tool, we must also be sceptical about its reliability as a foundation for blueprints of political action. To the extent that economies are complex systems, the best individuals and governments can hope for is to learn continuously how best to adapt to a dynamic and ever-changing environment. In our unpredictable world, rigid adherence to economic dogma is very unlikely to lead to certain benefits.

A more specific sense in which complexity theory undermines the equilibrium model of classical economics is the importance it places on increasing returns. Much of the theory of market equilibrium is based on the notion of diminishing marginal utility and diminishing marginal returns. In particular, for example, it is a critical condition of a truly free competitive market that no player gets large enough to distort the free operation of the pricing mechanism. Classical economists generally assumed that, as companies got bigger, they would be subject to diminishing marginal returns, and that size was therefore self-limiting; there were, in other words, important negative-feedback effects of size. In a genuinely free market, classical theory assumed that perfect competition would be self-sustaining; monopolies and oligopolies were seen as the unnatural result of interference in the market and of restrictive practices. By contrast, many would now argue that the conditions of perfect competition are inherently unstable, given the existence in reality of positive-feedback effects, i.e., the tendency for success to be cumulative; winners in the technology race, or the market struggle, often appear to be able freely to establish a dominant position, and then to control prices and raise barriers to entry in such a way as to frustrate competition.

The standard example of self-reinforcing success, or positive feedback, is the dominant position of the QWERTY keyboard for typewriters and computers. Initially introduced to slow typists down to a speed which the early technology could cope with, the irrational distribution of letters on the standard keyboard has become locked in, probably indefinitely, as a result of the huge investment in time, money and effort by all users of keyboards in every generation in learning to use the QWERTY distribution of letters. As a result, a policy adopted many decades ago by the then dominant typewriter manufacturer – a policy which has no modern relevance – still dictates the typing habits of many millions of people. In a similar way, a small initial advantage by one competitor in many high-technology areas can often be translated into a dominant position for the technology of that competitor. So, for example, Betamax video recorders lost out to VHS, and a myriad software packages lost out to those of Microsoft, not because of inferior technology, but partly at least because they lagged behind slightly in the very early days of competition owing to a particular combination of market circumstances, and consumers from then on opted for the 'safer' market leader (i.e., the one perceived as most likely to dominate the market in future).

Wherever increasing returns are important, and market positions become dominant, it cannot be proven – even theoretically – that a free market leads to an optimal outcome or equilibrium over time; for in such circumstances, that all-important condition of a benign free-market equilibrium, namely perfect competition, is quickly eliminated; early advantage becomes self-reinforcing and may solidify into a position of stultifying dominance. Increasing returns ensure that in many cases even the most free of free markets will not produce the best outcome; for good or ill, chance events or small initial advantages may result in one outcome becoming locked in, and in any prior harmonious balance being destroyed.

The existence of increasing returns appears to offer another chink of light to those who favour market intervention and oppose *laissez-faire* economics. For if early advantage is so important, then government help to secure such early advantage may be beneficial in the long term, without the need for continuing government support. This is particularly germane in high-technology, high-break-even industries, such as aircraft manufacture. Many would argue that US defence orders for Boeing, and European subsidies to Airbus, helped establish the dominant position of these two players at the expense of others without such help. In such cases, once the companies have achieved the all-important economies of scale in research and production, the direct and indirect subsidies may not be needed for sustained profitability. In many cases also, countries seek to protect so-called 'infant industries' behind tariff barriers to give them time to reach the scale required if they are to compete with previously dominant players. In a similar way, the tendency for companies of a particular industry or group of industries to be clustered together (e.g., pharmaceutical companies in Basle, Switzerland, or computer companies in Silicon Glen, in Scotland) can sometimes be attributed to government intervention (such as enterprise zones or targeted tax breaks), as well as to chance events. Once established, such clustering allows for a superior interchange of ideas and information, a strong support base of supplier industries, an impressive pool of local talent and fierce local rivalry – all factors which can help to reinforce a dominant competitive position for the cluster of companies concerned. But while the evidence of increasing returns in these and other examples may seem to strengthen the argument for government interference in the workings of the free market, there is a need – in this area as in so many others – for great humility about the capacity of government; it is fiendishly difficult to isolate the key determining factor in a complex situation, or to predict correctly the rising industrial stars of the next generation.

The radical uncertainty about the future in all complex economic systems, and the importance of increasing returns and threshold effects, make the invisible hand of the free market unlikely on its own to achieve an optimal solution for all market participants. At the same time, radical uncertainty also renders governments largely impotent in their attempts to achieve an optimal solution for their own country. This is true not only of intervention at the micro-economic level, such as the fostering of particular high-technology industries, but also of the decisions taken by governments in many macro-economic areas. It may be clear that the pursuit of a genuinely free market is not enough to ensure a harmonious equilibrium and balanced progress for society as a whole, and that, despite the workings of the invisible hand, the aggregate impact of the piecemeal decisions of free-market participants frequently involves unpredictable and unwelcome results. But similarly, carefully planned government intervention may also inadvertently lead to unforeseen problems and unpredictable results.

The complexity of our predicament is central to the dynamism of human activity, but it also introduces uncertainty into the very fabric of our economic life, and makes the future inherently unpredictable and uncontrollable. The complexity of our interactions with one another renders untenable any absolute faith that we can engineer progress in the future by relying, in Alexander Pope's words, on 'self-love to urge and reason to restrain'. Neither the pursuit of self-interest in conditions of economic liberalism nor human reason in the service of science and government can assure us of continued success. We live on the 'edge of chaos', overconfident of our ability to control and predict our future, and overconfident of the free market's ability to maximise the social good.

CHAPTER 11

Free Trade and a Global Destiny

Free trade and free capital movements are central to the debate about whether attempts to maximise economic growth by freeing the invisible hand of the free market from artificial restrictions in fact conflict with broader notions of human progress. In part, the debate concerns the speed of change envisaged; for the effects of a gradual liberalisation of trade or capital movements are likely to be much more positive than those of a sudden liberalisation. While there is little reason to doubt that the gradual lifting of trade restrictions since World War II has provided a significant boost to the economic wealth and welfare of almost all concerned, the rapid acceleration of globalisation since the 1980s promises to be more problematic. Aside from the problems associated with the shock of rapid liberalisation, however, the fiercest debate centres around the negative impact of the globalisation of trade and capital movements on the ability of democratic governments and nation states to exercise any effective control over the economic, social and environmental issues affecting their people. Even those who happily embrace the idea of a 'global village' and a common destiny for all mankind, and who are uninterested in the sovereignty of the nation state, tend to find some aspects of the evolution of a global free-trade zone troubling. For free trade threatens to render democratic governments impotent in their attempts to control or channel market mechanisms, and to make redundant their wish to set limits to the legitimate operation of the free market. There are many respects in which governments can only hope to intervene successfully in the market if their sovereign power is coterminous with the

extent of free capital movements and free trade. Since a global government is out of the question, a global free-trade zone is one where
mankind is increasingly powerless to use democratic means to redistribute wealth from rich to poor, to protect the environment, to safeguard
public goods or to reduce the social costs of economic growth. Global free
trade and free capital movements extend consumer choice and freedom
in one sense, but threaten to disenfranchise those without capital or skills
from any say in the future of their lives.

Many people, from the time of Johann Herder in the late eighteenth
century, have believed that true progress consists in the realisation of
nationhood – that is, in the improved ability of each people to control its
own destiny and sing its own national song. To such opponents of the
French Enlightenment belief that progress is the realisation of a single
global destiny for all mankind, there should be something deeply disquieting about the numbing uniformity of some aspects of the modern
global consumer market and culture, and something deeply troubling
about the growing powerlessness in the modern free-market world of
national self-determination over economic and social affairs. It seems
odd in this respect that the self-appointed guardians of national sovereignty on the right wing of the UK Conservative party should strenuously
oppose the pooling of sovereignty within the EU, and yet happily
embrace sovereignty-sapping global capital movements, global free trade
and the freedom of citizens to reduce their contribution to national rev-
enues by parking their money in offshore tax havens. For in the modern
era of globalisation, large regional units such as the EU or the USA are
the only political units which are sufficiently immune to international
trade (if not international capital movements) to maintain any effective
capacity to counteract the overbearing influence of the global free
market. Whereas the EU and the USA have only roughly 10 per cent of
their economies dependent directly on trade with the outside world, for
smaller countries the percentage may be between 30 and 60 per cent.
The destinies of small countries are hugely dependent on those of their
trading partners. Those who champion national (as opposed to regional)
sovereignty but also embrace free capital movements and free trade are
presumably quite content that globalisation will ensure that governments
are prevented from interfering effectively in the workings of the free
market. They may sincerely believe that globalisation will not only have
the obvious effect of allowing the rich to exploit their capital resources
more freely to their own best advantage, but that it will also help to maximise wealth for all. They must also believe that national sovereignty is

only of importance in such non-market areas as law and order and defence, and that the sole sovereign power in such essentially economic fields as employment rights or even cultural identity should be the global free market.

It was Adam Smith's *Wealth of Nations* which did much to establish the Anglo-Saxon presumption in favour of free trade, and it still represents one of the most passionate and cogently expressed arguments for the virtues of trade liberalisation. Smith argued that by expanding the opportunities for the division of labour and for specialisation, free trade could boost real wealth by allowing for a better allocation of resources:

> What is prudence in the conduct of every private family, can scarce be folly in that of a great kingdom. If a foreign country can supply us with a commodity cheaper than we ourselves can make it, better buy it of them with some part of the produce of our own industry, employed in a way in which we have some advantage. The general industry of the country, being always in proportion to the capital which employs it, will not thereby be diminished . . . but only left to find out the way in which it can be employed with the greatest advantage. It is certainly not employed to the greatest advantage, when it is thus directed towards an object which it can buy cheaper than it can make.[1]

Smith firmly believed that all attempts by a country to secure advantage for particular industries by trade restrictions would serve only to reduce 'the real value of the annual produce of its land and its labour'; for it would have the effect of reducing the total output for a given level of inputs, since capital and labour would be directed towards industries which were less efficient than their equivalents abroad, and away from industries which were more efficient than their equivalents abroad. Furthermore, because trade restrictions would reduce a country's 'revenue' (i.e., the value of its output), this would have the long-term effect of reducing the potential size of its industrial base, since capital investment can increase only in proportion to a country's total revenue. Smith argued that, by contrast, free trade would allow every country to specialise in its own areas of advantage, and to purchase the goods it wanted at the lowest available prices; this increase in efficiency would maximise the rate of future investment, which the invisible hand of the free market would then ensure was invested in the most productive way.

Smith's classic argument was taken a stage further by David Ricardo, in his theory of comparative advantage. This theory states that it is not merely beneficial for a country to specialise in those goods in which it has an absolute advantage over other countries, but also in those industries where it has a comparative advantage. One country may have an absolute productivity advantage in most or all of its products, but it will still be beneficial for it to engage in trade with less productive countries – by specialising in and exporting only those goods in which it has a comparative advantage (i.e., those goods in which its efficiency advantage over its competitors is greatest when compared with its efficiency advantage elsewhere) and by importing those goods where it has a comparative disadvantage (i.e., those in which its efficiency advantage is smallest). Similarly, it is advantageous for a relatively unproductive country (in absolute terms) to engage in trade, and to concentrate on those areas where its productivity disadvantage relative to other countries is smallest – thereby reducing the cost to it of being less productive. According to this theory, trade will allow all countries to improve their own internal opportunity-cost ratios; by allowing each country – after the necessary exchange-rate adjustments – to specialise in those industries in which it is relatively more productive, trade will boost the average productivity and hence the aggregate real wealth of every country.

The theory of comparative advantage remains the basis of the modern free-trade orthodoxy. Trade, like all other market exchange, is seen as mutually beneficial, while protectionism is thought to reduce efficiency and wealth. The costs of protectionism may be spread diffusely over all consumers, and therefore be less visible than the concentrated benefits of protectionism for the industry concerned; but at the aggregate level, it is generally believed that protectionism will reduce wealth. It is fair to assume that the huge growth in world trade since World War II, which resulted from the gradual liberalisation of trading practices, has indeed boosted world growth and raised living standards, as well as increasing the interdependence of trading countries. At the same time, trade has given consumers lower prices, by increasing competition, and – in some areas at least – has given them a greater choice of goods. It is unlikely, for example, that video recorders would have become either as cheap or as sophisticated in the European marketplace as they are today if European producers had not faced strong Japanese competition.

However, despite the compelling nature of Smith and Ricardo's theories, they have not met with universal assent. Throughout the last two hundred years, there has been an often fierce debate between those who agree that trade is beneficial on the whole but wish to manage it, and those who argue that it should be as free as possible. At various points many countries have sought to lower transition costs in their society by pursuing only a gradual and managed move to free trade. Some countries have also sought to protect infant industries with tariffs, subsidies or unofficial barriers to trade; and a prima facie case for such intervention can be made – particularly in high-technology industries – given the existence of increasing returns and imperfect competition. More generally, some commentators argue that the world as a whole would be better served at the end of the twentieth century by a system of regional trade blocs instead of global free trade; this, they argue, would combine many of the advantages of free trade within homogenous regional blocs with the advantages of managing trade between blocs which have radically different capital or labour structures.

There have always been three principal objections to all such managed or semi-protectionist policies. The first is the insistence by free-marketeers that no government can have the organisational capacity or detailed information necessary to manage the marketplace successfully. Adam Smith, for example, argued that under a system of natural liberty (and free trade):

> The sovereign is completely discharged from a duty, in the attempting to perform which he must always be exposed to innumerable delusions, and for the proper performance of which no human wisdom or knowledge could ever be sufficient; the duty of superintending the industry of private people, and of directing it towards the employments most suitable to the interest of the society.[2]

Secondly, free-traders following Smith argue that the pressures of free-trade competition are far more likely than protectionism to create the necessary conditions for success both in trade and in wealth creation, by fostering adaptation and innovation. Fear is a better nursemaid of enterprise than government help. The third general argument against managed trade is the manifest danger of its tipping into a retaliatory spiral of rising tariffs – a trade war. Even in the case of infant industries operating in conditions of increasing returns, intervention will only be successful if not matched by other trading partners. All too often, seemingly rational unilateral action sparks off tit-for-tat retaliation and a wasteful and inefficient spiral of tariffs or subsidies. Similarly a retreat to regional trade blocs protected by external tariffs may sound a good idea in theory, but any sudden erection of tariff barriers designed to achieve this could cause serious economic shocks, damaging both third parties and – when retaliation comes – those putting up the tariffs in the first place. It was an example of precisely this phenomenon in the 1930s which has since given protectionism such a bad name; a sudden surge in the level of tariffs worldwide, together with beggar-my-neighbour competitive currency devaluations, killed world trade, and was responsible for exacerbating (although not causing) the 1930s slump. There is little question that the uncoordinated and competitive erection of trade barriers can cause serious damage. It was to avoid this that the GATT (General Agreement on Trade and Tariffs) was set up after World War II, with the mission of coordinating the gradual international liberalisation of trade. This process was very successful in boosting trade in a way that, most agree, has been of net benefit to all concerned.

Several factors have combined since the late 1980s to rekindle the old debate, after forty years of successfully growing world trade and widespread consensus in favour of trade liberalisation. One was the new GATT agreement reached in 1993, which significantly increased the extent of free trade both geographically and in terms of the economic sectors within its scope. This would probably not have been very controversial had it not coincided with another factor, namely the seismic geopolitical changes of the years following 1988, when the fall of communism allowed Russia, Eastern Europe, Vietnam and even parts of China to enter the world economy, while other political and economic developments saw most of Latin America and India open up to the forces of globalisation. The free-trade zone, which previously included some 700 million mostly rich people, now included two to three billion more, many of whom were very poor. At the same time, and most crucially of all, exchange and capital controls in the OECD area had by 1993 been virtually eliminated, freeing capital to pursue the best investment opportunities wherever they were to be found. Free capital movements have raised the spectre of First World productive investment capital being increasingly diverted to high-return investment opportunities in the developing world, with a consequent reduction in productive investment in the developed countries themselves. The fear has grown that the combined impact of lower investment at home and increased cheap labour competition from the newly capitalist economies abroad may lead to further large rises in First World unemployment, or to large drops in the real wages of ordinary workers in developed countries. This process may be compounded by the simultaneous impact of new computer and communication technology, which is in itself lowering the requirement for labour while making it easier for multinational companies to spread their operations across the world. The multinationals are the main engine of the internationalisation of production; they have the capital and the corporate infrastructure to exploit the different advantages of a whole range of countries in their production. So the research for a product may be done in the UK, the electronics in the USA, and the physical product built in South-East Asia or Poland. As labour-intensive production moves out of the First World, the fear is that developed countries will be left with high unemployment and high government welfare spending – if the wages of the unskilled or semi-skilled do not fall sharply (i.e., in a regulated environment) – or, alternatively, with greater poverty – if wage-rates do fall (i.e., in an unregulated environment).

Adam Smith and David Ricardo argued that the increased wealth generated by an enlarged area of free trade would, in turn, generate increased investment (and hence jobs). It is crucial to note, though, that both Smith and Ricardo assumed that most of this extra investment would be in the capitalists' own countries, in their respective areas of comparative advantage; this would indeed make it likely that the greater wealth generated by trade would benefit the capitalists' own society as a whole. Increasingly, however, in the modern world, global capital flows allow productive investment to follow absolute advantage wherever it may be found. The danger for First World countries is that this may gradually transform them into *rentier* states, living largely off capital invested elsewhere, with home investment being directed only to a few high-value-added capital-intensive specialist industries which have a low general labour component of production. Those lucky enough to own the *rentier* capital, or to have the very special skills which remain essential to the rich countries' areas of absolute or comparative advantage, may do very well indeed. Those with fewer skills or capital may be left dependent either on welfare or on servicing the needs of the new global élite. Many middle-class occupations may be among those hit; for there are many pools of great talent in such areas as computer software and accountancy in populous, low-wage countries like India. Nor will exchange-rate depreciation necessarily come to the rescue of unskilled or semi-skilled First World labour, reducing the global price of this labour (and the purchasing power of its wages). For it may well be that, despite the absence of increased labour-intensive investment at home, the total wealth of the First World countries will continue to rise in aggregate, in the new larger free-trade area, given increasing returns on productive investment elsewhere, and new opportunities for the high-technology specialist industries that remain their areas of comparative advantage. This aggregate success may mask a serious maldistribution of the fruits of economic growth, as the wealthy get much richer and the poor get poorer; but despite this, the exchange rates of these rich though increasingly unequal countries may actually exacerbate the plight of the poor and unskilled by becoming stronger, owing to the persistence of strong current-account surpluses, based on specialist exports, investment income from abroad and very subdued demand at home from the millions of unemployed, under-employed and increasingly poor ordinary consumers. Many European countries, such as Switzerland and France, were (to differing degrees) in this position in the mid-1990s.

Trade liberalisation has, of course, always brought costs as well as benefits; in every country, those working in sectors in which their country does not have a comparative advantage will suffer, at least at first. Free-market economists argue that these short-term costs are far outweighed by the long-term benefits, and that as long as economies are not distorted by excessive labour rigidities and regulations, growth in the areas of specialisation resulting from trade will quickly absorb displaced labour. However, many economists hold that this faith in the efficiency and power of adaptation of the free-market system is only likely to be justified if the process of liberalisation is managed so as to reduce the speed of change and avoid economic shocks. Human beings adapt well, and markets clear efficiently, they argue, so long as the speed of transition is not too great. If the process is too rapid, there is a significant danger of hysteresis: capital stock may be quickly destroyed by sudden liberalisation when – given a little time to adapt – it might have competed well; furthermore, if unemployment rises too quickly, it may be impossible for people to retrain, and they may become discouraged and join the ranks of the long-term unemployed. The result may then be a smaller available pool of capital and labour, and hence a lower potential growth rate. At the same time, a fast change is more likely to necessitate socially and politically disruptive falls in wage levels in uncompetitive sectors and a widening of differentials in society. Even the great apostle of free trade, Adam Smith, allowed for the need for caution as to the speed of introducing liberalisation, arguing in *The Wealth of Nations* that: 'Humanity may in this case require that the freedom of trade should be restored only by slow gradations, and with a good deal of reserve and circumspection.' Observing that the money tied up in a newly disadvantaged industry might be lost to the owner for ever if liberalisation were introduced suddenly, Smith noted later in the same passage: 'The equitable regard, therefore, to his interest requires that changes of this kind should never be introduced suddenly, but slowly, gradually, and after a very long warning.'[3] It can be convincingly argued that the liberalisation of trade and capital movements after World War II was so successful and popular precisely because it was gradual, and because the countries which were party to it were, in the main, the large developed economies which all shared comparable economic structures and wage levels. By contrast, the liberalisation of the 1980s and 1990s is likely to have a much more dramatic short- and long-term impact, because of the sudden introduction into the free-trade system of so many developing countries whose workers in some cases earn less than 5 per cent of average European or US wages.

The standard economic assumption remains that these rapid latter-day moves to globalisation are in fact *un*likely to cause an economic shock in First World countries that would seriously damage growth *per se* and that, in practice, the problems of adjustment in developing countries are likely to slow the speed of change enough to ensure that liberalisation has a positive rather than disruptive impact on growth and profits. The converse may be true, however, if the difficulties experienced by developing countries in adapting quickly to the new global market are themselves significant enough to have a detrimental effect on world growth. The south-east Asian crisis of the late 1990s may be the first evidence that damaging shocks are more likely to come from this quarter than from within First World countries themselves. But fears on this score have not so far dented the conviction of the free-marketeers that trade liberalisation and the globalisation of capital markets will lead to higher growth rates, particularly in the economies with few wage rigidities (such as the USA and the UK).

Free-marketeers also argue that there is little direct evidence that greater free trade makes the distribution of wealth and income much more unequal. They point to a number of economic studies which purport to show that in the 1980s and early to mid 1990s the short-term direct effects of trade liberalisation on income differentials have been much less significant than the impact of supply-side reforms, such as lower marginal rates of income tax, cuts in welfare, and labour-market deregulation. However, this may be to miss the essential point. For while there is little reason to doubt that supply-side reforms have had a more significant impact in the short term on income differentials than has trade liberalisation itself, it is also clear that these supply-side reforms are themselves made all the more urgent by the increasing globalisation of the economy, and by the rigours of global competition; the social impact of these supply-side reforms therefore represents, to some extent at least, an indirect effect of trade liberalisation. Furthermore, it may still be legitimate to fear that these indirect effects of globalisation will in the long term be compounded by more direct effects of liberalisation, leading to a further socially dangerous widening of income differentials. Those with skills in the new technologies or in design or management should continue to do even better in a larger world and have more opportunity to exploit their skills to greater effect. Those with capital should also do well, as returns on new investment rise with the increased scope to exploit cheap labour in the developing world. By contrast, those without skills, or with outdated skills, will find themselves increasingly having to compete with labour from countries where wages are a small fraction of those in the developed world. This will be particularly true in the traded goods sector. But even in the service sector – the great white hope for employment – similar pressures will ensure that unskilled workers may not be able to command high wages; for it is in the service sector where the computer revolution is set to make the largest cost savings in labour from now on – partly because computers can perform many clerical functions more cheaply than people, but partly also because global computer networks enable many companies to transfer support functions to low-labour-cost regions on the other side of the world. Even in necessarily local and labour-intensive service sectors where computer technology is of little relevance, such as restaurants or road maintenance, the increasing numbers of workers displaced from other sectors, together with immigration pressures from low-wage countries, may ensure that the real value of unskilled wages tends to fall in developed countries. Over time, of course, skill levels in developed countries can improve, but this may not be enough to protect First World labour from an erosion of their wage levels; for skill levels will also improve in the developing world – in some cases more quickly, given superior secondary education.

The potential for a further significant widening of income differentials in developed countries over the next few decades, as a result of the recent step-change in the scale and impact of global free trade and free capital movements, is not simply a political and ethical issue. In continental Europe, where one-nation politics has dictated higher minimum wages, more employment protection and a more lavish welfare system than in the Anglo-Saxon world, the huge expansion of the global free-trade and free capital movement zone to include hundreds of millions of very poorly paid workers may exacerbate already seriously high levels of unemployment and government spending. Increased spending on unemployment may in turn result either in yet higher public debt levels and borrowing costs (thereby crowding out private investment and causing even more unemployment) or in yet higher taxes. The other possible course of action is sharp cuts in the level of government spending, and hence in the level of welfare protection. European countries may thus be faced with the choice between two unpalatable options: on the one hand, losing some of the growth dividend of increased trade, through being saddled with the high borrowing costs or high taxes that result from excessive government spending; or, on the other hand, increasing social tensions and divisions further by slashing welfare spending. Moreover, if European countries remain firmly embedded in the new global marketplace, they may have little choice but to take the second option. This is because, in the modern era of a mobile élite workforce and global capital flows, high taxes (particularly higher marginal tax rates) will lead to a damaging brain-drain, while high government borrowing will lead to penal rates of interest and lost capital investment. Governments have been left largely impotent in the new global marketplace – unable to answer their electorates' call for action to prevent the worst excesses of the free market.

The impact of the new freer trade and capital movements may also have negative consequences for many developing countries if the speed of transition is too great. In particular, the new global economy is leading to much more unequal – and in some cases politically explosive – distributions of income in developing countries, with fabulous wealth often living cheek by jowl with massive poverty. A particularly acute example of the problems caused by sudden liberalisation of markets is to be found in Eastern Europe where the shock therapy advocated by the West has meant enormous economic disruption, with the result that even by 1996 many countries had not yet got back to pre-1989 levels of output; but while many people in Russia and elsewhere have consequently become much poorer than they were before liberalisation, others in the same countries are nevertheless able to enjoy previously undreamed-of luxuries. In many former communist countries, dramatically widening wealth differentials are contributing to a rise in crime, and are increasing popular disaffection with liberal capitalism and even with democracy. At the same time, there is a danger in some populous developing countries that the extension of free trade in agriculture may hasten the demise of subsistence-level farming, and lead to a sudden and harmful large-scale migration of people from village to shantytown. In such ways, the head-long pursuit of growth and material progress – through rapid moves to free trade, global capital flows and free-market reforms – may indeed lead to what Joseph Schumpeter once called 'gales of creative destruction'.

Less than a decade after the momentous extension of the free market globally, it is still too early to establish conclusively whether or not the long-term impact on the welfare of most people in the developed and developing world will indeed be negative. But in trying to assess the nature and scale of the economic and social disruption likely to result from the sudden entry of so many emerging economies into a more com-prehensively free-trade system, it is illuminating to compare the situation now with that which pertained in the forty-five years before World War I. For that was the only other period prior to the late 1980s and the 1990s when the world enjoyed a boom in world trade predicated on rapidly growing emerging markets (chiefly, then, the USA), relatively free move-ment of capital and a general acceptance worldwide of market-oriented systems. Taking the period as a whole, the Old World (Europe) saw con-siderable growth. But the first twenty-five years of the period were characterised by serious deflation, high real borrowing costs and upheavals in the labour market. Deflation and depression began in the agricultural sector, as a result of a flood of cheap transatlantic grain in the 1870s from the low labour-cost and increasingly mechanised grain prairies of North America. The result was a dramatic drop in employment on the land in Europe. By 1914, the agriculture industry in the UK employed only 8 per cent of the working population, down from more than 25 per cent in 1870. Nor did these job losses and deflation allow cheap borrow-ing, for real interest rates were kept up by the high returns that could be made from investment in the New World.

If the parallels between the 1990s and the period from 1870 to 1914 are clear and disquieting, the differences are even more worrying. First, in the earlier period, Europe was able to cope with the employment shock resulting from the collapse of its agriculture sector by virtue of the mass emigration of the dispossessed to a sparsely populated emerging New World. Some 26 million people emigrated from Europe between 1880 and 1910.[4] Today, by contrast, First World countries are faced with immigration rather than emigration, potentially hastening the equalisa-tion of wages between developed and developing countries, and bringing additional social pressures. Secondly, Europe in the nineteenth century had little or no welfare system, so that deflation and unemployment did not lead governments to compete for scarce savings by having high public spending and high budget deficits, in the way they do now. Thirdly, Europe, and especially the UK, was a huge net lender to the emerging world in the nineteenth century, which assured it of a healthy return on capital invested in the growth opportunities elsewhere. Today, while some developed countries such as Japan, Switzerland and Holland are large net creditors, the major developed (G7) countries are in aggregate modest net borrowers from the world financial system. Lastly, in the late nineteenth century Europe responded to the economic dislocation which resulted from competition with the New World and Russia by introducing tariffs. Only the UK refused to go down this route, shielded as it was by earnings as financier and shipper to the world and, later, by the system of imperial preference. Today, the OECD area is, by contrast, still making progress towards tariff reductions. All these factors suggest that the dislocations may be even greater for the major developed economies in the coming years than they were for Europe in the late nineteenth century. The economies of today are more complex and less able to adapt quickly to change, in large part because the minimum protection thought acceptable for working people is now far higher.

It was following this period of upheaval in Europe and America in the late nineteenth century that there emerged a growing political consensus (coinciding with the advent of universal male suffrage) on the need for some protection for workers and help for the less fortunate, less successful and less clever. This led to the full legalisation of trade unions, and the gradual building of a welfare state based on redistributive taxation. It also helped pave the way – during the next economic depression (the slump of the 1930s) – for the Keynesian belief that government must try to find ways to improve the workings of the free market. In the area of free-trade theory itself, there were many from the nineteenth century onwards who were concerned about the distribution implications of free trade, and who doubted Adam Smith's contention that the invisible hand of the free market would ensure that new wealth cascaded down the social order from rich to poor – the elusive trickle-down effect.

As we have seen, the unequal distribution of the benefits of growth is one of the principal reasons for doubting that there is any exact equivalence between an increase in a society's wealth and a rise in its aggregate welfare or happiness. For it seems clear to most of us that an extra £1,000 will produce more happiness and additional welfare for a family on the breadline than for a billionaire tycoon. But if this common-sense proposition of diminishing marginal utility is true, it militates against the automatic assumption that just because a move towards greater free trade produces more wealth, it also leads to progress in the welfare of society as a whole. Indeed, if most of the new wealth accruing from a move to greater freedom of trade goes to the already rich, and the previously disadvantaged lose out further, the reverse is almost certainly the case. The problem remains, of course, that there is no way of calibrating scientifically the utility, happiness or welfare of one person against another, and hence no way of being sure that the extra wealth flowing from the liberalisation produces less utility etc. for those who benefit than the amount lost by those disadvantaged by the move.

Many economists wishing to avoid the unscientific imprecision of such interpersonal comparisons of utility in deciding between states of affairs have been drawn, as we saw in Chapter 6, to the Pareto criterion as a fairly uncontroversial guideline for judging the relative desirability of different outcomes. This criterion stipulates that a state is optimal or efficient when there is no alternative state in which any individual could be better off without someone else being worse off. We have seen that it is precisely this criterion which an equilibrium position can be shown theoretically to satisfy in the mythical 'perfect free market'. But although the Pareto criterion may offer some limited ethical justification for a theoretical perfect free-market equilibrium once established, it does not help free-marketeers to justify ethically a *move towards* a genuinely free market or free trade. It emphatically cannot be shown that the *transition* from a semi-protectionist system to a more genuinely free-trade system will constitute a Pareto improvement – in the sense of maximising the efficiency of the economy *without making anyone worse off*. For in any such transition from one system to a more free-market one, there will almost always be absolute losers as well as winners.

To get round this problem, some economists have followed J. S. Mill in proposing that compensation should be paid from those gaining from a transition to free trade to those losing out; so long as the gains from the transition are greater overall than the pre-compensation losses, the payment of compensation will allow a society as a whole to be better off as a result of a move to free trade without any individual being worse off. Such compensation payments are, of course, fiendishly difficult to devise in theory and to set up in practice; but this sort of reasoning did presumably underlie the general move earlier this century towards government-sponsored redistribution of income and wealth, through the tax system. A redistributive tax system, it could be argued, was a rough and ready way of ensuring that everyone benefited from changes which were in aggregate beneficial. In the 1980s and 1990s, however, the political consensus behind redistributive taxes has been unravelling. The new élite owners of capital and skills threaten to desert their countries and communities if any government dares to tax them heavily. As a result, the globalisation of jobs and capital has inflicted a potentially fatal blow to the ability of governments to ensure progress in welfare for all.

The dangers of hysteresis, of social dislocation and of growing government impotence in efforts to redistribute income and safeguard the welfare of the poor are not the only potential costs of sudden trade liberalisation. The move to global free trade also threatens to make it much more difficult, in the traded goods sectors of the economy, to set up the mechanisms required to combat environmental damage. If companies are subject to environmental regulations forcing them to adopt more costly production methods, they will – in a free-trade system – face competition from companies in other countries which do not impose such regulations. As a result, multinational companies may move production to areas not subject to strict controls, while companies too small to move production may go out of business. Some free-marketeers advocate dealing with the externalities of pollution or resource depletion by internalising them into the price mechanism, by means of pollution taxes or tradable quotas. But even this market solution (which might be workable within a regional bloc such as the EU or the USA) is rarely available in the traded goods sector of small countries in a global free-trade environment. For once again, companies which are made to internalise the externality will be disadvantaged in trade with those not being required to do so. As a result, free trade entails that measures to reduce the environmental costs of growth must be global (like the CFC ban) to create a level playing field. In practice, though, global agreements are extremely difficult to set up. It is particularly unlikely that sophisticated 'market' solutions like taxes or quotas can be used, since it is almost impossible to agree a global tax or quota regime. Furthermore, global free trade makes it more difficult for the EU or the USA to use trade concessions as a carrot to encourage environmental cooperation amongst all polluting countries. It seems clear that greater free trade is likely to make it significantly harder for mankind to reduce the environmental costs of economic growth.

The modern world has largely adopted a free-trade, free-market approach to the pursuit of economic growth and progress in human welfare. Much of the ultimate success of this strategy will depend on whether or not the large increase in liberalisation in the 1980s and 1990s does indeed produce higher economic growth. Even more will depend on whether any increase in economic growth can be bought at an acceptably low social and environmental cost. If the social and environmental costs of rapid liberalisation are deemed by the majority of people to be too high, the link between the achievement of higher economic growth and a widespread confident belief in human progress may finally be broken. Moreover, if governments are shown in the era of globalisation to be largely impotent in the face of these rising social and environmental costs, democracy itself may be a casualty of the free market. Our common global destiny may then be one of social strife and political turmoil. The invisible hand would finally have failed us.

CHAPTER 12

The Age of Self-Interest

The economy reigns supreme, determining political choices and the limits of social action. And the free market emerges as a leading ideology, fostering competition and an exaggerated, narcissistic individualism that equate the realm of values with the dictates of efficiency.

Fernando Henrique Cardoso, President of Brazil, UNDP
Human Development Report 1996

There is also the eternal question in economics of the relation of means to ends. Conscientious economists usually stress the point that their science is concerned with means only, and that it is for others to prescribe the ends. None the less it is hard to draw the line, especially when the economist concerns himself with practical issues. An idea as to what the appropriate ends are may lurk implicit in his recommendation.

R. F. Harrod, *The Life of John Maynard Keynes*

Ethics and Economics

Economics is the study of human behaviour in the production and distribution of wealth. Most economic analysis purports to be a scientific study of how the economy actually works, and of what the practical effects of any particular policy would actually be. Such 'positive' economics is concerned with the efficacy of the means society employs to achieve the goals, or ends, it has set itself. It is concerned with such questions as whether intervention or deregulation are the best means to the end of decreasing unemployment, and whether money-supply targeting is a credible means to the end of controlling inflation. Economists usually seek to draw a sharp distinction between positive economics and normative questions, in an effort to preserve their science from fraught ethical issues – such as what the aims of society should be and which means to these ends are morally acceptable. Economists wish to avoid making value judgements about what economic changes constitute human progress. Society's goals and the moral acceptability of different methods should, they argue, be determined by the political process or by social ethics; the economist's job is merely to expedite the goals set, within the constraint of using only those methods found morally acceptable.

Although such an analytical distinction between positive and normative questions is, in itself, intellectually valid, it is frequently misleading to assume that – when it comes to considering practical issues – the discipline of economics can be completely isolated from ethical questions. In the complicated reality of everyday issues, there can often be no sharp distinction between consideration of suitable means and of desirable ends, nor between the legitimate sphere of economics and that of politics and morality. This is not merely because so many economists, however objective their analysis claims to be, are in fact passionate advocates of particular goals. It is also because an objective scientific recommendation to adopt any given economic mechanism, with a view to meeting a particular goal efficiently, will often have very significant implications for the ability of society to meet other goals; quite apart from any differences in the efficacy of different mechanisms in reaching the particular goal, there may also be enormous differences in the knock-on effects of the respective mechanisms on other social aspirations and even the moral values of society. This is the case, for example, with different recommendations – such as for more deregulation or for more government intervention – which are made by economists when addressing the goal set for them by politicians of reducing unemployment and boosting economic growth; the deregulation of the labour market, the abolition of a minimum wage and the weakening of trade union power may indeed lower unemployment more effectively and efficiently than government intervention, but it may do so at the expense of social cohesion and solidarity, with a massive widening of income differentials and a deterioration in the security and working conditions of large numbers of people. Choices of economic method may masquerade as simple questions of efficiency, but they often have a fundamental bearing on the kind of society we live in. This is particularly true when the method chosen is a free-market policy, such as the globalisation of capital flows and global free trade; for then society becomes ruled by the goddess TINA – There Is No Alternative. The moral values of our society and the very goals of human progress become dictated by the obligatory quest for efficiency, as companies are forced into a spiral of ever more ruthless cost-cutting in order to remain competitive. It is this which makes the formal distinction between economics and ethics sometimes disingenuous and often dangerous.

For reasons explored earlier in the book, the eighteenth-century theories of Adam Smith and the separate philosophy of the utilitarians taken together helped to fashion an implicit acceptance in Western liberal democracies of the need to subordinate many overtly ethical considerations to the narrower considerations of economic efficiency. This was, however, no part of Smith's own intention. In *The Wealth of Nations*, he was acutely sensible, for example, of the potentially alienating effect of the division of labour on the minds and souls of working people, and he advocated compulsory education designed to give citizens the intellectual and moral wherewithal to withstand the pressures of industrialisation. Moreover, as the author also of *The Theory of Moral Sentiments*, which stressed the key role of sympathy and benevolence in creating a cohesive society, there is clear evidence that Smith implicitly assumed that the free pursuit by individuals of their own self-interest would serve the public interest only if it occurred within a cohesive and morally disciplined society. It was in this context that Smith argued that social cooperation and cohesiveness would be further reinforced by the motive of self-interest: for, thanks to the division of labour, it would indeed be in everyone's self-interest to engage in mutually advantageous cooperative transactions. Nevertheless, the assumption by Smith of such a social and moral background was of less lasting influence than his detailed account of the free-market mechanism; it was this account which, when taken out of the context of his other views, did appear to promise that the market expression by individuals of their own self-interest, in a framework of justice and perfect competition, would be sufficient to further the economic interests of society as a whole. The invisible hand of the free market could on its own ensure an outcome which fully exploited all the potential benefits from market exchange to the mutual advantage of all the participants in the market. Here, it seemed to many people, was a morally attractive outcome, brought about with maximum individual freedom, without government intervention and – in the sphere of economic activity at least – without the explicit need for moral motives. Indeed, self-interest and competition were shown to be positively beneficial, and a system of natural liberty for individuals was shown to be compatible with the good of society as a whole.

Over the one hundred and fifty years following the publication of *The Wealth of Nations* in 1776, the classical economic framework which Smith did so much to set up became ever more imbued with the methodology, and (implicitly at least) much of the ethical content, of utilitarianism. For the invisible hand had an obvious relevance for the utilitarian's desire to move from the supposed psychological observation that everyone freely aims at their own happiness to the moral principle that an action is morally good if it leads to the greatest happiness of the greatest number. The invisible hand seemed to show that the utilitarian moral principle would not demand too much of self-interested individuals, and – most important of all – that it could be compatible with a full measure of natural liberty. If happiness were defined as the satisfaction of desires, and if the key desires of all individuals were expressed in the marketplace, and if, further, the invisible hand promised the efficient maximisation of the desire-satisfaction of everyone within the confines of a process of mutually beneficial exchange, then surely the free market was an important tool in the armoury of the utilitarian. Moreover, if this was the case, utilitarianism's attractiveness as a moral doctrine could – to some extent at least – attach to the invisible hand of the free market. It was this symbiosis of classical economics and utilitarianism, together with the paramount value attached by nineteenth-century liberals to individual freedom from coercion, which was responsible for the implicit acceptance by many that the free-market system had genuine ethical content. Free-market liberalism came to be seen as a valid social ideology, as well as an economic methodology. The invisible hand appeared to go a long way towards squaring the circle between the moral requirement for individual liberty and the distinctively utilitarian moral requirement to pursue the greatest happiness of the greatest number.

Utilitarianism, however, has drawbacks as an ethical system, and some of these drawbacks were to be shared by free-market economics when elevated implicitly to the status of a moral ideology. Utilitarianism holds that only consequences matter, and that the moral content of the motivations of individuals is secondary to the moral content of the outcome of their actions. If, for example, the free market were genuinely to maximise the interests of the greatest number by harnessing the selfish motives of individuals, so much the better; it is the outcome that matters, not the moral attractiveness of the motivations of individuals. Utilitarianism also holds that ends can justify means, and that the sacrifice of some individuals' welfare for the good of the greatest number can be acceptable.

Individual rights and moral codes have only derivative status or instrumental value, and *can* be compromised if the total consequences of doing so, all things considered, are positive.

In classical economics, within a given structural framework or free-market system, a free-market equilibrium does *not* demand that the interests of any party to the process of exchange should be sacrificed; people only freely enter into a market transaction if it is to their own mutual advantage to do so. This means, of course, that a free-market equilibrium does not come close to maximising the utility or wellbeing of the greatest number; it can only maximise utility within the constraint of *not* being able to make anyone worse off. In this sense, the free market respects the autonomy of individuals far more than utilitarianism does, but at the cost of losing much of the attractiveness of the utilitarian doctrine; for those who are disadvantaged in the initial distribution of income, wealth or abilities may remain so even if some redistribution of income would maximise utility. However, while the mythical perfect free-market system does not entail that anyone operating within it will become worse off through the voluntary process of mutually beneficial exchange, it is important to note that, by contrast, the dynamic evolution of a free-market system (involving changes to the structural framework of law and tax within which the market operates) can entail that individuals become worse off than they were before – sometimes severely so. So, for example, when governments choose to move to a more genuinely free market (e.g., in trade), and choose not to intervene to safeguard groups which suffer from the consequent changes in supply and demand, they are in effect choosing to sacrifice the interests of the few to the interests of the many. In the liberal *laissez-faire* economic creed, intervention to safeguard the welfare of disadvantaged elements in society is seen as compromising the goal of greater efficiency, while deregulation (often the removal of protection for disadvantaged groups) is seen to improve efficiency; and since maximising average wealth has become (on implicit utilitarian grounds) the paramount moral goal, the efficient maximisation of wealth for society as a whole is given priority over safeguarding the interests or respecting the rights of the few.

Any discussion of the moral advantages and disadvantages of a free-market ideology must judge such implicit ethical positions against the explicit framework of pure ethical theories other than utilitarianism. For a number of other ethical systems challenge the maximising, consequentialist nature of utilitarianism and (implicitly) of liberal economics, with their lack of intrinsic interest in the moral motivations or the rights of individuals. Some moral philosophers, for example, attach paramount importance to the moral quality of individual motivations, and to the moral integrity of individual agents. They hold that it is vital not only that the results of our actions are in fact benign, but also that our actions are motivated by dispositions, such as altruism and benevolence, which are in themselves virtuous. They consider it important to have virtuous people as well as virtuous outcomes. Other philosophers argue that since ideal virtues, such as altruism and brotherly love, are unattainable on a universal basis, it is essential to recognise the importance of self-interest as a major part of individual motivation, the better to control it. To achieve this control, they may attach primary importance to individuals following an ethical code of practice which sets absolute boundaries both to the free pursuit of individual self-interest and to the maximisation of the welfare of the greatest number. Such ethical codes can be seen as embodying either objective moral truth or the collective wisdom of a civilisation. They ensure that individuals do not have to try to work out the particular consequences of each and every individual action, which is often an impossible task. They also require of individuals that sometimes they should consciously sacrifice their own self-interest, and require of communities that they should sometimes forgo the greatest good of the greatest number, in deference to the moral integrity of individuals, and the rights and welfare of the potentially disadvantaged.

Many moral philosophers place their primary emphasis on individual rights which operate as constraints on the maximisation by others of their self-interest. They may follow Kantian ethics in stipulating that people should never be treated as a means to an end, but should always have the right to be treated as important ends in themselves. If, for example, people are seen as having a right to wellbeing, as well as to life and liberty, such a principle implies that a minority should never have their own right to wellbeing sacrificed in order to promote the interests of the majority. This could entail that when a change is effected, such as a move to free trade or to a more advanced form of computer technology, which impacts negatively upon the livelihoods of some people while boosting the average wealth of most, those who gain from the move should compensate those who lose out. In this non-utilitarian view, progress for society as a whole should never be to the detriment of the minority.

Pure utilitarians do, of course, frequently argue for redistribution of wealth in favour of the disadvantaged on the grounds of the diminishing marginal utility of wealth (i.e., that £1,000 is worth more to a pauper than to a millionaire). But this utilitarian argument for redistribution is based on the desire to maximise the welfare or happiness of everyone taken together, not on any recognition of the rights of individuals to a particular level of welfare. Utilitarians do allow individuals the right to an equal weighting in the calculation of total utility, but this in no way implies any right to a certain share of utility. Free-market economics, moreover, has carefully denuded itself of even the diminishing marginal utility argument for redistribution. This is, in part, because the comparison of utility between individuals is held not to be sufficiently scientific; there is no scientific calibration of diminishing marginal utility, and no scientific proof, therefore, that redistribution would maximise welfare. Moreover, since redistributive taxation or regulations (e.g., a minimum wage) would potentially interfere with the efficient operation of the free-market mechanism, liberal economists have strong 'scientific' objections to redistribution as necessarily compromising efficiency and distorting incentives. As a result, even though liberal economics was elevated to the status of ideology because of its claim to further the interests of society as a whole, its ability to fulfil this claim is in fact severely limited by the self-imposed constraint of being unwilling to intervene actively to reduce initial disparities of wealth. It may be that this limitation is often ignored in political debate precisely because liberal economics has the useful attribute as an implicit ideology of claiming to have proven scientifically that the free pursuit of self-interest should never be compromised. As Keynes expressed it, liberal economics has the advantage, from the point of view of the wealthy and the business community, that it can 'explain much social injustice and apparent cruelty as an inevitable incident in the scheme of progress, and the attempt to change such things as likely on the whole to do more harm than good'.[1] Liberal economics is a very convenient ideology for the lucky few.

A further crucial feature of utilitarianism is that it purports to provide a common currency for all moral judgements; it suggests that moral conflicts can be solved simply by calculating the effects of the different possible choices on the total amount of what is valuable – e.g., happiness or desire-satisfaction. Most people would agree that it is a patent misconception that all desires are directly comparable, and that the satisfaction of all desires can be placed on a one-dimensional scale of quantitative value and summed arithmetically. But on this point, economics appeared to come to the rescue of utilitarianism. For here, surely, was a system which did assign a comparable value in a single unit of account (i.e., money) to all goods and services purchased to satisfy market-expressed desires. Now, if all important desires were efficiently expressed in a free market ('the market knows best') and efficiently catered for by the operation of the free-market mechanism through economic activity, then measures of economic growth might seem genuinely to represent the growth of the total level of anticipated desire-satisfaction, with an aggregate valuation objectively derived from the prices paid by the consumers of the relevant output. If, furthermore, the satisfaction of desires were to be acceptable as an adequate definition of welfare or happiness, then we would be free to conclude that measures of economic growth do genuinely represent measures of progress in welfare or happiness. It is essentially such a conclusion which implicitly underlies the exaltation of economic growth in modern Western societies to the status of paramount political and even moral goal.

However, as this book has demonstrated, the simple equation of economic growth with progress in welfare is a fallacy for many reasons; it is a fallacy because so many important human desires are for non-traded goods (e.g., the absence of pollution or the presence of community spirit), and because desires which are not expressed in the marketplace are more likely to be compromised than satisfied by economic growth in a free-market system; it is also a fallacy because – even among those desires which are expressed and satisfied in the marketplace – we do not wish to accord moral weight on the same scale to rational desires (e.g., for food), irrational or antisocial desires (e.g., for pornography) and created desires (e.g., for fashion accessories) merely on the basis of their relative financial weight in the market; furthermore, equating economic growth with progress in welfare is a fallacy because the financial weight given to desires in the marketplace is a function as much of the wealth of the purchasers as of the strength of the desires of the individuals concerned, so that economic growth is primarily a measure of the desire-satisfaction of the rich; and, finally, it is a fallacy, more generally, because the existence of market failure, of coordination problems and of radical uncertainty limits the connection between the market expression of preferences and the meeting of people's true social preferences. And yet despite all this, the fallacy that 'the market knows best' and that economic growth is essentially synonymous with progress in welfare lives on, and is responsible, in part at least, for the tragic narrowing of our conception of human progress. In our scientific and money-driven age, desires for goods which are not valued in monetary terms are increasingly ignored and left out of the social and economic equations of life. The only ultimate value we recognise is that implied by market price.

Individualism and the Death of Society

Much of the focus of this book has been on the limitations of the free-market mechanism. We have explored the lack of connection between market efficiency and distributive equality, the failure of the free-market system to cater for public goods (such as clean air), and the difficulty of making the free market inclusive of externalities such as pollution, congestion and resource depletion. We have also sought to understand why, on so many important occasions, the market fails to reach the optimal equilibrium promised by classical free-market economics. For many commentators, however, it is not these limitations and failures of scope of the invisible hand which most threaten to turn the free-market mechanism from being a powerful generator of progress into a threat to human welfare and the public interest. Nor is it directly the mistaken elevation by some people of free-market economic methodology to the status of moral ideology, underwritten by the ethical doctrines of utilitarianism and of natural liberty. Instead it is the connected tendency of free-market economies to undermine the time-honoured moral and ethical framework of society itself. The insistence by free-market economists and politicians that the unbridled pursuit of self-interest is crucial for the generation of wealth and economic progress can foster an exaggerated emphasis on selfish individualism which, in turn, damages the traditional social fabric which has held together our societies for generations.

Some utilitarian philosophers have argued that all individuals do in fact pursue their own happiness as the sole goal of all their actions, and this narrow picture of individuals as self-interested utility maximisers is the central assumption built into free-market economics about what constitutes the 'rational' behaviour of 'economic man'. Moreover, as we have seen, free-market economics claims to prove that such self-interested behaviour furthers the public interest, so long as it is exercised in conditions of unfettered competition. This narrow view of self-interest as the only important motivation of individuals is unconvincing even in the analysis of the workings of the economy. For there is plenty of evidence to show that other types of motivation and emotion are also important to economic success. A sense of duty and a solid work ethic, for example, are usually features of successful capitalist economies, such as

nineteenth-century Britain and twentieth-century Japan. Thrift and fru-
gality, as Adam Smith emphasised, are important for the generation of a
healthy rate of savings and capital investment. Trust is crucial to the success of economic relationships, such as that between managers and
workers or between companies and their suppliers, and honesty is the
essential lubricant to a system of exchange. If trust and honesty mean anything, it is that individuals will be motivated by them to suspend the
continual quest for personal advantage in certain key situations. Where
trust and honesty break down, society and individuals will have to spend
a large part of their energy and resources in formulating detailed prescriptive rules and contracts, and then even more resources in enforcing
them. Francis Fukuyama argues, in his book, *Trust – The Social Virtues and
the Creation of Prosperity*, that the growing absence of trust and honesty in
society is directly responsible for the huge rise in legal costs and in spending on crime prevention, security guards and prison maintenance, all of
which constitute a form of tax on other economic activity. Fukuyama
argues that, in future, it will be those countries with the highest levels of
trust and social cooperation which will do best economically. To many
observers, though, the maintenance of such social and moral attributes in
a modern society ruled by free-market ideology appears increasingly difficult to engineer. There is growing evidence to support the prediction
made by Schumpeter in 1942 that the ideology of capitalism would gradually undermine the 'pre-capitalist' social and moral supports on which
capitalism itself was founded, and upon which it relied for success.

The damage caused to the social fabric of society by the cult of individual self-interest is of greater concern to most people than its
detrimental impact on the capacity for economic growth. It is, of course,
a highly contentious question whether the growth of antisocial behaviour
and the gradual breakdown of community values is primarily the result of
the rhetoric and reality of free markets, or the result of a quite separate
breakdown of the religious and moral framework of society. But it would
seem strange if the all-pervasive free-market ideology of the last twenty
years had not had some effect. The glorification of the free pursuit by
individuals of their own gratification, together with the frequent insistence by free-marketeers on the need for the liberation of the individual
from artificial social bonds (such as a redistributive tax system, or trade
union membership), has made respectable, as never before, the selfish
and single-minded quest for individual advantage. Even the British
prime minister, Margaret Thatcher, found her role as apostle of the free
market more compelling than her position as figurehead for a cohesive

society when she expressed the view that: 'There is no such thing as Society. There are individual men and women, and there are families.'[2] Would it be surprising if such rhetoric indirectly contributed to individualism in areas other than legitimate economic activity? If individual material success becomes seen as the principal goal, and if social duty and collective obligations come to be seen as largely irrelevant to the creation of that material success, can we wonder that more and more individuals have seen fit to further their own interests through antisocial behaviour or crime? If redistributive taxation is seen to be an unnecessary and immoral evil rather than a contribution by the successful to the nation that nurtured them, can we wonder at the growth of the black market and of tax evasion and avoidance by the wealthy?

It is likely, of course, that economic realities have had a more damaging effect on the social fabric of society than has the rhetoric of free-market apostles and politicians. But, as this book has attempted to explain, many of these realities have also become increasingly deleterious. The growing importance in affluent societies of the relative income advantage required to secure status and positional goods (such as weekend cottages or golf club membership), and to buy relief from the ill-effects of physical and social congestion, has had the effect of transforming economic activity from a cooperative to a competitive venture. Our fellow market participants are no longer seen as the mutually dependent partners in wealth creation that Adam Smith envisaged, but as rivals to be defeated in the race to succeed. Our fellow citizens have become the obstacles to our success and happiness. During the 1980s and 1990s, as the advent of new technologies and global competition has increased unemployment, particularly in Europe, work has also been transformed from a cooperative venture into a competitive struggle by individuals to outdo their colleagues and so be left out of the next wave of redundancies. Furthermore, the rise of long-term unemployment among the unskilled, at a time of financial pressure to reduce the social welfare net, has resulted in the creation of an alienated underclass of poverty and despair. In France these unfortunate people are given the name '*les exclus*' – an apt description of their effective disenfranchisement from society and from the market process which was supposed to optimise their interests. At the same time, globalisation is further weakening the social ties between companies and their communities, and between the wealthy élite and their countries. Companies, if they are to survive, are having to close long-established factories in their traditional neighbourhoods and shift the work to cheap-labour emerging countries.

Meanwhile, the élite few with the mobile capital and skills which are ever more valuable in the global environment are increasingly able and willing to evade the tax obligations of their home countries. The so-called global village is not a community, but an asocial void in which individuals and companies have no duties but their own self-interest, and must compete vigorously to survive.

It would be quite wrong, of course, to succumb to nostalgia for a mythical past when people were motivated not by self-interest but by altruism, brotherly love and solidarity. It is much more valid, though, to mourn the passing of strong communities and feelings of civic duty and corporate loyalty. As J. L. Mackie points out, in his book, *Ethics – Inventing Right and Wrong*, people have always been motivated by a mixture of egoism and 'self-referential altruism' or 'confined generosity', in other words, not only by their own self-interest, but also by the interests of those with whose fate they empathise – family, colleagues, local people and even (to some extent) fellow countrymen. Social behaviour and generosity thus depend on individuals belonging to communities. But modern life, and the modern global economy, demands a mobile workforce and mobile capital that break up long-standing companies, sunder communities and split families. Very few people work with their neighbours, as they did in the old agricultural, mining and mill communities of the past. The motor car, too, must take some of the blame for the breakdown of communities, for it has allowed people to live much more atomised lives – not using the local shop but the hypermarket ten miles away, not sharing the bus and chatting together but inching forward in traffic jams, hooting and swearing at one another. It is this loss of community which is one of the salient features of the late twentieth century, and it is this loss which must take much of the blame for the breakdown of the social ethos. Human society has for generations resembled – from an individual's point of view – a series of concentric circles: individual, family, extended family, colleagues, village, region and country. But now many people have no meaningful circles around them, apart from the globe itself. They are alone, with selfishness their only relevant creed.

Some of the blame for the disintegration of a clear social and moral framework in which individuals can pursue their business must attach to the growing secularisation of our society. For it is only in the last two generations that a majority in many Western societies stopped being practising believers in organised religion. Religions provide an objective framework of moral codes and personal rules. They buttress the individual conscience against the temptations to dishonesty or antisocial behaviour, and they provide a spiritual and non-material dimension to people's aspirations. The avowedly secular J. M. Keynes himself wondered whether the slow demise of religious belief would not weaken the moral fabric of society, as revealed in this entry from Virginia Woolf's diary, dated 19 April 1934:

> Morality. And J. M. [Keynes] said that he would be inclined not to demolish Christianity if it were proved that without it morality is impossible. 'I begin to see that our generation – yours and mine V., owed a great deal to our fathers' religion. And the young, like Julian, who are brought up without it, will never get so much out of life. They're trivial: like dogs in their lusts. We had the best of both worlds. We destroyed Christianity and yet had its benefits.'[3]

It was a core belief of most Enlightenment and Bloomsbury intellectuals that mankind would flourish when human reason was liberated from the prejudices of religious dogma. But Keynes increasingly appears to have been right to suspect that the benefits of such freedom were greatest in the period of transition from a religious to a secular age, when reason was liberated but the individual conscience was still schooled in the lessons of guilt and people's aspirations were still tinged with a hint of the spiritual.

Coincident with the slow demise of religion in the twentieth century has been a gradual collapse in the humanist belief in the objective status of moral values. It is not just faith that no longer promises to reveal a simple transcendent truth; reason and intuition, too, increasingly seem powerless to map out an objective system of moral truth which exists entirely independently of our subjective views. G. E. Moore defined 'good' as a 'non-natural quality' which can be known only by intuition, and held that the only things that were good in themselves were 'the enjoyment of beautiful objects' and 'the pleasures of human intercourse' – a typically Bloomsbury definition. But any such definition can be objected to by someone who claims that their intuition reveals to them that the fundamental premise of ethics should be quite different – based, perhaps, on inalienable rights or classical utilitarianism. Reason can, of course, be applied in ethical debate to make arguments coherent and consistent, but it does not appear any more able than intuition to establish beyond doubt the basic premises of morality. Reason can analyse what the different results of applying different moral principles would be in different real-life situations, and assess these results with reference to customary values, but it cannot seem to provide an ultimately objective and irrefutable action-guiding justification for one system over another. The recent shift in the ethical consensus from a belief in the objective reality of moral truths to various shades of subjectivism must also have played its part in undermining the importance attached to strict moral codes. At its extreme, some people have adopted a relativist position – that moral beliefs depend on particular social practices and norms, and that there are no absolute criteria by which alternative views can be criticised. Others have adopted the less extreme position that, while there are some basic moral principles and obligations which have the quasi-objective status of accepted canons of behaviour (i.e., which – to a great extent at least – we all share and jointly affirm), these principles and obligations can nonetheless never be established beyond doubt by reason, nor even be reduced to a single, complete and logically coherent whole. Our aims, our rights and our duties are irresolvably diverse, and the goals we value often clash with each other. If this is true, then it would seem rational to let democratic governments decide on the detail of our social obligations, and arbitrate between the conflicting requirements of our various shared social goals, while letting the free-market mechanism cater for our diverse individual goals.

It is not, however, only the moral framework in which we live our lives and pursue our self-interest which has fragmented in the twentieth century. The capacity for government action to further certain social goals and enforce social obligations has also been increasingly called into question. In the field of macro-economic demand management, particularly, there has been a growing awareness of the need for humility about the capacity of government to engineer a particular market outcome. But even where there seem to be relatively straightforward roles for government in the areas of social welfare or environmental protection (for example, in agreeing a redistributive element to taxation or setting up pollution taxes), the globalisation of markets threatens to emasculate our elected representatives. In a global free market, the rich, if taxed heavily to help their less fortunate fellow citizens, will go elsewhere; the polluters, if made to pay for the damage they cause, will either go out of business competing with those in countries where they do not have to pay, or will move their factories. When the geographic reach of a democratic government's sovereign power is no longer coterminous with the extent of the free movement of the capital and goods of its people, elected politicians are left powerless to constrain many of the worst excesses of the free market. As a result, at the same time as the moral framework for society is fragmenting, the ability of democratic governments to design and implement a rational framework within which the free market can safely operate is also being reduced.

For some people, the erosion of religious dogma and prescriptive moral codes, and the advent of 'small government', is a cause for celebration. Individuals are free once more – free from coercion by priests or the nanny state, free to pursue their own self-interest, free to live according to their own chosen morality and free from the suffocatingly cohesive social and moral order of the bygone era. But freedom has always been an ambiguous concept, in theory and in practice. Many people would argue that freedom has no meaning unless it includes an element of empowerment. Those disadvantaged or ignored by the new liberal order may have little or no effective freedom of choice if they are poorly educated or are left penniless as a result of changes outside their control. More generally, one person's right to freedom of action may clash with another person's right not to be harmed. Indeed, in our increasingly interconnected and congested world, surprisingly few actions by individuals are without important consequences for others. As a result, particularly if we cease to be self-motivated to consider the interests of others, and cease to follow customary social codes and moral etiquette, the state will increasingly be forced to legislate or arbitrate in order to prevent the pursuit of our conflicting self-interests descending into a Darwinian struggle for survival and into social anarchy. So, for example, if people do not consider the effect of building extensions to their houses on their neighbours' access to light, or if unscrupulous landlords feel no compunction about maximising returns by converting pubs situated in quiet residential areas into noisy all-night discothèques, then society has no choice but to adopt a cumbersome and intrusive planning and noise-abatement bureaucracy to protect its citizens. So too, if the self-interest of newspaper journalists and proprietors frequently dictates that they break normal codes of decency and integrity and invade the privacy of ordinary citizens to sell stories of no legitimate public interest, then the state may be forced to curtail the ancient liberty of free speech. In this age of self-interest, the decline of community spirit and codes of moral decency can often necessitate 'bigger government' and greater state interference in our lives.

In the 1980s and 1990s, the most significant extensions of state power and erosion of individual liberties have been in the area of law and order. The causes of the huge crime wave in North America and Europe, from Los Angeles to Moscow, are, of course, very complex. Some of the blame, though, must surely attach to the substantial increase in income and wealth differentials, and the simultaneous decline in the absolute incomes and job prospects of the poorest sections of society, which have been the inevitable result of the rigours of global competition and rapid deregulation. To the extent that this is true, the very enlargement of the economic freedom of individuals to pursue their own self-interest, without interference, has had the direct corollary of restricting personal liberty outside the marketplace. Even the wealthiest in society have their lives increasingly hedged about by the need for more and more personal and domestic security; some of their wealth must be spent on panic alarms, locks and grilles for every window, anti-burglar devices for every car, and even private security guards.

The crime wave is also due, in part, to the decline of a strong moral code backed by religion. An active individual conscience and the eye of God are always the most effective policemen. When the state is increasingly forced to take over the role that was formerly performed to a large extent by religious sanctions and by each individual's moral conscience, it can only do so by assuming considerable powers of surveillance which intrude further and further into our everyday lives. A modern state often resorts to such devices as closed-circuit television cameras and phone-tapping, to an extent which brings modern reality closer to George Orwell's *1984* than we would like to admit. Because of the decline of social ethics, and the increase of relative and absolute poverty, we all have to accept organised intrusion into our privacy, and watch as the state arms itself with weapons which could allow an unscrupulous government grossly to abuse our individual liberties. At the same time, traditional peer-group pressure to conform to moral standards, and the practical support of tight-knit communities in times of hardship, is gradually giving way to a society reliant on impersonal 'sneak' telephone lines which enable one neighbour to report another to the authorities without even knowing his name. As communities and social ethics have crumbled, the state is left to enforce an ever-growing body of laws designed to control the worst excesses of our individualistic and selfish behaviour. It is far from clear that 'big government' will be any more successful in the area of law and order than it has been whenever government has attempted to control every nuance of our economic lives.

Progress in Doubt

Belief in progress has been a salient feature of most of the period since 1776 – the year of the American Declaration of Independence and the publication of Adam Smith's *Wealth of Nations*. The enormous strides made by human reason in scientific understanding and by human ingenuity in technological advance have seemed to promise man almost unlimited scope to understand and control his predicament. At the same time, the ability of the free market to harness self-interest in the pursuit of economic growth has seemed to promise an everlasting improvement in material prospects and welfare for society as a whole. All that was additionally required to assure us of success was a strong framework of morality and social cohesiveness, and strong enlightened democratic government. With such a framework firmly in place in Western liberal democracies at least, there seemed every reason to believe that both the growing power of reason to control nature and the creative power of self-interest to promote wealth would serve the interests of all.

Since 1973, however, the prevailing mood of optimism has gradually become tinged with doubt, anxiety and pessimism. As the frontiers of science advance into ever more specialised compartments, there are doubts about the nature and scope of progress in knowledge itself, and about the ability of mankind fully to understand and predict the effects of tampering ever more comprehensively with the complex systems of life. There is a growing fear that we have neither the wisdom nor the moral capacity to use the enormous extension of power granted by science to good effect and to the benefit of the majority. Moreover, as the limitations of the free-market mechanism as a generator of human progress are becoming more apparent, and the dangers of an ideology of self-interest become clearer, we are suddenly discovering that the framework in which the free market was supposed to operate – that of strong democratic government and a cohesive social and moral fabric – is crumbling. The free market is devouring the social, moral and institutional supports on which our future depends, just as remorselessly as it is squandering our resources and threatening the physical environment. Man, for all his brittle sophistication, stands on the edge of chaos.

As the belief in progress ebbs, there will be many who chastise the pessimists and doomsayers, and accuse them of sapping the energy of human endeavour. It is often argued that a belief in progress is an essential prerequisite for progress. It is the secular equivalent of the Christian belief in the Second Coming; our minds and our sense of duty are engaged in the project of preparing for the glorious salvation to come. J. B. Bury concludes his history of the idea of progress with this thought:

Consideration for posterity has throughout history operated as

a motive of conduct, but feebly, occasionally, and in a very limited sense. With the doctrine of Progress it assumes, logically,
a preponderating importance; for the centre of interest is
transferred to the life of future generations who are to enjoy
conditions of happiness denied to us, but which our labours
and sufferings are to help to bring about . . . [If] it is held that
each generation can by its own deliberate acts determine for
good or evil the destinies of the race, then our duties towards
others reach out through time as well as through space, and
our contemporaries are only a negligible fraction of the 'neighbours' to whom we owe obligations.[4]

Such a viewpoint might have been valid in 1920 when the language of
sacrifice and collective duties to one another was commonplace. But in
the age of self-interest and the frantic pursuit of short-term material
advantage, it may be essential that we embrace the idea that future
progress is actually in doubt. For increasingly, a belief in inevitable
progress into the future represents an excuse for ignoring the interests of
posterity and our duty to the generations to come. We like to assume that
our children will – thanks to the progress of science and ever-increasing
wealth – be able to sort out any problem we bequeath to them. As the
world becomes more crowded, vital resources become more depleted
and the disparity of wealth and poverty grows more extreme, such a faith
that all will be well in the end looks more like staggering complacency
than well-founded optimism.

The problems facing the modern world are legion. If we continue to
resign ourselves to the accelerating quest for economic efficiency implied
by globalisation and deregulation, and continue to regard all calls for
gradualism as misguided, then countries, institutions and individuals
alike will have to learn how to adapt to a speed of change which is quite
unparalleled in human history. Furthermore, as environmental limits are
breached and new ecological thresholds are crossed, mankind must find
ways to cooperate on a global scale in order to husband resources and prevent environmental catastrophe. In a global free market it will not be easy
to provide the legal framework required to prevent some countries from
free-riding on the environmental restraint of others; nor will it be easy to
build the required global consensus for the necessary changes in environmental policy. As technological change and the globalisation of the
economy also take their toll on the employment and earnings prospects
of tens of millions of people in the old democracies, ways must be found

to share the still considerable spoils of economic growth across the whole spectrum of society. This could include more job-sharing and voluntary or enforced limits on the number of hours worked, in order to avoid the patent madness of much of the population suffering the stress of over-work while others endure the scourge of unemployment and poverty. It is only if some way can be found to share the available better-paid work more widely that there is any hope of curing the social cancer of an alien-ated underclass of inactivity and poverty, or any hope that technological change, rather than boosting unemployment, can fulfil its early promise of allowing those in work to have greater leisure time. But the prognosis at present is not favourable. For such changes would require a reordering of social priorities away from the frenetic search for ever more material goods, and away from competition for social prestige, towards an appre-ciation by successful individuals of the benefits of having more time to pursue inexpensive pastimes and enjoy the pleasures of friendship. Such changes would also require a renewed faith in the role of government. In the 1990s, on the contrary, our societies seem to have grown still more obsessed with fulfilling exclusively material aspirations, and the post-World War II consensus behind the need for strong collective action to benefit society as a whole appears to be unravelling fast.

Nowhere is such dislike of collective action more evident than in the vexed area of income redistribution. In the 1950s and 1960s, most Western governments operated with a consensus behind levying high marginal rates of income tax. This was despite the fact that there was then a cogent intellectual argument against incentive-reducing and growth-sapping redistribution, since the wonders of exponential growth and its trickle-down effects did serve the interests of the poor at a time when there was full employment and high wage growth across the income spectrum. Even without the redistributive taxation of those decades, the poor of Western countries would still have had a stake in the strong economic growth, and the march of progress would still have been inclusive of all but a tiny minority. In the 1980s and 1990s, by contrast, the benefits of growth have become much more concentrated. The very rich have got much richer, while the very poor have often become even poorer. In the relatively successful US economy, there are finally signs, in the later stages of the economic up-swing of the 1990s, that the poor are once again sharing some of the benefits of growth; but this comes after a twenty-year period (up to 1995) during which the real incomes of even the average worker had changed little. Over the long term, the trickle-down flow of wealth appears to have slowed or even stopped in many economies, as growing technological unemployment, deregulation and the globalisation of the labour market (as well as welfare cuts) have put pressure on the incomes and jobs of the poorest in the developed world. Moreover, as environmental constraints on the relentless pursuit of ever more economic growth tighten, and as positional goods and relative income advantage become more important in affluent societies (thereby reducing the welfare content for society as a whole of any given increase in income), there are additional reasons to doubt that the lot of the poor can improve significantly unless there is a process of income redistribution. But the redistribution required if further economic growth is to provide progress in welfare for all now appears virtually impossible, given the current taxpayer revolt. The burgeoning cult of individualism and narrow self-interest and deepening popular scepticism about the right or ability of government to undertake social engineering have fuelled an abject refusal by a blocking majority of voters to countenance rises in income tax. This refusal has left governments increasingly powerless to design a collective response to many of the social and environmental challenges that lie ahead.

Ever since the eighteenth-century Enlightenment, there has been creative tension between different traditions, and a fertile mix of conflicting ideals. There has been a shifting balance between the belief in collective action and in individual liberty, between faith in cooperation and in the creative power of competition, between faith in rational planning and in *laissez-faire* policies, between respect for civic duty and for the pursuit of individual self-interest, between the ideal of equality and of personal freedom, and between belief in the unity of mankind and in the unresolvable diversity of human goals and aspirations. The secret of human success during the last two hundred years has been precisely that, for most of the period, there was a genuine balance between all these elements. Aristotle held that virtue lay in a 'mean between two vices, that which depends on excess and that which depends on defect',[5] and it was a commonplace in Ancient Greece that moderation in all things (or 'nothing in excess') was the key to wisdom and success. Modern progress has also implicitly relied on the virtues of moderation and balance. It has depended above all on respect for liberty and the right of individuals to pursue their own self-interest being balanced by respect for a supportive, though not over-intrusive, framework of rational planning, and by a strong sense of civic duty. Whenever the creative balance between individual liberty and a framework of government has given way to the total hegemony of one over the other, the result has been either anarchy or totalitarianism. The successful economies and progressive societies have been those which have maintained a measured pluralist approach.

As we near the third millennium, the pluralist balance of different ideals and traditions we have witnessed in Western culture for most of the period since the Enlightenment seems to be breaking down, perhaps irretrievably. The long-term survival of cohesive communities, effective government power and fruitful social cooperation has been called into question by the growing triumph of globalisation and free-market dereg-ulation, and by the spreading culture of rampant individualism. It will be difficult to rebuild the necessary creative tension between a sense of duty to our fellow citizens and the energetic pursuit of legitimate self-interest. Indeed, we must face the disquieting possibility that the essential balance between the collectivist and individualist traditions which has existed for most of the last two hundred years may have been an historical accident. It may be the case that such a balance was only possible during the transitional phase between the religious pre-capitalist era and the secular capitalist age. If that is so, the prospects for continued human progress are bleak indeed.

Notes

Source Notes

Chapter 1

1. Tolstoy, L. N., *Anna Karenina*, trans. Rosemary Edmonds (Penguin, 1954).
2. Berlin, Isaiah, *The Crooked Timber of Humanity – Chapters in the History of Ideas* (John Murray, 1990). From the essay 'The Pursuit of the Ideal'.
3. Collingwood, R. G., *The Idea of History* (Oxford University Press, 1994, revised edition). Originally published 1946.
4. Carr, E. H., *What is History?* (Penguin, 1990). Originally published 1961.
5. Gombrich, E. H., *The Story of Art* (Phaidon, 1984). From the preface to the original edition, published 1950.
6. Sassoon, Siegfried, extract from 'Attack', from *Collected Poems of Siegfried Sassoon* (Penguin USA, 1946).

Chapter 2

1. Lucretius, Carus Titus (c.99BC–c.55BC), *De Rerum Natura* (On the Nature of the Universe), V.1412f., trans. R. E. Latham (Penguin, 1951).
2. Ibid., V.1430f.
3. Kenny, Anthony, 'Aristotle on Happiness'. Originally published in Proceedings of the Aristotelian Society 65 (1965–6). Revised version

published in *Articles on Aristotle, Vol. 2, Ethics and Politics*, ed. Jonathan Barnes, Malcolm Schofield and Richard Sorabji (Duckworth 1977).

4. Russell, Bertrand, *History of Western Philosophy* (George Allen & Unwin, 1946).

5. Collingwood, R. G., op. cit.

6. Theocritus, *Idyll* 7.141f., ed. with a translation and commentary A. S. F. Gow (Cambridge University Press, 1950).

7. Homer, *The Iliad*, 14.346f., trans. Richmond Lattimore (University of Chicago Press, 1951).

8. Ibid., 12.278f.

9. Sappho, 2 LP.1f., trans. Moses Hadas and James Willis, in *Early Greek Poetry and Philosophy*, Hermann Frankel (Blackwell, 1975).

10. Ibid., 96LP. 8f.

11. Arapooish, 'The Crow country is a good country . . .' in *Adventures of Bonneville*, Washington Irving (G. P. Putnam, New York, 1849). Reprinted in *Native Heritage: Personal Accounts by American Indians 1790 to the Present*, ed. Arlene Hirschfelder (Macmillan USA, 1995).

12. Satanta, 'I love the land . . .', Office of Indian Affairs, National Archives, 104 (Medicine Lodge Creek Treaty Meeting, 20 October, 1867). Extract reprinted in *500 Nations, An Illustrated History of North American Indians*, Alvin M. Josephy (Hutchinson, 1995).

13. Beckermann, Wilfred, *Small is Stupid – Blowing the Whistle on the Greens* (Duckworth, 1995).

Chapter 3

1. Dodds, E. R., *The Ancient Concept of Progress and Other Essays on Greek Literature and Belief* (Oxford University Press, 1973).

2. Edelstein, Ludwig, *The Idea of Progress in Classical Antiquity* (The Johns Hopkins Press, Baltimore, 1967).

3. Thucydides, *History of the Peloponnesian War*, I.6.6, trans. R. Warner (Penguin, 1954).

4. Ibid., I.71.

5. Aeschylus, *Prometheus Bound*, L.447f., trans. H. Weir Smyth (Loeb Classical Library, 1922).

6. Xenophanes, Frag. 18, Diels-Kranz/Frag. 16, Diehl-Beutler, in *Senofane di Colofone, Ione di Chio*, ed. Antonio Farina (Libreria Scientifica Editrice, Naples, 1961).

7. Sophocles, *Antigone*, L.332.f., L.354f., trans. Hugh Lloyd-Jones (Loeb Classical Library, 1994).

8. Lucretius, op. cit. V.1448f.

9. Homer, op. cit. 24.9f.

10. Ibid., 24.507f.

11. Ibid., 24.525f.

12. Herodotus, *The Histories*, I.5.4, trans. Aubrey de Sélincourt (Penguin, 1954).

13. Ibid., I.32.7f.

14. Ibid., I.32.1.

15. Aeschylus, *Agamemnon*, L.763f., trans. H. Weir Smyth (Loeb Classical Library, 1926).

16. Ibid., L.773f.

17. Sophocles, op. cit., L.604f.

18. Ibid., L.1348f.

19. Horace, *Odes*, I.3.37f., trans. James Michie (Penguin, 1967).

20. Hesiod, *Works and Days*, L.90f., ed. with Prolegomena and commentary M. L. West (Oxford University Press, 1978).

21. Ibid., L.108f.

22. Plato, *Laws*, 679, trans. B. Jowett (C. Scribner's, New York, 1883).

23. Horace, *Odes*, 3.6.45f., trans. C. E. Bennett (Loeb Classical Library, 1914).

24. Ibid., 3.6.33f.

25. Virgil, *Aeneid*, VI.791f., trans. H. R. Fairclough (Loeb Classical Library, 1916).

26. Austin, R. G., *Virgil Aeneid VI – With a Commentary* (Oxford University Press, 1977).

27. Plato, op. cit. 676f.

28. Aristotle, *Metaphysics*, 1074b10f., trans. Jonathan Barnes, *The Complete Works of Aristotle – The Revised Oxford Translation* (Princeton University Press, New Jersey, 1984).

29. Ibid., 993a30f.

30. Seneca, *Natural Questions*, VII.25.4–5, trans. Thomas H. Corcoran (Loeb Classical Library, 1972).

31. Pliny the Elder, *Natural History*, II.13.62, trans. H. Rackman (Loeb Classical Library, 1938).

32. Lucretius, op. cit., V.1430f.

33. Tarnas, Richard, *The Passion of the Western Mind – Understanding the Ideas That Have Shaped Our World View* (Ballantine, New York, 1991).

34. Ibid.

35. St Augustine, *City of God*, V.17, trans. W. M. Green (Loeb Classical Library, 1963).

36. O'Donnell, James J., *Augustine* (Twayne Publishers, Boston, 1985).

37. Markus, R. A., *Saeculum: History and Society in the Theology of St Augustine* (Cambridge University Press, 1970).
38. Bury, J. B., *The Idea of Progress – An Inquiry into its Origin and Growth* (Macmillan, 1920).
39. O'Donnell, op. cit.
40. Hale, John, *The Civilisation of Europe in the Renaissance* (Fontana Press, 1994).
41. Fontenelle, Bernard le Bovier de, *Entretiens sur la pluralité des mondes habités* (The Plurality of Worlds), *Oeuvres Complètes II* (Fayard, France, 1991).
42. Hampson, Norman, *The Enlightenment – An evaluation of its assumptions, attitudes and values* (Penguin, 1990). Originally published in 1968.
43. Holbach, Baron d', *Common Sense, or Natural Ideas Opposed to Supernatural* (1772), trans. from *The Portable Enlightenment Reader*, ed. Isaac Kramnick (Penguin USA, 1995).
44. Bury, op. cit.
45. Turgot, Anne-Robert-Jacques, *On the Successive Advances of the Human Mind* (1750). Trans. from Kramnick, op. cit.
46. Franklin, Benjamin, letter to Joseph Priestley, 8 February 1780. Reprinted in Kramnick, op. cit.
47. Bury, op. cit.
48. Franklin, op. cit.
49. Condorcet, Marquis de, *Sketch for a Historical Picture of the Human Mind* (1794). Trans. from Kramnick, op. cit.
50. Priestley, Joseph, Letters to the Right Honorable Edmund Burke (1781). Concluding chapter reprinted in Kramnick, op. cit.
51. Rousseau, Jean-Jacques, *Discourse on Arts and Sciences* (1751). Trans. from Kramnick, op. cit.
52. Hampson, op. cit.

Chapter 4

1. Fukuyama, Francis, *The End of History and the Last Man* (Penguin, 1992).
2. Bury, op. cit.
3. Berlin, op. cit.
4. Kant, Immanuel, 'Idea of a Universal History from a Cosmopolitical Point of View' (1784). Trans. W. Hastie, *Kant's Principles of Politics* (T. & T. Clark, 1891).
5. Shaw, G. B., *Man and Superman: A Comedy and a Philosophy*, 'Maxims for Revolutionists' (Archibald Constable & Co., 1903).

6. Pope, Alexander, 'An Essay on Man, Epistle II' (1733). From *The Poems of Alexander Pope Volume III*, ed. Maynard Mack (Methuen & Co., 1950).

7. Berlin, op. cit., from the essay 'The Apotheosis of the Romantic Will'.

8. Tarnas, op. cit.

9. Rousseau, op. cit.

10. Ibid., *The Social Contract* (1762). Trans. from Kramnick, op. cit.

11. Russell, Bertrand, op. cit.

12. Fukuyama, Francis, 'On the Possibility of Writing a Universal History', in *History and the Idea of Progress*, ed. Arthur M. Melzer, Jerry Weinberger and M. Richard Zinman (Cornell University Press, Ithaca, 1995).

13. Yeats, W. B., extract from 'The Second Coming', from *The Collected Poems of W. B. Yeats* (Macmillan, 1933). Originally published in *Michael Robartes and the Dancer* (1921).

14. Beckett, Samuel, *Malone Dies, The Unnamable* (Calder and Boyars, 1966). First published in French by Editions de Minuit as *Malone Meurt* (1951), *L'Innomable* (1952).

Chapter 5

1. Bowler, Peter J. *Evolution: The History of an Idea* (University of California Press, Berkeley, 1983).

2. Tarnas, op. cit.

3. Waldrop, M. Mitchell, *Complexity – The Emerging Science at the Edge of Order and Chaos* (Penguin, 1994).

4. Rifkin, Jeremy, *The End of Work – The Decline of the Global Labor Force and the Dawn of the Post-Market Era* (G. P. Putnam's Sons, New York, 1995).

Chapter 6

1. Lasch, Christopher, 'The Age of Limits', in Arthur M. Melzer et al., op. cit.

2. Smith, Adam, *An Inquiry into the Nature and Causes of the Wealth of Nations*, I.ii (Oxford University Press, 1976). Originally published 1776.

3. Ibid.

4. Ibid., II.iii.

5. Ibid., IV.ii

6. Smith, Adam, *The Theory of Moral Sentiments*, IV.i (Oxford University Press, 1976). Originally published 1759.

7 Smith, Adam, *The Wealth of Nations*, IV.v.

8. Ibid., IV.ii.

9. Ibid., IV.ix.

10. Ibid., V.i.

11. Bentham, Jeremy, *An Introduction to the Principles of Morals and Legislation* (Oxford University Press, 1948). Originally published 1789.

12. *Independent on Sunday*, 21 July 1996.

13. Smith, Adam, *The Theory of Moral Sentiments*.

Chapter 7

1. Todaro, Michael P., *Economic Development*, fifth edition (Longman, 1994).

2. Hirsch, Fred, *Social Limits to Growth* (Routledge, 1977).

3. *Independent on Sunday*, 21 July 1996.

4. *Financial Times*, 29 August 1996.

5. Nordhaus, William, and Tobin, James, 'Is Growth Obsolete?' National Bureau of Economic Research General Series, No. 96E, Columbia University Press (New York, 1972).

6. Daly, Herman E., and Cobb, John B. Jr, *For the Common Good – Redirecting the Economy Towards Community, the Environment and a Sustainable Future* (Green Print, 1990).

7. *Financial Times*, 30 August 1996.

8. Corry, D., Hawkins, R. and Webb, J., 'Sense of Well-Being' in *New Economy*, Spring 1996 (Institute of Public Policy Research, Dryden Press).

9. Jacobs, Michael, *The Green Economy – Environment, Sustainable Development and the Politics of the Future* (Pluto Press, 1991).

Chapter 8

1. Price, David E., 'Is Man Becoming Obsolete?' US Public Health Reports, Vol. 74 (1959), No. 8.

2. Huxley, Aldous, quoted by his brother Julian in his preface to the UK edition of Rachel Carson's *Silent Spring* (Hamish Hamilton, 1963).

3. Todaro, op. cit.

4. Brown, Lester, et al., *State of the World 1996* (Earthscan, 1996).

5. Todaro, op. cit.

6. Brown, op. cit.; and article, 'A New Era Unfolds', in *Leading Economic Controversies of 1995*, ed. Edwin Mansfield (Norton, New York, 1995).

7. *Independent on Sunday*, 12 November 1995.

8. Jacobs, op. cit.

9. Daly, Herman E., *Steady-State Economics*, second edition (Earthscan, 1992).

10. Carson, Rachel, *Silent Spring* (Houghton Mifflin, New York, 1987). Originally published 1962.

11. Brown, Lester, et al, *Vital Signs – the trends that are shaping our future, 1995, 1996* (Earthscan, 1995); and Brown, et al, *State of the World 1996*.

12. BBC, *Panorama*: 'Fish Wars', 5 February 1996; Brown, Lester, et al., 'A New Era Unfolds'; *The Independent*, 31 May 1996.

13. BBC, *Panorama*, op. cit.

14. *Independent on Sunday*, 18 February 1996; Segar, Douglas A., *Introduction to Ocean Sciences* (Wadsworth, Belmont, California, 1998).

15. Carson, op. cit., quoting Paul Shepard, 'The Place of Nature in Man's World' in *Atlantic Naturalist*, Vol. 13 (April–June 1958).

16. Calthrop, Edward, in dissertation results quoted in *The True Costs of Road Transport*, ed. David Maddison et al. (Earthscan, 1996).

17. Ibid.

18. Todaro, op. cit.; Brown, et al., *Vital Signs*.

19. Daly, op. cit.

Chapter 9

1. Lucretius, op. cit., V.1117f.

2. Horace, *Odes*, 3.6, trans. C. E. Bennett (Loeb Classical Library, 1914).

3. Mill, John Stuart, *Principles of Political Economy*, Book IV.6 (University of Toronto Press, Canada, 1965). Originally published 1848.

Chapter 10

1. Keynes, John Maynard, *The General Theory of Employment, Interest and Money* (Macmillan, for the Royal Economic Society, 1973). Originally published 1936.

2. Ibid.

3. Ibid.

4. Ibid.

5. Lipsey, R. G. and Lancaster, K. J., 'The General Theory of Second Best' in *The Review of Economic Studies* Vol. XXIV No. 63, 1956–7.

6. Waldrop, M. Mitchell, *Complexity – The Emerging Science at the Edge of Order and Chaos* (Penguin, 1994).

7. Ibid.

Chapter 11

1. Smith, Adam, *The Wealth of Nations*, IV.ii.

2. Ibid., IV.ix.
3. Ibid., IV.ii.
4. Roberts, J. M., *Europe 1880–1945* (Longman, 1967).

Chapter 12
1. Keynes, op. cit.
2. Thatcher, Margaret, quoted in *Woman's Own*, 31 October 1987.
3. Woolf, Virginia, *The Diary of Virginia Woolf, Volume IV: 1931–1935*, ed. Anne Oliver Bell (Hogarth Press, 1982).
4. Bury, op. cit.
5. Aristotle, *The Nicomachean Ethics*, 1107a, trans. with an introduction David Ross (Oxford University Press, 1925).

Other Reference Works

In addition to the works listed above, the following may prove as helpful to the reader as they were to the author.

Begg, David, Fischer, Stanley and Dornbusch, Rudiger, *Economics*, fourth edition (McGraw Hill, 1994).

Brennan, Geoffrey, 'The Contribution of Economics' in *A Companion to Contemporary Political Philosophy*, ed. Robert E. Goodin and Philip Pettit (Blackwell, 1993).

Chadwick, Henry, *Augustine* (Oxford University Press, 1986).

European Commission, 'Towards Fair and Efficient Pricing in Transport – Policy Options for Internalising the External Costs of Transport in the European Union' (Green Paper, 1995).

Fukuyama, Francis, *Trust – The Social Virtues and the Creation of Prosperity* (Penguin, 1995).

Gleick, James, *Chaos* (Heinemann, 1988).

Griffiths, M. R. and Lucas, J. R., *Ethical Economics* (Macmillan, 1996).

Harrod, R. F., *The Life of John Maynard Keynes* (Harcourt Brace, New York, 1951).

Henderson, Hazel, *Paradigms in Progress – Life Beyond Economics* (Adamantine, 1993).

Hobsbawm, Eric, *Age of Extremes – The Short Twentieth Century 1914–1991* (Abacus, 1995).

Irwin, Douglas A., *Against the Tide – An Intellectual History of Free Trade* (Princeton University Press, New Jersey, 1996).

Krugman, Paul, *Peddling Prosperity – Economic Sense and Nonsense in the Age of Diminished Expectations* (Norton, New York, 1994).

Mackie, J. L., *Ethics – Inventing Right and Wrong* (Penguin, 1977).

Mill, John Stuart, *Utilitarianism* (Fontana, 1962). Originally published 1861.

Mishan, E. J. *The Costs of Economic Growth* (Weidenfeld & Nicolson, 1967).

Nisbet, Robert, *History of the Idea of Progress* (Heinemann, 1980).

Ormorod, Paul, *The Death of Economics* (Faber & Faber, 1994).

Raphael, D. D., *Adam Smith* (Oxford University Press, 1985).

Roll, Eric, *A History of Economic Thought* (Faber & Faber, 1938).

Sen, Amartya, *On Ethics and Economics* (Blackwell, 1987).

Sen, Amartya and Williams, Bernard (eds), *Utilitarianism and Beyond* (Cambridge University Press, 1982).

Sharples, R. W., *Stoics, Epicureans and Sceptics – An Introduction to Hellenistic Philosophy* (Routledge, 1996).

Skidelsky, Robert, *Keynes* (Oxford University Press, 1996).

Smart, J. J. C. and Williams, Bernard, *Utilitarianism: For and Against* (Cambridge University Press, 1973).

Telfer, Elizabeth, *Happiness* (Macmillan, 1980).

Tobin, James, 'The Invisible Hand in Modern Macroeconomics' in *Adam Smith's Legacy*, ed. M. Fry (Routledge, 1992).

United Nations Development Program, Human Development Report 1996 (Oxford University Press, 1996).

Werhane, Patricia H., *Adam Smith and his Legacy for Modern Capitalism* (Oxford University Press, New York, 1991).

Williams, Bernard, *Morality – An Introduction to Ethics* (Cambridge University Press, 1972).

Yovel, Yirmiahu, *Kant and the Philosophy of History* (Princeton University Press, New Jersey, 1980).

Credits

For permission to publish copyright material in this book grateful acknowledgement is made to the following:

Samuel Beckett: for extracts from *Malone Dies* and *The Unnamable*, to Calder Publications Ltd; Isaiah Berlin: for extracts from *The Crooked Timber of Humanity*, to John Murray (Publishers) Ltd and Alfred A. Knopf Inc.; Fernando Henrique Cardoso: for an extract from Human

rights in which are vested in the Crown, to the Crown's Patentee, Cambridge University Press.

Every effort has been made to obtain permission from all copyright-holders, but in some cases this has not proved possible at the time of going to press. The publishers therefore wish to thank those authors whose work is included without acknowledgement, and would be grateful to be notified of any omissions or corrections which should be incorporated in the next edition.

Index

HITLER'S BANKER

John Weitz

Hjalmar Horace Greeley Schacht was a genius, an eccentric and an enigma. Single-handedly halting Germany's runaway inflation and freeing her from the crippling reparation debts imposed by the Treaty of Versailles, he gained worldwide fame as the economic guru of Nazi Germany. Yet while he financed Hitler's military regime, he held most Nazi's in contempt and frequently clashed with its hierarchy – and Hitler himself – over anti-Jewish laws and war spending. Before the war was over, he had been imprisoned in Dachau; later, he was one of only three defendants to be acquitted at the Nuremberg trials.

John Weitz's riveting biography brings this complex figure, a skilled manipulator of money, men and governments, to life against the chilling, brutal but often grimly fascinating history of twentieth century Germany.

'Weitz is perhaps at his best in the details of the floundering Deutschemark … and in the well-placed reminders of the way in which the Americans, British and French were prepared to overlook the increasing thuggery of Nazi Germany so long as their own interests were safe'
Daily Telegraph

'A good, vivid read … Weitz's judgements are often shrewd'
Literary Review

THE GENERAL AGAINST THE KREMLIN

Alexander Lebed: Power and Illusion

Harold Elletson

The General Against the Kremlin is not simply an account of the
life of Alexander Lebed, the man who, in the year 2000,
hopes to become the next President of Russia. Placing his
story firmly in the context of the power struggles and
conflicts which have riven Russian over the last forty years
– many of which Lebed has experienced at first-hand, even
directly contributed to – Harold Elletson has written an
authoritative, illuminating and thought-provoking
exploration of the politics of a country which is still far
from democracy.

'Impressive ... a brave attempt at pinning down the elusive
Lebed ... he has also, in passing, written an excellent
concise history of Russia's past two decades'
TLS

'an entertaining, thought-provoking and unsettling read ...
his insider knowledge and long historical perspective
provide valuable insight and a welcome,
informed corrective'
Time Out

Other bestselling Warner titles available by mail: